The Tulips Are Red

The Tulips Are Red

Leesha Rose

South Brunswick and New York: A. S. Barnes and Company
London: Thomas Yoseloff Ltd

A. S. Barnes and Co., Inc.
Cranbury, New Jersey 08512

Thomas Yoseloff Ltd
Magdalen House
136-148 Tooley Street
London SE1 2TT, England

Rose, Leesha, 1922-
    The tulips are red.
    1. Rose, Leesha, 1922–   2. World War, 1939-1945—Personal
narratives, Jewish.   3. Holocaust, Jewish (1939-1945)—
Netherlands   4. Netherlands—History—German occupation, 1940-1945.
I. Title.
D810.J4R6537   940.53′1503′924 [B]   77–89649
ISBN 0-498-02176-9

PRINTED IN THE UNITED STATES OF AMERICA

DEDICATED TO:
My dearly beloved parents, Yeshayahu and Chanah Bornstein, and my dear brothers, Paul and Jackie, Martyrs of the Holocaust, of Blessed Memory — whose lives were snuffed out in the Nazi concentration camps of Auschwitz and Sobibor.

IN TRIBUTE TO:
Reinier van Kampenhout, friend and mentor, who fought courageously while endangering his life in the performance of Underground rescue and Resistance operations. Five months before the end of World War II, he was captured and tortured to death by the Nazis.

IN TRIBUTE TO:
The courage and fortitude of the many Dutch Gentiles who took the risk of hiding Jews in their homes and who performed great acts of resistance out of the conviction that it was "the Christian thing to do."

ACKNOWLEDGMENTS

I wish to acknowledge my indebtedness to: Dr. Hyman Frank, who originally suggested that I undertake the writing of my experiences during World War II and for whose subsequent help I am forever grateful; to my good friend Mr. Zvi Caspi, the Israeli Consul General in Montreal, Canada, for his great interest; to Mr. Sam E. Bloch, Director of Publications of the World Zionist Organization in New York and General Secretary of the World Federation of the Bergen-Belsen Associations for his recognition of the importance of my manuscript and to Yad Vashem in Jerusalem for extending their library facilities to me. Above all I am beholden and grateful to my dear husband, who stood by me in my many agonizing periods of writing, who counseled me so wisely in the editing of the manuscript, and for whose moral support and infinite patience I am deeply thankful.

The Tulips Are Red

1

A crash of thunder disrupted the quiet stillness of the dawn. I turned over in bed, pulling the covers over my ears. My body, longing for sleep, quivered with the intruding roar as fear enveloped me, running through my body like an electric current. I closed my eyes tightly and I lay there tense with the hope that the noise would not be repeated.

Suddenly there was a tremendous roar followed by a series of small staccato shots, one following the other in rapid succession. Simultaneously, I heard people's voices coming from the gardens in back of the houses, talking and shouting.

"Look, over there! Look. They are jumping from airplanes! My God! What is this? Parachutes? Is this our Dutch army on war exercises? If it is, then why all this shooting by antiaircraft guns?"

I jumped out of bed, and ran to my parents' bedroom. They too were up, looking startled. My brother Paul, who had also been awakened by the noise, opened the French doors to the patio and ran out to the garden. We followed him and the sweet air of spring touched us with its gentle aroma. It appeared to me that the early Friday morning sun on that fatal day of May 10, 1940, was nearly obliterated by a squadron of German planes dropping hundreds of parachutists.

Again the rapid put-put-put of sounds . . . .

By now there was no doubt. It certainly was not a thunderstorm!

"Quickly, turn on the radio!," someone said.

Our neighbors were all standing on their lawns or on their balconies, pointing up to the sky, talking and shouting excitedly. The children looked up at the spectacle with their mouths open. The grownups shook their heads, unbelievingly. Some cried openly with terror in their eyes.

The news started with a special statement by Queen Wilhelmina vehemently protesting the German invasion and calling it "the most flagrant breach of conduct practiced among civilized nations." The Netherlands government had been reassured repeatedly by the German Foreign Office that her neutrality would be respected.

As we heard the news we realized the tremendous tragedy that had befallen us.

"The Germans have invaded Holland! It is war and we are being attacked."

The radio spelled out the awful tidings.

"Nazi air-borne troops have parachuted onto the airfields of Holland and have overpowered the Dutch airforce; German armies have driven across the southern provinces of Limburg and Noord-Brabant into Belgium and are advancing along the Rhine and Maas rivers toward Rotterdam."

The playing of the Dutch national anthem, the "*Wilhelmus*," ended the broadcast. We were as if rooted to the ground, standing in shock.

"Where were our defenses? What happened to our Dutch antiaircraft forces and to our fighter planes? How could the Germans have broken through the obstacles of 'Fortress Holland,' the central section of the country, which was protected by trenches, inundations, and fortified defense positions?" Everyone speculated and guessed, but all of us were seized by a feeling of disbelief and paralysis.

"It cannot happen here—not in Holland. During World War I we were neutral, we want to remain that way now. Holland does not want war! The Germans promised they would not harm us. Why did they attack us? What wrong did we ever do to them?"

After the first shock of the German attack we sat day and night near our radios, our lifeline to the world of reality. We followed

12

all the Dutch government instructions concerning blackout and curfew at night.

The whole country was in a state of turmoil. Shelling and bombing could be heard constantly. We were warned about possible acts of treason by the N.S.B. party—the Dutch Nazi party, which might have taken on the role of a fifth column—and we were asked to be on the lookout for German parachutists in disguise. It was difficult to trust anyone because so much treason and confusion was going on. No one was allowed to walk with his hands in his pockets or with his hands behind his back. These warnings increased our nervousness. Between the news broadcasts the radio played military marches.

We remained in the house as much as possible. The food shops were open and people performed only their most necessary activities, rushing home immediately. They hurried down the streets, hugging the sides of the houses for protection, ducking into a doorway when the German planes were heard overhead.

All Dutch theaters and movie houses, schools, offices, and places of business were closed. There was no mail delivery. Trains, buses, streetcars, and taxis were not in operation. The telephones did not work. Only doctors, hospitals, and military service personnel could use the telephone. Newspapers had only a few pages and contained very little news. Sirens were screeching at intervals to warn of impending air attacks. A curfew from 8:00 P.M. to 6:00 A.M. was put into efect.

In our home our feelings were those of tension, fear, and apprehension of the worst to come. In the Jewish communities of Holland the synagogues were filled to capacity on the first Sabbath, and the fervent prayers of the worshippers could be heard in the streets.

That Friday night, May 10th, 1940, normally would be the beginning of our holy day of rest, the cherished Shabbat, the day we anticipated all week with such eagerness. But now my family gathered around the diningroom table in a very different mood: my father strong and determined; my delicate mother, my fifteen-year-old brother Paul, my little brother Jackie, four years old, and myself, a high school senior of seventeen. We knew

13

each other's feelings, we did not dare raise our eyes. Our thoughts were submerged within ourselves, fearful of giving way to our emotions.

Father raised the silver goblet filled with wine and just as on any other Friday night began to chant the Kiddush, the Sanctification, his eyes closed, full of devotion and concentration. But when he came to the passage *"Ki vahnu vaharta v'otanu kidashta ..."*—"Almighty God, You have chosen and sanctified us"—his voice broke and tears streamed down his face. This was the first time that we had seen Father cry, and a sense of foreboding and an ominous feeling of impending grief and disaster descended upon us.

For the first time that I could remember we did not celebrate the Shabbat with the customary singing and good cheer. Our throats were too constricted with sorrow to enjoy our traditional Shabbat dinner, and my father barely murmured the Zmirot, the traditional Shabbat songs.

As strict Sabbath observers we did not turn on the radio, and our Gentile neighbors came in and gave us the latest news:

"The Dutch army is fighting bravely. The German armies in the North have driven up to the Ijsselmeer without encountering much opposition. Bitter fighting has developed along the defense lines of the Rhine and the Maas rivers. Communications with Belgium have been cut off." That first Sabbath in May 1940 was a sad day for us all.

Mrs. van Heeren, our neighbor, showed us a leaflet that the German planes had dropped. We looked at it with horror as we read:

"The city is surrounded by German troops. Any resistance is senseless."

"England won't permit this to go on any longer!," Paul called out angrily. "The Allies can see that we need them desperately now to save Holland. You'll see they will strike so fast, the Germans won't know what hit them!"

My girlfriend Kitty, who lived across the street, ran into our house. We were so happy to see each other, we hugged each other and cried, there was no need for words, we understood and

14

felt alike. She brought us another piece of news from her neighbor Mr. Jansen:

"The three airfields around The Hague—Valkenburg, Ockenburg, and Ypenburg—have been bombed by the Germans and they have dropped paratroopers in great numbers. Our Dutch troops fought them courageously and drove them off the airfields. This battle success has saved The Hague and the Dutch government. One of the major goals of the invaders was to capture the royal family and the ministers on the first day of the invasion."

On May 11th the Cabinet recommended to the Queen that she take measures for the safety of the royal family.

On May 12th Crown Princess Juliana, her husband, Prince Bernhard, and their children sailed for England on a British destroyer. The Prince immediately returned to join the Dutch troops who were fighting in Zeeland.

On May 13th General H. G. Winkelman, Commander in Chief of the Dutch armed forces, advised Queen Wilhelmina that he could no longer be responsible for her safety. At her request she was taken to England by another British destroyer. The government followed her later in the day.

Upon arriving in London, the Queen released a statement explaining the reasons for her departure from Holland. From England she could best protect the interests of her country and retain a measure of freedom of action. Had she fallen into the hands of the enemy, all would have been lost. She vowed that the fight against the invaders would be maintained from London until victory was achieved. She proclaimed London as the seat of government of the Netherlands.

We felt lost.

On Tuesday, May 14th, the military situation had become hopeless. The Dutch airforce had been practically wiped out. The British Airforce was engaged in desperate battles over France and Belgium. The Germans had been informed about our fortifications by means of espionage and their own aerial observations. The Germans had cut off fortress Holland from Belgium and had established themselves solidly near Rotterdam. A threat was issued to bomb each of the cities of Holland, beginning with Rotterdam, if Holland would not surrender. Negotiations dragged on beyond the deadline stipulated in the German ultimatum. At 1:30 P.M. the German air force, in wave after wave of deadly *Heinkel* bombers, devastated the greater part of the city of Rotterdam.

Like shooting at a sitting duck! It was an easy task! Unhindered, the German bombers flew low over the city and sought out their targets with precision. All at once the center was transformed into a flaming hell of thick, black and orange suffocating clouds. Thousands of terrified inhabitants ran through the streets, trying to avoid the collapsing buildings and the pursuing flames. Twenty-one churches and four hospitals were burning!

Later that afternoon, General Winkelman announced his decision to surrender to the Nazi invaders with a proclamation to his officers:

"Germany has bombed Rotterdam today. Utrecht is threatened with destruction. To save the population and avoid further bloodshed, I believe I am justified in ordering the troops under your command to stop fighting."

The following morning the capitulation papers were signed. Suddenly everything was over. All our hopes, our prayers for a Dutch victory were shattered.

May 15th, 1940, the German armies paraded through the cities of Holland and took possession—lock, stock, and barrel.

The Dutch citizens, their faces stern, black, immobile with inner rage and disfigured with shed and unshed tears, watched the grand entrance of the German war machine. Along the streets we stood huddled together, shivering in the bright May sunshine watching, watching . . . endlessly.

We saw armored cars, powerful guns, panzerwagons, trucks, and then rows upon rows of marching soldiers, like automatons, their boots lifting and falling on the pavement in minutest cadenza and precision, their arms swaying up and down like a machine.

I, too, stared at this frightening spectacle. I felt myself hypnotized by this rythmic movement. The falling and lifting of the boots became more vigorous, the arms swayed higher and higher, the noise reverberated louder and louder—fear and rage rose in my throat.

This relentless pounding of the boots on the pavement became for me the symbol of impending danger, of fear and of hatred.

What was in store for us now? What kind of life awaited us?

2

Finally the dust had settled. It was hard to realize the situation we were in. The proud Dutch nation was subjugated and overrun by the brazen German enemy. We stared around us with unbelieving eyes not knowing what to expect. The shock and grief of our military defeat was felt deeply by everyone.

What would become of our beautiful, peaceful country? Would we be able to continue our comfortable, relaxed, and orderly way of life? How would the Dutch, who for so long did not know of oppression or of war, be able to withstand tyranny? Would we be able to continue to be masters of our own private destiny?

Thoughts, questions, doubts, and emotions such as these were common. People were unsure and afraid to make hasty decisions.

Was it advisable to try to escape? Either by boat across the North Sea to safety in England, or to flee via Belgium and France to neutral Switzerland?

Mr. and Mrs. Prinz, friends of my parents, came back from the harbor of Ijmuiden in a state of turmoil. Mrs. Prinz cried as her husband related what had happened: ''We, together with thousands of people, were rushing on the highway by car and by bicycle. Some highways were blocked by the Germans, so the people tried to escape via Katwijk or Scheveningen on the North Sea coast. The spectacle in Ijmuiden was unbelievable, devastating! Just like the end of the world! The German planes were circling above the sea and shooting at the full boats and we saw people falling into the water. People were clamoring impatiently to escape, offering money and jewelry for a place on a boat. But only a few boats got away. The Ijmuiden harbor was blocked by a liner that had struck a mine and by other ships that were sunk. We did not succeed, we had to come back. We are desperate!''

My father tried to calm them down: ''Maybe the Germans will not be as bad as we anticipate. Holland is a peace-loving country. The people will be treated decently. Holland is not Poland or Austria or Sudetenland. Have faith!''

''How about the Jews,'' Mrs. Prinz retorted. ''You know how Hitler treats the Jews? We come from Germany, we have been through all this before. The burning of synagogues and prayer-books and scrolls of our holy Torah. The special sanctions and regulations were in effect only against the Jews. My God, it is so frightening! To think that we have to suffer again the degradations and persecution. I cannot bear it any longer! What shall we do?''

What could one answer? Her words echoed in the room. ''God,'' I prayed, ''did you hear this? Help us, please, help us.''

The following day we heard that Mr. and Mrs. Prinz were found dead. They had committed suicide.

Many people took suicide as a way out—feeling trapped and not being able to face the future under the Nazi regime.

Toward the end of May 1940 the Netherlands were put under the ''exalted rule'' of a *Reichskommissar* who was under the direct orders of Hitler in Berlin, Germany. Dr. Arthur Seyss-Inquart began his rule at a ceremony that took place at the historic Ridderzaal—the Hall of Knights in The Hague. It was the very place where the Queen used to officially open the States-General of the Dutch government on the third Tuesday in September of each year. In his speech to the Dutch people he promised that our laws and basic rights would be respected. The Dutch would not be obligated to accept the Nazi creed. But he warned the judges, civil servants, and other functionaries to obey the German regime.

Seyss-Inquart, originally an attorney in Vienna, Austria, walked with a limp, but otherwise looked quite ordinary, stocky, of medium height, and wore glasses. He was the man responsible for Austria's *Anschluss* into the German Reich after which he was appointed the Chancellor of Austria. Prior to his coming to the Netherlands he was the deputy Governor General of Occupied Poland. His devotion and servitude to Hitler knew no bounds. The Dutch called him *zes'n quart*—"six'n quarter"—and that, not lovingly.

After a few weeks people resumed their daily activities. Life continued with its necessary routine. The Germans were visible but in those first days and weeks of the occupation they did not make themselves felt to any great extent. Theaters and movies opened. We could see the Germans enjoying themselves in the cafes, restaurants, and nightclubs often in the company of some willing Dutch Nazi sympathizer girlfriends.

We sighed in relief. Could it be possible that the Germans, contrary to their way of behavior in their own land and in other occupied countries, would act like gentlemen here in the Netherlands?

My father's friends, the so-called armchair politicians' club, had a field day. I enjoyed listening to them:

"Maybe it won't be that bad. The Germans need Holland as a base closer to England. They may not harm the civilian population."

"Of course, we hate it, but we have to accept the realities and try to live with them as best we can."

"The Allies will rally together and in no time they will chase out the Germans and it will be all over before long."

"Do you think the Nazis will treat us Jews like the other Dutch citizens?"

They listened to the news from England and were up to date on the political and military situation. The daily broadcasts were the highlights of their present existence and were thoroughly discussed afterwards.

Stores opened up and soon everyone returned to their previous activities, which had been so brutally interrupted.

My father, who owned a drygoods business, immersed himself totally, trying to make up for lost time. For my brothers and myself, it was back to school. I was graduating from high school that spring and I had to pass finals in all subjects. Cramming sessions in mathematics, chemistry, physics, history, geography, Dutch, German, French, and English were my daily diet. I dreamed of blowing up the German armies with Bunsen burners and wiping Germany off the map. Finally, the ordeal was over. I had graduated. Normally this would have been an occasion of great excitement and rejoicing, but under the present war circumstances it was all subdued.

I felt happy—happy and relieved and grown-up suddenly. Awed with the responsibility for my next step in life.

"Why don't you take a well-deserved vacation with your friends? You've worked so hard," my mother suggested.

Amazed, I looked at her. "You think it's safe, with the Germans all around? Oh, it would be wonderful to go to the lakes. Kitty and Sofie would be delighted to join, I'm sure."

I looked at her while she talked to me and it seemed as if I saw my mother for the first time. She was so beautiful, my love for her made me almost ache inside. The oval face with its regular features, surrounded by dark-brown wavy hair. Her nose finely chiseled, under it the sensitive mouth, closing with lips resembling two myrtle leaves. But the most striking were her Garbo-esque and almost shy dark-brown eyes. All this balanced on a swanlike neck. Her slender body moved lightly and softly.

Could she have read my thoughts? Her love for me lit up her face. I was almost embarrassed, for we usually did not display our affection—we felt our love for each other so deeply.

"Look, as long as we can live and enjoy, let's do it. So far nothing has been forbidden. We'll talk it over tonight. Now, help me, please, to pack some food packages to send to the family in Poland. They are worse off than we are at the present time."

The sending of food packages to our grandparents and other relatives in Poland had become a standard procedure in our house. Since the Germans conquered that country and drove all the Jews into ghettos with no means of sustaining themselves, every week my parents sent between seven to ten food packages to Warsaw and Lodz. For two years everything arrived in good order, but then we heard from our relatives that the packages were opened by the Germans and most of their contents were stolen. We tried to secure the safe arrival of the packages by sending them by registered mail, which was much more expensive and required the recipient to sign a card, which was returned to us. We could thus verify the signatures of our relatives.

The whole family was involved in the buying of food, packing, wrapping, addressing, filling out numerous papers, and mailing these packages. We felt we could not eat as long as our relatives did not share with us. My father had many requests for food from noted Rabbis in the ghettos, which he could not refuse.

My brothers and I were in great awe of our father. We loved and respected him immensely and we would not think of doing something of which he might disapprove. He was a handsome and proud-looking man with dark-brown hair and eyes and above-medium stature. His clever personality exuded purpose, strong will, and decisiveness. We felt safe and secure in his presence—we could count on him. People told me I resembled him a lot outwardly. Before marriage he had devoted every waking moment to studying at a talmudical academy and throughout his life he kept on devoting time to his sacred studies whenever he could free himself from business responsibilities, which he took very seriously. When a young man in Poland in his twenties, his zeal, idealism, and love for establishing a Jewish homeland in Palestine led him together with other young Zionists to smuggle themselves illegally into Palestine after having covered half the distance on foot. Palestine was at that time under the British mandate and did not allow free immigration of Jews. Hard physical work and fighting off Arab attacks was the only meaningful way of life for a lover of Zion. He worked very hard, planting orchards and building roads. After a few years he contracted a liver ailment and his family insisted on his returning to Poland.

After his move to Holland he suffered greatly from a feeling of frustration at not having realized his dream to live and work in Palestine. He was always talking to us about going to live there in the future and we were sure that this would be our ultimate goal.

That night we sat together around the table. We closed the

blackout curtains and this closed out the world outside—the enemy. Inside we had the family—the familiar cosy feeling, the Dutch *gezelligheid*, the good talk and togetherness.

My brother Paul, two years my junior, was a high school student. His boyish, good-looking face resembled his mother's. He wore eyeglasses, which hid his dark-brown intelligent eyes. He could do anything he set his mind to, but because mathematics was his forte, he chose to major in engineering, after finishing high school. At the same time he continued his talmudic studies with a private teacher who came to the house.

And the whole family just adored our "Prul," the little one. Jackie was born to my parents after they thought they had finished raising a family. He was the cutest four-year-old, a delicious ball of energy, forever talking and running and busy with everyone and everything. In short he was our playtoy. We all indulged him terribly. I felt much more toward him than a sister. Actually the whole family joined in bringing up Jackie.

"I also want to go to the Reeuwijk Lakes," Jackie implored us, "I want to go with you."

Mother promised to take him to the beach in Scheveningen. It was decided that I could go to Gouda with my friends, where we would rent a few rooms at a farmhouse near the lakes.

"Paul, please come with us," I said. "You can make contact with the boys at the Hakhsharah." This was a farm where the religious Zionist youth groups were preparing and training to become members of an agricultural settlement in Palestine.

Our so well-planned vacation on the Reeuwijk Lakes turned out to be a self-imposed house-detention in a large farmhouse room, because of the constant rain that fell during the entire week.

Between my friends Kitty, Sofie, Iris, my brother Paul, and two of his friends and myself, we consumed loads of food and coffee at all hours of the day and night. We had marvelous discussions to the musical background of records of Shubert's *Unfinished Symphony*, Mozart's *Eine Kleine Nachtmusik*, and *Scheherazade* by Rimsky-Korsakov, which were played ad nauseam on our manually operated phonograph. On the one day we ventured out to go boating we were anxiously aware of the many German soldiers patrolling the area.

But despite the bad weather and anxiety we enjoyed being young and vigorous and looked forward with great anticipation to a self-determined future—the right of every young person.

Would we be allowed to exercise this right under Nazi domination?

3

If we had any illusions that the Germans would continue to refrain from force and threats, and give the impression that they were not so bad, that they were occupying Holland only for military reasons—very soon the increasing clutch of terror shattered that hope.

The *Reichskommissar,* Dr. Seyss-Inquart, appointed Hans Albin Rauter, one of his deputies, to become the "Higher S.S. and Police Chief" for the occupied Netherlands, to be in complete charge of the German security mechanism, including the feared *Gestapo*, the police, the S.D.—the *Siecherheitsdienst*, the security service. Very soon we came to know the feared terror of the *Gestapo*, the German Secret Police, and the "Green Police," a special *Gestapo* unit, so called because of the color of their uniforms.

Even more, if that was possible, we hated the "Black Shirts"—the Dutch N.S.B.—Nazi police of the National Socialist Movement.

The sight of the skull and bones insignia on the Nazi uniforms sent a shiver of fear through all of us. Soon we began to hear of atrocities being committed against innocent citizens by the elite guard of the Nazis, the S.S.—the *Schutz Staffeln*.

The German soldiers marching and singing in the streets in utmost precision and harmony: *"Wir fahren gegen England"*— "We are sailing to fight against England"—evoked bitterness and resentment against the intruders. "Falderie, Faldera, Faldera, ha, ha, ha to you, you hated *MOFFEN*! This was the word we used for the hated Germans.

Father came home incensed: "There is bad news today. The Germans are shipping tremendous quantities of food and cattle off to Germany. You know what this means? Very soon there won't be very much left here in Holland. And furthermore, listen to this. Here is the first blow against us, as Jews: Ritual slaughter is forbidden as of July 31st!"

"But Daddy, you said that they would treat us differently here in Holland," Paul said indignantly.

We knew this decree was but the beginning of more to come.

One day, Jackie came running in with his friend: "You know, the *Moffen* are yelling at Mr. Venema on the Stationsweg, because he has the Dutch red, white, and blue flag in the window of his store. Inside they found a picture of Queen Wilhelmina. We saw him take it all out and then the Germans left. Isn't that right, Manny?"

We could not even display our own national colors or the orange flag of the Royal House of Orange. But the proud Dutch defied that decree by wearing orange flowers on their lapel or dress on the occasion of a birthday of a member of the royal family.

We were forced to read and observe the anti-Jewish decrees on the special bulletins plastered on the walls and in the newspapers. They were especially directed at gradually isolating the Jews from public life. We began to feel that we were being set apart from the rest of the Dutch people.

By the end of September 1940 all Jews were discharged from positions they held in the government and in the municipalities. It was shocking but revealing to us that even a Jewish personality like the president of the Supreme Court, Mr. L. E. Visser, was dismissed.

A stunning blow was dealt to the educational system when in the Dutch universities Jewish professors were ordered dismissed. This action aroused a furor. In Leiden University, Prof. R. P. Cleveringa and two other professors were sent to a concentration camp after they fearlessly expressed their indignation and protested against the dismissal of Jewish professors and students.

In response against the decrees the students went on strike. As a result the German Security Police dissolved the student organizations and imprisoned some professors and students. Leiden and Delft Universities were forced to close. After the closing, Leiden U. did not open again for the duration of the war. It chose not to function at all, rather than to become untrue to the principles of the university that were adopted at her founding in 1573: "Service to free science in a free country."

My plans to continue with my education and my dreams to follow the example of Dr. Albert Schweitzer went up in smoke. What should I do now? Kitty and I discussed this and other problems during one of our long walks in our favorite park, De Haagse Bosjes, a large wooded park area stretching along the outskirts of The Hague, our city. The memory of these walks evoke in me even now feelings of great pleasure and nostalgia. Neither rain nor wind would stop us. We would cut across the busy shopping district in the center of town and the streets filled with many large department stores and numerous elegant specialty shops offering a wealth of goods.

I never failed to become excited at the sight of the ancient government buildings and De Ridderzaal—the Hall of Knights. Alongside was De Vijverberg, a large, square pond with stately swans and quacking duck families gliding by, with islands of trees and spouting fountains lit up at night. Bordering this was a public park area with tall, ancient trees forming a cathedrallike passage.

We would pass the Royal Palace on Noordeinde, now empty. Although an imposing structure, it was an integral part of the street and was not isolated from it, just like the Queen, who showed she was a part of her people and lived close to them.

When we reached De Haagshe Bosjes, our park, we felt we were in our private paradise. We gloried in the different colors and hues of the foliage at the different seasons of the year. The park was structured along a series of ponds of various shapes surrounded by flowers and shrubs connected by quaint little bridges and interspersed with rose gardens. At the very end there stood a small palace of the Queen Mother.

It was a revitalizing experience for both of us because of the quiet and harmony around us. We could think and talk clearly. Kitty and I were much attuned to each other. Our attitude to each other was honest and straightforward, and we had respect for each other's opinions. We had been very close friends for many years and our parents were amazed that we still weren't "talked out." We had many things in common: a mutual love for music, hopes for a future in a Jewish homeland, deep enjoyment of aesthetic things in life, of good and inspiring discussions, and an aversion to the vulgar.

"You could work in an office like I do," Kitty suggested. "I'm not excited about it, but I earn a salary and that comes in handy. How long we'll be able to continue to work is not certain. There are rumors that soon all Jews will have to give up their businesses."

"Kitty, I think there is still time for me to do what I really want most of all. I would like to prepare myself for a life on a collective farm, a kibbutz in Palestine. I want to apply to the Hahkshara, the training farm, and work there. I heard that even now the Hehalutz pioneer movement has ways of getting to Palestine illegally."

"Yes, so I heard too," Kitty said. "As a matter of fact at our next meeting, which will be combined with all Mizrahi [Religious Zionist] youth groups, one of the organizers will speak about this project."

I detect a pensive hesitation. "Are you thinking about it too?," I asked her. "That would be wonderful. We will go together!"

I was carried away by the idea.

"Well it is not that easy. I cannot leave my sister, Iris, here. She would not be able to come because my father needs her in the business. Besides, you know, Mother is not a well person. Oh, you are such a daredevil! Do you think your parents will let you go?"

"You know, Kitty," I answered, "if you don't dare, you don't win, the saying goes. What other alternative is there? What if our fears come true and the *Moffen* start persecuting us physically. You have no idea, how much I want to realize my dream, to help build up Palestine! That's the place where we all should be!"

Kitty jumped up and rays of sunshine filtering through the trees illuminated her deep-set blue eyes and made her blond hair sparkle like spun gold. Laughingly she said: "Nobody will be able to resist you when you talk with such fire and enthusiasm."

As we were leaving the park, a group of German soldiers walking on the other side of the lake started calling to us. The fear of being confronted by them made us run as fast as our feet could carry us. We heard their laughter and shouts: "*Mädchen, schöne Mädchen*" — "Girls, lovely girls."

When we reached the street we managed to lose ourselves among the many pedestrians. Kitty said breathlessly: "We can't walk to the park anymore. It isn't safe. What a close call, they could have come upon us while we were sitting there!"

"Kitty, we were very lucky. They could have shot after us, when we started running." I shivered as I spoke.

In the weeks and months that followed we began to feel what the Germans meant when they stated in the press: "The orders against the Jews are not an interference in internal Dutch relations. They are only directed against the Jews, who are considered enemies of Germany."

A gloom settled over us and we felt that our very existence was threatened. Our earthly possessions, earned by hard work, were confiscated. Suddenly we were made to feel as if we were not entitled to own anything because we were considered inferior. The decrees and orders against us were meant to destroy our pride and self-esteem. In this regard, unfortunately, the Nazis succeeded only too well. To refuse to carry out the Nazi decrees would be at the risk of being punished, imprisoned, or killed. Some Jews tried to evade the decrees but few succeeded. It was the individual Jew against the mighty Nazi military power. With keen psychological precision they gradually stripped us of our rights, our social standing, and our worldly possessions until we were reduced to frightening, hungry, downtrodden creatures with only one instinct—to remain alive, no matter how.

All Jewish businesses had to be registered with the Germans and then the Jewish owners were forced to sell at a pittance of the real value. Real estate owned by Jews was confiscated outright. My father was terribly upset:

"What am I to do? If I don't register the business, it will be liquidated anyway and I'll be punished. But how will we survive without a source of income? My worry is not only for us. We have to continue sending food packages to our relatives in Poland as long as it is permitted. Our rations will not suffice to fill the packages. I must assure myself of an income in order to buy on the black market, which has become terribly expensive."

We had complete faith in Father, for he always knew how to handle a difficult situation. He sold the business to a Gentile friend, Mr. de Groot, with whom he had been associated for some time and who was willing to risk safeguarding some of father's capital.

In October of that year the Dutch Christian churches began protesting against the anti-Jewish measures taken by the Nazis.

The news spread like wildfire. We felt comforted by the fact that the Christian communities cared and were raising their voices against the invaders. Ministers of churches encouraged their congregants to help the Jews.

The situation in the land became increasingly tense. Supplies of vital necessities were becoming scarce and expensive and no hope for improvement was in sight.

At home, despite all this, mother was ready to cope with the difficulties: "As long as they leave us in peace even under these circumstances. So we'll do our own housecleaning if Gentile maids cannot work in our homes anymore. Rika, our maid, is such a good girl and so attached to us. I'm sorry to see her go and I know she, too, is unhappy about the situation."

Little Jackie asked: "Mommy, what will happen to us?" He held her face in both his hands so that she would give him her undivided attention. She hugged him close to her and he did not see the tears filling her eyes as she answered him: "We have to keep faith in God. He will take care of us."

I thought to myself: "Is that all that we can do?"

4

We were listening with rapt attention to the dynamic young speaker at the Mizrahi youth meeting:

"Friends, I am telling you, our last and only hope for survival is to go to Palestine. If we Jews would have been wise enough to learn our lessons from past experiences, we would not have waited until the Nazis conquered Holland and the other Western countries. We would have left long before! Some people still cannot believe that the Nazis are determined to make our lives unbearable."

"Have you heard of the Warsaw and Lodz ghettos? The Nazis are forcing people out of their homes and crowding them together in ghettos under the most deplorable of conditions, slowly starving them to death. There are certain channels of information available to us that tell us what is going on. They speak of deporting Dutch Jews to concentration camps to do forced labor."

The crowd gasped.

"For us here there is still a chance," he continued. "You can leave for Palestine through our Hehalutz movement. We know of illegal ways to smuggle people out of Holland, either through Belgium, France, and Switzerland or through Spain and then to Palestine. What you have to do, and there is still time, is to prepare yourselves for work on a farm so that you can take your place in a kibbutz in Palestine. This is your great chance! You can still do it!"

31

I felt as if every word were directed at me personally. He was pointing to me and directing me to the right way. Surely, if I followed his advice, I could not go wrong. That would be the only way in which to realize my long-cherished dream to go to Palestine. Naturally I had to go! I only had to tell my parents of my decision.

I was sitting there transfixed, deep in thought, determined to carry out the plan suggested by the speaker. As I looked up and gazed across the room, I met a pair of blue eyes belonging to a young man. Our eyes held and held and held. It was as if for the first time in my life I was aware of myself. The blood rose to my cheeks and I shivered. Then I turned my face because tears sprang into my eyes. What was it that I felt? Why did I react that way?

I could not remember what I said or did afterwards. I was not aware of the others in the crowded group of our Mizrahi youth meeting in our clubhouse. It was as if a cloud had picked me up and had isolated me. People talked to me and I heard myself reply, but it was as if I were in a dream. As we went outside he came over to me, his blue eyes fixed on mine: "I am David, I saw you were totally absorbed in what the speaker said. Are you interested in going on Hakhsharah?"

I nodded, unable to bring out a word. David continued to speak, with each of his words falling on me like drops of soft rain. The only thing that penetrated the fog around me was his promise that if I needed more information and help, I should get in touch with him.

I walked home together with a large and talkative group of friends. Kitty noticed that I was unusually quiet.

"Is there anything the matter?," she asked.

"Kitty, I feel a terrible urgency to go and prepare myself for a life in Palestine. That's the right thing for me to do. However, what about my family, my parents, my brothers, Paul and Jackie? I'll have to leave them here in Holland. Maybe Paul would want to go, too. Is fifteen too young? I have such mixed feelings, but of one thing I am convinced. I must go! I cannot think of anything else to do now."

That night at the supper table, still under the glow of that afternoon's experiences, I announced to the family:

"I have decided to go on Hakhsharah now. Within a few months the Movement will find ways to smuggle me into Palestine. They have assured us that there are ways to enter without being detected."

My mother dropped the platter of food on the table and the clatter echoed throughout the room. It was as if I had exploded a bomb. I smiled innocently:

"What's the matter? What did I do?"

My father got up suddenly, his chair noisily scraping the floor. He spoke to me in sharp terms:

"As long as you are in our charge and not married, you will not go alone anywhere. You don't know what it's like for a girl to be all alone in a strange country and to have to work under difficult conditions."

He went on and on, with Mother helping him in her emotional way. But I was determined and the argument that ensued in our house was unbelievable.

"And you call yourself a Zionist," I said, and I knew I hurt him deeply. "I want to help build a country for the Jews so that we will be free and not at the mercy of the Nazis or any other persecutors. I don't want to be afraid anymore. I don't want to be told what to do and what not to do just because I am a Jew."

I felt I could not hold back my tears, I ran out of the room and slammed the door behind me.

The atmosphere in our house became heavy with tension. I no longer talked to my parents. My father walked about with a stern face, and my mother cried constantly. Paul and Jackie did not know whose side to take. It became so depressing in our house that I asked permission to stay with Kitty for a few days. She and her sister, Iris, commiserated with me and we talked all night long.

The confrontation made me very sad and unhappy, especially since it came at a time when new Nazi decrees, issued against the Jews, cut painfully into our social lives. Jews were not allowed in theaters, cafes, or restaurants. All public places had a sign:

"Verboden voor Joden"—"Forbidden for Jews." We were treated like outcasts.

My thoughts of David overwhelmed me with feelings that I had never experienced and whose meanings I did not understand. I yearned to hear his voice again and to be in his company, but I was too shy and proud to get in touch with him. However, a few days later chance brought us together.

The Mizrahi youth movement conducted a leadership seminar and David was the teacher of the Hebrew class for which I had registered. For five years I had studied the Hebrew language privately with a wonderful teacher, Mr. Grabel.

The sight of tall and dark David standing in front of the class made me tremble inside. Under his tutelage I actually started to love the language. After class, David inquired whether there was any progress in my Hakhsharah plans. We started talking and soon we became close friends. The fact that he had studied medicine and played the piano made him even more attractive to me, since I loved and needed music in order to be fulfilled. Also, for some time I had been thinking about making my career in the field of medicine. All these commonly held interests made us gravitate toward each other. I told him about my problems at home, about my determination to go through with my plans for Hakhsharah and then going to Palestine and about my parents' refusal to give me permission.

Suddenly I had lost my shyness. It was such a wonderful feeling of relief to be able to talk so freely and to have his complete attention and sympathy. David encouraged me:

"Why don't you explain the situation to your parents in the same way you related it to me? They surely will see your point and your sincerity."

Nothing would have pleased me more. The strain of being locked in argument with my parents was hard on me. I missed the close affection and love of my parents. I hated the situation as it had developed.

That afternoon I went home and pleaded with my father and mother as if my life depended on convincing them:

"This is my future and my goal. I am already eighteen years of age and I have the right to make my own decision. I want to work the land, to feel the soil of Palestine with my own hands. I want to sense the ground under my feet, to be in the country that belongs to me and my people by virtue of our historic and religious rights. It will be my country, which I am prepared to defend with my life in order to assure its existence. Please, let me go.''

Father still held to the same determined stand. If anything, his opposition was stronger. My mother agreed with him and tried to persuade me:

"When the war is over, we'll all go to Palestine. We promise! It is too dangerous for you to go now. You'll be a girl all alone in the land, with none of your family there. I know what I'm talking about. Life is very hard there. Let's stop this aggravating argument. We have had enough of disagreement. Come dear, give up your plan.''

When I heard these words from my mother, something snapped in me. Excitement and anger began to shake my whole body and tears of frustration and disappointment streamed down my face.

Father, Mother, and I were all talking, shouting, pleading, and crying at the same time.

"This is not a childish prank. You don't believe me, but for the first time in my life I am convinced that this is the right decision for me to take!," I asserted strongly. "I'll go ahead with it anyway, no matter what and you can do nothing to stop me!''

To emphasize my outburst I banged my right fist on the table with all my might and broke a crystal bowl in the process. The pieces of crystal flew about the room and blood from a severe cut in my hand began splashing everywhere. I felt pain and when I saw a piece of bloody flesh hanging from the side of my right hand I almost fainted. Father held me firmly, mother wrapped a towel around my hand, and they took me to the clinic of the nearest hospital where my hand was stitched and my arm put in a sling.

For many days afterwards I was subdued and quiet. My parents were helpful and loving, but did not mention the word *Palestine* again. They understood that it was a sore spot for me, and left it alone. Mother started talking about plans for me to attend medical school after the war, knowing how much I was inclined in that direction. In the meantime she suggested my looking into the possibilities of enrolling in a private school for fashion design. I followed her advice and it turned out to be a very interesting and practical course, especially since clothes were being rationed and the stores had few things to sell.

Thus my first and only resistance to parental authority ended. I had no regrets that the argument had happened and I was still convinced that I was right. However, it hurt me that so much anger had been aroused. I loved my parents deeply and an eruption like this had never occurred before. But I felt that I had established my personality in the family. I was now recognized as a grownup whose opinion was to be consulted. How I loved being part of the family again!

It was important for all of us to maintain the closeness of the family unit, now more than ever, in order to endure the degradations and increasing social isolation that the Nazis imposed upon us with their anti-Semitic propaganda and their ever-tightening sanctions and decrees.

5

"Franklin Delano Roosevelt, a great friend of Holland, has been reelected President of the United States of America! He will make an end to the war!"

My father was excited at the news as he busily discussed politics with his friends who came to listen to the B.B.C. or the Radio Oranje in Dutch, which was forbidden. Anyone caught listening to the news could be deported to workcamps with "destination unknown."

But we took the risk. Father had made a special hiding place for our Phillips radio inside a closet, and we listened constantly. The daily broadcasts from England were the highlights of our shrinking sources of pleasure.

"The British have won a victory in the Libyan desert in North Africa!"

"Mussolini, the Italian ally of Hitler, attempted to invade Greece and failed!"

"Let the Nazis try to cross the Channel now! They have been threatening for such a long time. Now England is ready to meet a German invasion. They are in a much better state of preparedness than ever before. Their bombing missions every night are shooting up the entire Ruhr industry area! Naturally, the Germans claim that the Allies are bombing only nonmilitary, civilian positions and that they themselves attack only military targets. It's all lies! Look at what the Nazis did to London with their bombardments! Because of this, thousands of English children are being shipped to Canada in order to safeguard their lives."

Father kept saying: "The war will be over soon! The Nazis will lose out on all fronts! Roosevelt will come to our aid, certainly to the aid of Britain and France, even if they have not declared war on Germany. We just have to be patient, the best thing is to be inconspicuous and the Germans will leave us alone."

On another occasion he exclaaimed:

"Look at this! I found a mimeographed news sheet in the mailbox. Do you know what it is? News from the B.B.C.! It's printed and distributed by an underground organization. That's what I call daring! If they are ever caught in the act . . . I hate to think of the consequences . . . ."

As a counterpoise to my father's optimism we heard that the mayors of most large cities had been dismissed and replaced with men who were members of the Dutch Nazi party. The Germans started urging unemployed men to go to Germany to work in the armament factories. When they realized that the men were unwilling to go, the Germans began to use pressure by withholding unemployment checks. Even non-Jews started to feel the oppression.

Dockworkers in Amsterdam were accused of sabotage. Many were arrested and there were rumors of forced deportation. Dutch hatred against the Germans, which had started with the invasion, began to grow more deeply and strongly with each passing day.

Our hopes of waiting quietly and inconspicuously until the end of the war were finally crushed with the proclamation of a new system of identity cards. We were required to have a three-part complicated card that contained all our personal data, a photo and fingerprints in two places, a special stamp, and a permanent address. This identity card had to be obtained at a special registration office. Everyone above fifteen years of age had to carry an identity card at all times. Inspections could be conducted at any time on streets, trains, and public places, and anyone caught without his identity card was subject to arrest. Apparently, the Germans were planning something drastic—otherwise why all this identity procedure?

Another very important item that everyone was required to have was a ration booklet. This could only be obtained by presenting one's identity card. This ration booklet contained stamps for food, coal, shoes, and clothing, which were issued either weekly or monthly. As time went on the size of the rations became smaller and smaller as the Nazis continued to rob Holland of its produce and raw materials for civilian and military use in Germany. The Dutch, seeing what was going on, grumbled and cursed but were powerless to stop the vandalism.

In most homes people tried to maintain the normalcy of everyday life. The German and British planes overhead, the sound of antiaircraft, the sirens, the nightly blackouts and curfews became accepted facts and parts of an existence to which they had to adjust as best as they could.

My father was only partially occupied, helping Mr. de Groot, to whom he had sold his business. Mother, like all other housewives, tried to manage her household within the possibilities of rationing and black market. My brother Paul went to high school and little Jackie went to kindergarten.

My time was filled with designing and sewing at the School of Fashion Design and attending the Hebrew seminar sponsored by the Zionist organization.

That was only the tip of my iceberg. The greater part of my being was totally absorbed by a never-before-experienced, dreamy, sweet and strong feeling in connection with David. The sound of the pounding waves of the North Sea on the beach of Scheveningen reverberated within me, on our frequent trips along the boulevard, while fighting the wind and the rain. Above us the fearsome storm clouds, chasing each other, formed a frighteningly magnificent panorama. I felt an exhilaration as never before of being part of the elements, which included David riding beside me. We passed the many outdoor cafes, the exotic restaurants, and the shops that attracted so many visitors during the summer. The stately hotels and beach clubs were empty now.

For security reasons, this coastal area was closely patrolled by the Germans, and before long, we were forbidden to ride along the boulevard, to our great regret. Our beautiful beaches were dug up and studded with ugly and dangerous fortifications that became part of the "Atlantic Wall" stretching for miles along the entire North Sea coast.

David introduced me into a new world of art, philosophy, and music. When his long, sensitive fingers touched the keys on the piano, I felt as if the caresses were meant for me. We talked about the sculptor Rodin and admired his works, while his eyes spoke to me a language of their own. We never touched or even mentioned love, but the unspoken tension between us was stronger than physical contact.

I admired his clear, intelligent thinking and broad knowledge in so many areas. He never became excited, but spoke quietly with authority and tried to logically analyze a problem without forcing his own opinion upon the listener.

At home I was quiet, absent-minded, and lived in a world of my own. My family thought that I was unhappy about not going on Hakhsharah. I was indeed, but that was not what was uppermost in my heart.

Suddenly, there was a change! Everything around me took on vibrant colors. That year, nature was painting with the most glorious hues of fall. David and I were treading softly on the fallen leaves of red, gold, magenta, russet, and green of all shades, drinking in the pungent smell of earth, trees, burning leaves, and cold air. It seemed to me that this was the first time that I experienced fall and I wanted the whole world to be happy and joyful.

But the cruel reality of the times in which we lived slapped me down from the heights of my euphoria.

It was February 1941 and I visited Kitty.

"It has begun," Kitty's father announced with bitterness. "The Nazis are following the same pattern wherever their hob-nailed boots make their bloody course."

"What's the matter?," everyone was talking and asking. Kitty's mother looked pale, I thought she was going to faint. Iris explained: "The Dutch Nazi blackshirts—the N.S.B.—together with the German police have started anti-Jewish riots in the Jewish quarter of Amsterdam. They claim that the Jews shot at them from their windows. This is a lie!"

"Then the Nazi *Moffen* and the N.S.B. ran through the streets smashing windows, attacking people in the streets, dragging Jews from the streetcars, and setting fires to synagogues."

Soon other friends joined us. Kitty's mother was sighing: "*Oy, gevalt*, woe upon us!"

40

"But wait, that's not all," neighbor Mrs. van Houten exclaimed. "The Jews did not allow themselves to be overpowered. At first they were so shocked, that they did not know what to do or how to react. Then, what do you think? They fought back! Not only that, but Dutch Christians joined the battle too. They got hold of some crude weapons and iron pipes and together they fought like savages and chased the N.S.B. away. At night the Nazis came again in even greater force. The Dutch workers from the Kattenburg raincoat factory on the Waterloo plein ran to help the Jewish fighters. Together they defended the Jewish shops. Christian women took care of Jewish children during the fighting.

"It was some battle! The Nazi mob struck again, but again they were fought off by the Jews and their friends.

"Finally the Germans sent in three battalions of police with tanks and automatic weapons and began to fire indiscriminately into the crowd. Unfortunately, there were many killed and wounded. Now the Jewish section is closed off."

We were frightened and astounded at these horrifying developments. At the same time pride flooded our hearts at the fact that the Dutch population was with us. They were helping us — fighting side by side with us and defying the Nazis.

"Do you think this will spread throughout the country?" I asked. "Maybe if everyone joined ranks we could beat the Nazis and push them out of Holland."

"That's wishful thinking," said Kitty's father, "You heard what the *Moffen* did in one section of Amsterdam. You can just about imagine what they would do if the whole population would revolt. They could bomb and devastate the entire country!"

"But at least we would show them that we do not tolerate these brutalities and that we do not submit to this persecution without even lifting a finger!" I was boiling mad.

February 22nd 1941 became known as the black Sabbath. Iris came back, very distraught, from Amsterdam with a grueling report of what had happened there:

"The feared German 'Green Police' again raided the Jewish quarter. In one home the Nazis met with resistance and vitriolic acid was thrown into their faces. In reprisal, Hans Rauter, the higher S.S. and police chief, a villain in love with violence, ordered the arrest of hostages. Over four hundred fine Jewish young men were caught in the streets and forced to kneel there for hours. They had to perform gymnastics on the Waterloo plein, and were brutally beaten while Dutch citizens looked on horrified. Then the Nazis loaded them on to wagons and they were deported.''

The Dutch population became outraged and bitter. The events in Amsterdam brought their anger to the point of explosion. So the Dutch decided to fight back!

Pamphlets were distributed urging a one-day strike in protest at the treatment of Jews. Gentiles were encouraged to help the Jews to resist the Nazis. Dutch workers on their bicycles rang house-bells and stopped cars, calling out:

"We are striking on behalf of the Jews, will you join?" On the main street, the Rokin, the Dutch strikers forced passengers to leave the streetcars.

February 25th, Amsterdam was on strike! Life in Amsterdam came to a standstill while the people of Amsterdam protested!

Employees of the streetcars and the sanitation departments went on strike first. Then the whole city followed. Shops closed, factories emptied, offices were locked, and everyone went home. Newspapers were not published, utilities did not function. The shipyards were deserted, and in the streets of Amsterdam it was quiet. Only the big raiding trucks, the *overvalwagens* of the Nazis' Green Police, drove about in the streets. In the trucks the hatchet men were sitting like ramrods, back to back, their combat helmets tight under their chins, their rifles near their feet, hand grenades tucked into the cuffs of their boots, and another gun on their laps, ready to shoot.

Amsterdam was still.

Rauter was furious. He declared a state of siege and ordered work to be resumed immediately.

But the strike continued and spread to Hilversum, Haarlem, and Zaandam.

The Germans were stunned and perplexed. They had never before experienced such behavior. This was the only time in

Europe that the Gentile population had reacted so violently against the deportation of Jews.

This open demonstration against the Nazis was unprecedented. Rauter sent in his death-head battalions and ordered them to fire mercilessly into the crowds on the streets, thus killing and wounding many innocent people. Soon the strikes and demonstrations were crushed.

Workers were arrested and sent to concentration camps and heavy fines were imposed on the guilty cities.

The following day there was a "notification" by the *Reichskommissar* in all the papers ordering all work to be resumed. All demonstrations, assemblies, and political meetings were banned, and strike instigators would be punished severely.

We felt grateful to the strikers and proud that they had responded so strongly and had fought on our behalf. The entire population gloried in this display of courage and defiance against the enemy.

At the same time the Dutch had witnessed the murderous inhumanity of the Nazi police. The senseless loss of innocent lives discouraged any further open demonstrations.

But if the Germans thought that they had crushed the fighting spirit and morale of the Dutch, they soon found out that they had to deal with the even tougher elements of the Dutch Resistance, which was operating underground.

The harder the barbaric Nazi fist pounded at the suffering victims, the more determined the Dutch became in their solidarity and inventiveness to save the persecuted people.

6

People were confused and worried. They asked:

"Why create another separate Jewish Council—the *Joodse Raad*? We have our Jewish Community Organization in every city with a Rabbi at the head. Where does this leave the Coordinating Committee, representing all Jewish national organizations that already function?"

I, too, asked David:

"What is happening? First we had to register as Jews. Now they have established a *Joodse Raad*, a Jewish Council. What function will it perform that our Jewish Community Organization and the Coordinating Committee cannot perform? I don't understand it."

David replied in his usually clear manner:

"From what I understand, this is how it came about. After the February strike and the bloody fighting, the Germans were infuriated and ordered an 'Advisory Council' to be set up. Mr. Abraham Asscher, the wealthy diamond industrialist, together with Professor David Cohen, who had been professor of ancient history at the Amsterdam University and chairman of the committee for Jewish refugees, met with other Jewish leaders and set up, what became known as the Jewish Council—the *Joodse Raad*."

"The existing roof organization, the Coordinating Committee, could have become the *Joodse Raad*. Why do we need yet another council?," I argued.

44

"That is so true," David agreed. "But their chairman, Mr. L.E. Visser, the very respected president of the Supreme Court of Holland, who was dismissed by the Germans, refused categorically to have any dealings with the Germans. He thinks the *Joodse Raad* will not act on behalf of the Jewish people, but will be a tool of the Nazis in order to harm the Jews. As a matter of fact, as soon as the *Joodse Raad* came into being the Coordinating Committee disintegrated."

"Maybe if Mr. Visser would stay on, he could accomplish more on behalf of the Jews," I said thoughtfully. "But then, we don't know the Nazis yet. I'm afraid that even the strongest of our leaders would have to either submit or resign. It is frightening to think about it. I think we should either escape or fight the Nazis. My father says that the *Joodse Raad* will become the mouthpiece of the Germans!"

"Well, they have to cooperate with the Germans, issue their orders to the Jewish population, and keep law and order in the Jewish communities. They are to be the governing body of all the Jews in Holland, centralizing and deciding all functions and activities. They are supposed to give legal and financial advice, issue permits, organize educational facilities, and supervise the distribution of food. We don't know what else will come, but we are sure of one thing: we cannot make a move without consulting the *Joodse Raad*!" The situation was also getting under David's skin.

I was sitting quietly in the corner on the wide windowsill, listening to an outburst of David's emotions, which he expressed with the help of his piano. He made the tones sound sharp and hard and painful as he played a mazurka by Chopin.

"David, do you see a clear future for the Jews with all the restrictions and regulations?," I questioned desperately.

He looked at me, his facial expression softening while his fingers strung one arpeggio after another, as if he were caressing the notes on the piano.

"Do we have another way out? We have to live day by day and hope that it will be over soon. The Allies will eventually launch an offensive and Hitler will be defeated quickly."

It was so good to listen to him. It seemed as if nothing else mattered. Just being near him made me feel reassured and safe. There was such a vast difference between my two worlds. One world was being with David and the other was a cruel and cold reality that was enforced upon all of us.

Shortly afterwards, another decree was directed against Jews: "Jews are forbidden to go to the movies." "Well," my father joked, "at least the Nazis are doing their best to promote better family relations. Instead of going to the movies we'll spend our time with the family. We'll learn together, talk and play. It should not ever be worse!"

My mother expressed her favorite proverb: "When you get used to suffering and misfortune, you live with it in peace. We can do without going to cafes and restaurants and movies. We'll even give them our radios, which they requested we turn over to them—we can get used to all that, if only they would leave us in peace."

Of course, my father did not give the Germans our hidden radio. Instead he brought them an old radio that no longer worked.

The official radio broadcasts and newspapers were all Nazi-oriented, thoroughly one-sided and unreliable and full of lies and propaganda.

That night as my father entertained his friends in the back room with the news from England, the family had to stand guard to watch for N.S.B. traitors who were out to catch Jews with hidden radios. Paul was in the hall listening at the front door for footsteps outside the street. Mother was posted in the kitchen, ready to intercept his signal in order to forward it to the backroom. I had to be with the group in order to help translate the B.B.C. broadcast from English into Dutch. In case of suspected, unwanted visitors the radio could be returned to its special hiding-place within seconds.

Soon the news came on:

"The United States is helping the war effort of the Allies as much as possible without being in the war officially. She is making her production available for the democracies. Many new arms factories are being built to supply the Allies' armed forces."

"The English are victorious in North Africa, Benghazi has fallen and the Italians have been pushed back."

"Here in Holland eighteen hostages have been shot on charges of espionage and sabotage against the Germans."

"The Battle of Britain is on! The English are bombing strategic installations in Germany."

"The Balkan States are entering the war. They are now being invaded by the Germans and Italians."

After the broadcasts there were always heated discussions and speculations as to the outcome of the war. Most of the news was not promising and usually I would leave the room in a state of depression and fear.

I went to my room to try to get away from it all. On my way home I had treated myself to a big bunch of yellow daffodils, which I had arranged in a vase on my desk. I cranked up my record player, put on a Bach record, closed the door and fell onto my bed. I lay there, letting the music wash over me. In my line of vision were the tender and tall yellow daffodils, catching the light of my favorite delft-blue tablelamp. They stood there so beautifully, wearing their crowns with pride. I could not take my eyes away from this scene of perfection—the miracle of nature, the harmony of music, and the feeling of peace. A prayer of thanks for experiencing such beauty welled up in me:

"This is real life, not the ugliness outside! Oh God, when will this be over? I want to do so many things yet. I still want to see so much of the world we live in, I want to find my place in it. I want to do so much and leave something worthwhile behind."

I heard a modest knock on my door and Paul entered. Mother's birthday was approaching and we planned to surprise her with a nice present. It was very difficult to select a suitable gift, because after several shopping expeditions we had found everything to be so expensive. The only people who could afford it were the Germans, who bought up everything in sight. We ended up buying her a beautiful scarf.

Paul was worried about something else: "We were talking about it in school. There are a lot of people unemployed. Even more now that the army has been demobilized and many Dutchmen are forced to work in Germany. Do you think they will send Jews, too?''

Jackie came in and in one second he stirred up a storm. We roughed him up playfully to his great delight until Mother put him to bed.

We were very busy with our ongoing project of sending packages to our relatives in the Warsaw and Lodz ghettos in Poland. Communication with them was not regular and sometimes even in the open postcards we could read hidden meanings. One message was very disquieting to us. My uncle wrote:

"Our friends are going on a visit to Uncle Joseph." We knew that Uncle Joseph had been killed in Palestine during the Arab riots in the twenties. Did this mean people were being killed?

"Well," said my father, "as long as the signed red card is returned to us confirming receipt of the food package, we know they are alive and we will continue sending food, especially now before the Passover festival."

It became difficult to send all our packages from one post office. New instructions limited the sending of only one package per person a day from a particular post office. We had to run around to various neighborhoods in order to send the usual quantity every week.

In 1941 we celebrated the first Passover of the war. Mother amazed us all. Even in a time of rationing and shortages of so many items she prepared a wonderful holiday feast. I helped her whenever I could because we had no help in the house. Although Passover required a great deal of physical effort in cleaning and preparing, it was my favorite holiday. I loved the sight of the clean curtains all over the house, the smell of the waxed floors. The unpacking of the special Passover dishes was a yearly delight.

The bouquet of cooking chicken soup, borsht, and the baking of sponge cakes was a very special one. My father's annual job was grating the horseradish, (the bitter herbs for the seder plate), which he did with zeal while the sharp aroma induced tears to stream down his face.

Everyone in the family had a job to fulfill and there was that atmosphere of joy and anticipation in the air—of knowing that we would sit down to a wonderful family seder ceremony, which commemorates, with its many ceremonies, the religious celebration and observance of Passover.

We tried as much as possible to camouflage our feeling of trepidation and insecurity in order not to interfere with the spirit of the holiday. Even before we sat down to the seder ceremony the house shook and windows rattled with the drone of waves after waves of English planes on their way to bomb Germany. We could see the searchlights and we heard the staccato shots of the antiaircraft installations.

Although we did not get a new spring wardrobe as was customary in past years, everyone was dressed in fine clothes in honor of the festive occasion. Mother promised us:

"This year we will let the hems down and wash and iron everything neatly. Next year, with God's help, when the war will be over, we will buy everything new."

The presence of my little brother Jackie, his youth, joyfulness, and innocence regarding the war situation, helped us overcome the great sadness we all felt when we remembered the Passovers celebrated in peace in years past. For his sake mostly, we pretended cheerfulness, as we recited and sang from the Haggada. With joy we anticipated my father's traditional explanations of every part of the story of Passover. His spirit caught us up with him, as he related God's redemption of the Jewish people from the bitterness of slavery in Egypt and assured us that with His help we will be freed from the yoke of the Nazi invaders and we will live again in peace. And when, at the end of the seder we all sang "Next year in Jerusalem," we all felt it deeply with all our hearts. Father came over to me after we finished and hugged me. Did he feel guilt because he had interfered in my plans to go to Palestine or did he see my sudden tears? It did not matter anymore—it comforted me to feel his love.

Our family unit and our circle of friends were the only centers in which one could experience real sociability. Since our entertainment depended on our own inventiveness, our world became more and more limited. All this, as a consequence of the special Nazi decrees against the Jews in Holland.

"Now we have more time to enjoy our philosophical discussions," remarked Bram, one of the members of an intellectual discussion group to which I belonged. We met weekly in each other's houses, where we read and discussed the author Achad Ha'am's *Al parashat drahim (At the Crossroads)* under the guidance of a learned teacher or professor. The stimulus and enjoyment provided by these sessions lasted from meeting to meeting.

The Hebrew seminar, which offered a variety of courses, proved to be most popular. Participants studied diligently and applied themselves most seriously.

There was no point to recalling "the good old times"—we were too realistic for that. We tried as best as we could to adjust to the situation and to make our daily lives bearable physically and mentally within the limitations of the decrees. But no sooner did we become accustomed to a new way of life, when the Nazis cruelly imposed new decrees upon us.

The latest one struck at the professionals. Jewish doctors and dentists could treat only Jewish patients. Jewish lawyers and druggists could have only Jewish clients. Jews were forbidden to be members of the Stock Exchange.

Under these conditions how could we survive economically? The Nazis expressed it openly:

"The Jews are not part of the Dutch people. They are the enemy, they must be destroyed."

Any Dutchman who was not for the Germans was automatically considered to be against them.

The Dutch became increasingly bitter. Their wonderful way of life was being disturbed. The Queen and the government had been driven out. The repeated promises *Reichskommissar* Seyss-Inquart announced to preserve the Dutch national tradition and her form of government turned out to be a pack of lies. The country was being plundered of everything of value. Dutch workers were being sent to work in Germany as slave laborers. Staple items were either rationed or not available at all. There was the constant blackout and curfew; streetcars ran only until dark. The bombing and dogfighting between English and German planes overhead continued to shatter our nerves.

All this, one year after Germany had so brutally and unexpectedly invaded Holland. Sadness and resentment were felt throughout the country.

How long could this continue unavenged?

7

One morning we woke up to some exciting news that spread like wildfire:

"Rudolf Hess, the second in line-of-command after Hitler, has fled to England. He parachuted down near Glasgow!"

"Is it true?," people exclaimed hopefully. "Is there some great change taking place in Germany? Is Hess about to betray the German plans to the English? Is there a rift in the German camp?"

"You'll see, they are going to kill each other! The war will be over soon. Did you hear that Hitler and von Ribbentrop have fled Germany?"

Such wishful thinking!

From the B.B.C. newscast we heard the sad news that:

"The Germans have bombed London and damaged Big Ben, Westminster Abbey, and the Parliament Buildings."

"The Balkan States, including Greece and Yugoslavia are in German hands. They have bombed Belgrade to ruins."

"Our only hope is the United States. For all intents and purposes they are already in the war," my father insisted. "The U.S. has closed the German Consulates, the German library, and the travel agencies in New York in order to put a stop to German propaganda. In Germany and the occupied countries they have terminated U.S. consular services. There is no better proof that they are planning to enter the war on our side."

The spring of 1941 was a very cold one with people still

huddled around stoves in warm clothes contemplating whether they would have enough coal to heat their homes next year, if the war would continue another winter, God forbid.

The Nazis, however, had vacations and good times in mind, when they came out with their new plans for the Jews. From now on we were forbidden to attend public bathing clubs, public parks, and races. We were not permitted to rent rooms in any hotels, pensions, and boarding houses in vacation areas.

Kitty and I were frustrated and angry.

"Farewell to vacations and good times at lakes and beaches! Goodbye to beautiful times at our favorite park! Do we contaminate the air with our very presence?" Kitty exploded in anger.

"We are as healthy and clean as anyone else and not any different. What do they want from us?" I felt deep resentment that such simple pleasures were being denied to us. This was another strategy for completely isolating us from the outside world.

Although these infringements on my personal freedom angered and frustrated me and curtailed my movements to a minimum, still my inner feelings soared, blossomed, and awakened with my newly found world of love and emotion.

I had never before seen spring so beautiful and majestic. The sprouting green shrubs and trees had never been so tender in their early growth. The wonder of budding flowers had never before brought out my tears of gratitude for witnessing God's miracle of creation. The smell of earth and rain evoked within me a feeling of deep yearning that was both painful and delirious.

During one of our many bicycle outings, David presented me with a print of Rodin's sculpture, *La main de Dieu (The Hand of God)*—a strong, slim, alabaster hand rising up from a marble pedestal, holding within its palm a slab of marble, engaged in the process of the creation of mankind. I was touched by its symbolism, beauty of form, and realism of sculpture.

While completely absorbed by it, I suddenly picked up David's hand and said:

"You know, I was wondering why this hand on the print was

so familiar to me. It resembles yours. Look, it is also slim, long, strong, and tender. *La main de David* I shall call it—the hand of David.''

I felt David taking my face in both of his hands, we looked at each other for what seemed an eternity. I felt our heartbeats join through his fingers in an almost earshattering crescendo. I saw his lips forming the words "Thank you." Then the moment was gone. It was the first time he touched me.

This was my world. Nobody could take it away from me, nobody could intrude into this sweet privacy. I was suspended, at one with the universe.

That mood was still with me when I was called by my father to assist in translating the latest B.B.C. broadcast. But my mind was not on the news:

"What are they saying? Come now, it sounds important. Please concentrate. What's the matter with you?" My father was impatient with me, and after listening intently I reported:

"Germany has attacked Russia. The German armies are waging an offensive on a front 3,000 km. long from the borders of Finland to the Black Sea. Churchill has promised to help Russia; they'll bomb Germany day and night."

My father's friends of the armchair "war council" became excited. This news was like new fuel added to the fire of their imaginations.

"Well, if Hitler is fighting the Russians, the invasion into England is probably postponed for this year. And with the U.S.A. getting stronger all the time, he'll never make it to England. Thank God for that."

"Can you imagine the nerve, to attack Russia, after they signed a nonaggression pact? Not that Russia is such a great friend of ours but as of now, they are on the side of the Allies."

As the battle progressed we heard how strongly the Germans were forging ahead into Russia on their way to Moscow, Stalingrad, and Kiev. While the Russians were withdrawing they destroyed and burned everything behind them, forcing the Germans to resupply their armies from Germany and not from their spoils in Russia.

54

The Germans called this outrageously criminal. But when they did the same thing it was for the sake of the war effort.

Evidently there was a great lack of raw materials in Germany, because in Holland everyone was forced to hand over objects made of copper, tin, bronze, nickel, and lead.

"I bet you all this is going to be smelted down and recycled into weapons to be used against the Allies." Paul was figuring out. "Our copper vase may kill one of our friends. Mother, I am against handing over anything to the Germans. Let's bury it. Let it rather get corroded in the ground, as long as it doesn't get into the hands of the Nazis."

Father agreed: "First they want all our gold coins, now this."

"Next they'll demand silver. They are robbing the nation of all goods. I also heard they are sending Dutch boys to fight at the Russian front. Why don't they recruit their loyal followers, the N.S.B.ers? Let them fight! They are only a small percent of our population, yet these Nazi-minded Dutch sympathizers are a danger to our freedom. Sometimes they even try to outdo the Germans. They curse Churchill, Roosevelt, and Stalin as being representatives of capitalism, the Jews, and communism all at one and the same time. That is some combination!"

If the Jewish population were appalled and frustrated by their gradual segregation, isolation, and confiscation of their properties imposed by Nazi decrees, their fears of impending doom grew even stronger when in July 1941 a letter "J" had to be entered on the identity card of every Jew.

The B.B.C. reported one depressing piece of news after another. "The Japanese have occupied Indo-China. The German *Moffen* have broken through the Stalin line."

Now my father's friends were not in the mood to sit in council and discuss the war. It became increasingly apparent that more serious things were being planned for us by the Nazis.

Business associates of my father were in constant touch discussing the situation, advising each other about finances; but ultimately everyone had to decide for himself.

It was a black day for every Jewish breadwinner when we were informed that all bank accounts were frozen and Jews had to deposit all stock and bonds, all valuables, and foreign currency at the firm of Lippman & Rosenthal, who were to handle this spoliation for the Germans.

"How can we live on fl.250 a month? That's all they will allow us to draw from our frozen bank accounts! Without money we are lost altogether!"

Father must have made some arrangements financially because we were still sending food packages to our relatives in the Polish ghettos of Warsaw and Lodz.

People found all kinds of devious ways to hide their valuables, so that they would not fall into the hands of the Nazis.

One night our family became involved in an important project. Father owned a fine library of talmudical books. Only sheer desperation prompted him to make use of the beautiful, large, thick, leather-bound volumes for other than learning purposes. Very gingerly he opened the leather covers, slit a pocket lengthwise in the thick cardboard and then inserted stock certificates of Anaconda and Bethlehem Steel and some American dollar bills. It required skill to stretch the leather over the edges and to paste it to the inside page so it would look untampered. Father instructed all of us to memorize the numbers of the stock certificates and to reclaim them after the war, in case the books were lost.

It was the first time that we had ever done something against the law and we all felt like conspirators. Later on, we heard that everyone hid money and valuables.

We became more and more depressed as we realized that the war was not going to end so quickly. The Germans were now bombing Moscow and Japan was becoming more brazen with each day.

It was only when I was with David that my mood changed. His music worked wonders for me and as he played my obstinate and unhappy feelings gradually disappeared and I calmed down. I felt so at ease with him. Our souls touched and we found comfort in each other's presence, no matter how much pressure was imposed on us from the outside world.

He was playing the beginning of Beethoven's *Fifth Symphony*, which had become the symbol of freedom and victory. The first four notes of this symphony and the "V" for victory were synonymous with Churchill's sign that promised a sure victory for the Allies and freedom from oppression for all of us.

"David, why are Roosevelt and Churchill meeting, now, somewhere in the Atlantic Ocean? What's all this talk about the Atlantic Charter?"

I just had to ask, for I was convinced that he knew everything. Indeed, in his analytical and precise manner he explained to me:

"The purpose of this three-day conference is to discuss a constructive plan for cooperating against Nazi and Japanese aggression. America and England are not at war to achieve territorial gains for themselves, for they have agreed upon restoring freedom to conquered lands. Each nation has the right to self-government and self-determination. They are committed to freedom of the seas and to the destruction of Nazi terror, so that people may live without fear. They want to put an end to threats and oppression and to bring about a full and lasting peace. This can only happen when the Axis nations, Germany and Japan, will be totally disarmed."

"Oh, David, it would be Utopia, but it sounds so far away. Perhaps their decision will be the beginning of action for peace and of a promising future for us all! Will it come soon?"

He did not answer right away, but lit his pipe and looked out the window into the rain-drenched street.

"Do you know what damage this rain is doing? The harvest is rotting on the land. It will create even greater hardships; next winter will be a hard one. Our country, which has provided so well for us, has now become lean and poor. Will the war be over soon? *Ach meisje*, dear girl, let's hope so. So far the Allies are good at talking. And in the meantime, we Jews are treated like pariahs by the Nazis." I had never heard him speak so bitterly and it affected me deeply.

"It cannot go on forever! After the war we will be free people again. In the meantime we'll make the best of our situation and live quietly and inconspicuously, so that the Nazis won't pick on us. David, we will live through it, no matter what obstacles will be put in our way!"

I went over to him and very naturally he put his arms around

57

my shoulders. My head rested on his chest. I was overcome by emotion, by a mixture of excitement at his close proximity, and by the utter misery and helplessness we felt. I didn't dare move, it was almost unreal. I wanted to remember this forever. But I had to go. David helped me with my raincoat—tying my belt. I had the feeling he didn't want to let me go. Finally we said goodbye. We shook hands with warmth and deep affection and we promised to see each other soon.

The members of the Jewish community were still licking the wounds inflicted upon them by the financial calamity when a new Nazi decree struck at their educational system. Jewish children were no longer permitted to attend public schools and Jewish teachers were forbidden to teach there. The *Joodse Raad* was instructed to organize separate schools for the Jewish children in which Jewish teachers would teach, as part of a separate Jewish system of education.

My mother tried to see the positive factor of the situation: "We have some excellent Jewish teachers and the students will not be deprived of a good education. Maybe it's all for the best. It will be possible to impart some positive Jewish values to students who are not consciously Jewish. This presents a great challenge to our religious teachers and students to influence and help those who need spiritual guidance in times like these. There is a great job to be done and I hope they'll succeed."

The nightly crossings of the English bombers continued. Their droning noises, the antiaircraft firing and dogfights of the fighter-planes kept us awake and nervous for many an hour. The Germans complained in the newspapers that the English had bombed hospitals, churches and schools, while the Germans only hit military targets, ammunition factories, and harbor installations.

A terrible restlessness took hold of me as I became aware that something was missing. I had not heard anything from David for a number of days.

"I'll wait a while longer until I call him," I thought. "He must be busy and that's why he can't come to see me."

My powers of concentration on my studies went down to zero,

but I did not want to reveal my apprehension to my friends and my family.

One night after the B.B.C. newscast one of father's friends mentioned:

"Did you know that David and his family have left? They smuggled themselves to Switzerland. They must have arrived there safely, otherwise we would have heard to the contrary.

"After the financial freeze and the printing of a 'J' on the identity card, many more people are trying to run away. They make contact with a smuggler who finds a place to cross the heavily guarded border illegally between Holland and Belgium. They either stay there in hiding for a few days or they go on to France after crossing another dangerous border. Once in Paris they have to find the right person to show them the way to cross the most difficult border into neutral Switzerland. Sometimes the Swiss police refuse entry into Switzerland and send the people back into the Nazi hell, after they have successfully managed to overcome all the dangerous obstacles up to that point. It is a very risky undertaking, not to mention the fee of the smuggler and other expenses."

The room slowly started to spin around me. I heard a whistling in my ears and the words of the others began to fade away. I was conscious of groping my way into my room.

"How was it possible that he did not tell me? Why didn't he mention a thing about it? He didn't even say goodbye to me!"

I fell down on my bed, and held the pillow to my face, rocking in grief, disappointment, and utter unhappiness.

The questions tumbled around and around in my head. I could think of nothing else. The impact of David's leaving was like an unexpected physical blow below the belt.

My family was not aware of my deep feelings for David and did not realize what I was going through. I tried to behave as usual. My pride, although hurt, sustained me and prevented me from weakening and giving in to self-pity. The nights were the most difficult and I hated going to bed knowing that I would go through the familiar agony of trying to cope with unanswered questions.

"Didn't David trust me? Didn't he know that I wished him only the very best in life and that I would have encouraged him to flee into safety? I would rather be punished than give away a secret. Why had he been afraid to tell me? Didn't he feel close enough to me? Perhaps I had read too much into our friendship. But I couldn't be wrong in that respect! I had felt the love, tenderness, and concern for me in his eyes, in his words and in his whole behavior. No, I could not possibly have been mistaken about that!"

I trusted my sensitivity and my keen perception as I would a most accurate instrument. Even a slight hesitation in his feelings toward me would have made me shy away and withdraw immediately. "Could it have been his parents who strictly forbade him to mention their departure to anyone? Perhaps he didn't know until the last minute."

I thought to myself: "How would I have reacted if I were in his position?"

The rush of emotion at the thought of leaving him assured me that I would have moved heaven and earth in order to see him and talk to him just once more.

The days passed in agony and the nights were tortured. I knew that this was no way to live but I could not shut off my mind and feelings from him as yet. My heart pounded when I saw a tall, dark person walking in the street. I was sure it was David. A feeling of weakness overcame me each time I heard a piano playing, and I was touched to tears.

The reality of life demanded immediate action. This was no time to nurse my pain. I felt cold and empty inside. My feelings for David and our friendship had formed a soft, defensive bumper against the hard knocks that the Nazis had administered to us. The impact now was hard and raw.

"How will I make it on my own?"

8

"For the safety and protection of the Dutch population the following activities are forbidden to Jews: to visit a museum, to stay in hotels, to eat in restaurants, to use a sleeper-berth on a train, to eat at a stationcounter or to buy at a marketplace."

My father read this proclamation with mounting indignation. "For the protection of the Dutch people! We have been living side by side peacefully and amicably in this country for centuries. What a way to put it!"

Mother tried to calm him down. "Don't get so angry, dear, it won't help you. Those *Moffen* will say it anyway they want it. The Dutch people, too, are incensed about what the Nazis are doing to us. I only pray that they should not break up the family! For as long as we stay together here, we'll manage. We don't need hotels and restaurants and we can do without a museum until the war is over. Oh God, let's only stay together! So long as the Nazis will leave us in peace we'll make do with the minimum."

Paul told us about the Jewish high school he was attending. The *Joodse Raad* had organized it and it seemed to be satisfactory. Jackie was in kindergarten for the first time and he enjoyed it to the full. I registered for the second term in the School of Fashion Design, but since there were no materials available, we redesigned old dresses into skirts or combined two old dresses into one. My interest in the course declined as our Jewish misery increased. The leadership seminar sponsored by the Zionist organization had been terminated the previous spring and had not been resumed.

We dreaded the approach of cold winter, for we knew that the Germans had shipped away the coal we needed to warm our homes. The B.B.C. called on people to move out of the military target areas that were being bombed in Rotterdam. Some people slept outside the city to avoid the nightly danger, while others moved out permanently.

It was amazing to see how people were bearing up under the gradually increasing hardships and difficulties. It was a constant but gradual process that prevented us from realizing how much we were actually suffering, how much we were giving up, and ultimately what little resistance we were offering.

The underlying reason for this lack of awareness was the fear of punishment that was held over our heads in case we did not obey the decrees to the letter. Many, like my mother, kept praying:

"As long as we can be together. So we'll eat less and we won't go to the theater and other entertainment, but we will live through it until it ends and I hope to God the end will come soon."

People started reading the Jewish weekly published by the *Joodse Raad,* which informed us of the details of the Nazi decrees.

Once, Jackie asked father: "My friends were talking about a concentration camp. What is that? Are people going on vacation to Buchenwald camp? Where is it?"

How could father answer his question? None of us knew exactly what was the fate of the people who were sent to a concentration camp. We knew that Westerbork was a transit camp in Holland near the German border. We also heard of Vught, Amersfoort, Ommen, and the "Orange Hotel" prison in Scheveningen. Also that postcards were received from the hostages who had been taken to Mauthausen during the February demonstrations. Later on, their relatives received notices that they had died of "pneumonia" and they could collect their ashes for fl. 75 from the *Gestapo.* Did they really die of "pneumonia"?

One day there was an announcement of the opening of a "Central Office for Jewish Emigration" headed by Captain Aus der Funten in Amsterdam. Did this mean we could get out of

Holland and go where we wanted? Or was it the beginning of some new developments for the Jews?

At the Mizrahi youth meeting a light and joyful note was injected by our friend Nettie Weil:

"Something remarkable happened in Amsterdam. I am very excited about it. At the initiative of the Jewish community, the Hollandse Schouwburg is being used as a Jewish theater where dismissed Jewish artists give concerts and performances only for Jewish audiences and where they are permitted to play music by Jewish composers only. I attended a concert and it was really wonderful. You must go and see it, too, to believe it!"

Her report gave our meeting an appropriate opportunity to discuss the resilience of the Jewish people. Elie deJong, one of our most dynamic leaders, encouraged us:

"This is an example to be followed everywhere. If the Nazis forbid us to participate in public cultural events, we will organize our own. You just read that Jews are not permitted to belong to certain public organizations and societies. True, that is sad. But instead we will form our own Jewish societies. The Nazis will not defeat us spiritually. We will draw on our own rich cultural resources and our own wonderful teachings. We are proud of the many Jewish people who have labored, created, and contributed to the arts and sciences of the world. Our history with its tradition of strength and perseverance during the difficult times of adversity and oppression is a shining example for us now. The Nazis will not break us with their decrees. They may isolate us from public life, but we will live a cultural life until the war's end."

We had many such wonderful, idealistic meetings of the Mizrahi group and they helped us muster our courage for the moment. We never talked precisely about the future, we only mentioned hopefully "when all this is over . . . ."

That year, the High Holidays of Rosh Hashana and Yom Kippur were indeed solemn Days of Awe; and prayers were never uttered so fervently, so urgently, and so pleadingly. Young and old stood together in the synagogue, as never before, to express belief in the Almighty and to beg for salvation from tyranny.

"Heavenly Father, heed our cry. Accept our words, our fervent prayer. Lord, forsake us not, we pray, nor leave us . . . ."

"On New Years' day the decree is inscribed and on the Day of Atonement it is sealed; how many shall pass away and how many shall be born; who shall live and who shall die; who shall perish by water and who by fire; who by hunger and who by thirst; who shall have rest and who shall go wandering . . . ."

"Our Father, Our King, annul the cruel designs of those who hate us . . . ."

"Our Father, Our King, frustrate the counsel of our enemies . . . ."

"Our Father, Our King, destroy the power of every oppressor, and adversary. Silence the mouths of those who accuse us falsely . . . ."

We understood the meaning of our prayers with our bodies and souls. We cried out of the depths of our misery:

"Our God and God of our fathers, sound the great Shofar for our freedom . . .!"

Freedom? While Hitler lashes out against the "international" Jew as the most dangerous instigator to revolution?

Freedom? When our right to travel has been taken away from us and we must apply for a permit from the Germans every time we want to travel out of town?

Freedom? When Jewish clothing shops and stores selling silver and gold were forced to close down and sell their inventory to the Germans at a loss?

Everywhere there was so much damage and destruction; so much suffering and agony.

"God help us! We need You so!"

While we expressed the hope that we would meet again in peace, we wondered whether we would be together again next year, at this time.

During the following few weeks we heard that young Jewish men were being taken to prison and then deported to Germany. Young Jews no longer ventured out into the streets. Many slept at their Gentile friends', because the Germans would come to their own homes and take them out of bed.

Rumors spread that many of the deported young men had died

after a few months due to the medical experiments the Nazis tried out upon them and due to the miserable working conditions in the tin and mercury mines to which they were sent.

This news shook our family terribly. We were so afraid for Paul.

The Germans ordered all the Jewish people from the provinces to leave their homes and to move to Amsterdam, where they were forced to live in close quarters in special ghetto sections of the city.

The familiar sounds of the street—the noise of the traffic, the churchbells ringing out the hour and the half-hour, the calls of the fishmonger, the window-washer announcing his services, the music of the street organ were now intermixed with the frightening echoes of speeding Nazi trucks sounding their sirens and with the pounding of hobnailed German boots.

One evening Father came home so excited that he could hardly wait until the time for the B.B.C. news. His friends assembled. They too had heard snatches of some disquieting news that they found impossible to believe. Finally, we all listened to our hidden radio:

"Japan has attacked Pearl Harbor in a sudden surprise attack!

"The U.S.A. is at war with Japan and also with Germany!

"Hong Kong and Singapore have been bombed by Japan. Many ships have been sunk and many lives lost. The damage is unbelievable."

We were heartbroken. "Now it's a world war! Almost every nation is involved. The war will not be over so quickly!"

"What a cowardly and outrageous thing to do! The Japs are just as vicious as the Nazis!"

It seemed that we passed from one calamity to another. The latest decree was that we were forbidden to send packages to our relatives in the Warsaw and Lodz ghettos. We feared the worst for them, especially since we had not received their acknowledgements. I could see how this affected my parents. My mother would not eat and was losing weight.

"What will happen to them?," she worried. "How will they survive the war without the little extra food?"

My father looked as if he carried a very heavy burden. There was no mail from the ghetto and we could not find out what was happening there.

The only slight ray of light in that darkness was the fact that the Russians had withstood the German attacks. The German armies had started to withdraw from the frozen Russian front, leaving weapons and supplies behind and suffering great losses.

My friendships with Kitty and other girls sustained me to some degree. Each one was occupied with personal problems and tried to make the very best of the situation under the circumstances. Our Mizrahi youth organization met in small groups in secret in different people's homes since it was not advisable to have large meetings.

At night we sat around our large, coal-burning stove in the kitchen and economized on the use of coal and gas. Mother could cook on the stove at the same time we kept warm. Despite the blackout and our fear of Germans and the droning of the bombers overhead, it felt wonderful to be together so intimately. We were totally dependent upon each other.

The appetizing smell of food, the gleaming hot stove, the feeling of concern we all had for each other created an island of infinite sweetness and belonging.

We talked about Paul's safety: Should he hide in Holland or should he try to escape to Switzerland in order to avoid the workcamps in Germany and Poland?

I, too, wanted a change. I was disenchanted with the School of Fashion Design and I felt I wanted to do something more constructive. An idea began to germinate in my mind.

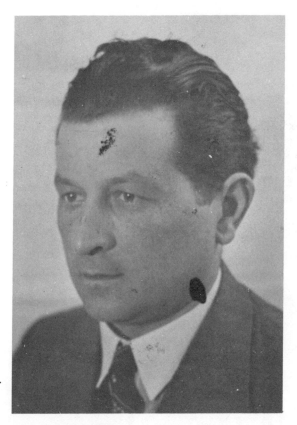

Father, 1941.

Mother, 1941.

67

My brother Paul, 1941.

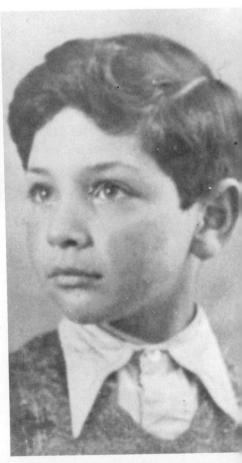

My little brother Jackie, 1942.

Leesha, 1941.

My yellow star with ''Jood,'' Jew, within. It had to be worn on the left side of each garment.

My friend Jules Godefroi, engineer in the Jewish Invalid Hospital. He was involved in rescue work and underground activities in the hospital.

9

In early 1942 I applied for the position of a student nurse at some of the Jewish hospitals in Amsterdam, in order to salvage some of my hopes to serve in the medical profession. I received a positive answer from the Joodse Invalide Hospital, which served the needs of invalid and chronically ill patients and I was asked to report for training in early April. Both my parents and I were overjoyed, since becoming a nurse was the fulfillment of my prayers at that moment. My friends, too, were happy for me, because they knew how much this move meant for me.

It was to be my first flight from the security and protection of my parental nest and I would be achieving an independence that my friends envied. Little did I know that this severance of the umbilical cord would be so final. Little did I dream that I would never again feel the loving warmth of my home and the protective wings of my parents: I wanted so eagerly to flee the security of my home in order to strike out on my own.

De Joodse Invalide (The Jewish Invalid) Hospital, was located in the Jewish section of Amsterdam on the Weesperplein. The narrow street leading to it was the Jodenbreestraat, which was intersected by canals and bridges and which was the nerve center of the Jewish quarter. On it there were many stores and stands where Jews were allowed to shop during the day at assigned hours. But at night, after the eight o'clock curfew, the streets were empty. The Germans concentrated as many Jews as possible from outlying districts, neighboring cities, and villages into this area and it was one of the sections of the Jewish ghetto in Amsterdam.

The day finally came when I had to report. As I approached the hospital building, I was impressed by its modern, all-glass facade shimmering in the sunlight. The heavy valise and other packages I was carrying did not dampen my rising excitement. For the first time in my life I was aware of a cold and unknown future staring me in the face, something that I would have to meet on my own.

I entered the lobby and was referred to the hospital director, Dr. J. H. Buzaglo, who made me welcome and explained the procedures I would have to follow. I was then introduced to the head nurse, Sister Oppenheimer, who assigned me to the third floor, where I was to work under the division head, Sister Hartog.

I unpacked my valise in the nurses-in-training quarters on the sixth floor, with its rows of single- and double-decker beds, and tried to stuff all my meager earthly possessions into the small wardrobe. Eagerly, I put on my uniform for the first time. It consisted of a light-blue dress, a white apron, a stiff Peter Pan collar and white cuffs, and a starched white cap. I looked at myself in the mirror and remarked: "Not bad—if only I could get rid of the frightened expression in my eyes and the hard-to-swallow lump in my throat, it might be better."

As I walked down the stairs, I held on to the banister, and kept thinking:

"I must not show my nervousness. I must succeed. I am just as competent as any of the other nurses-in-training walking around so busily and officiously, who appear to know exactly what they are doing."

The staircase formed a dizzying spiral from the sixth floor down to the ground floor and I had to grasp the banister with both hands in order to steady myself. Later, this staircase well became the most efficient means of relaying speedy communications between the ground floor and the upper floors during the many nocturnal visits of the German *Gestapo* deportation officials.

I took to nursing as a duck takes to water. In no time at all, I managed to make beds with very tight and neat hospital corners. I felt grateful that I could help the patients with their various needs.

No job was too menial and difficult for me. Even the inevitable washing and cleaning of bedpans and spitoons became an almost pleasant chore. My friend and colleague, Ann, often sang and chatted with me in the bathroom while we discharged our unglamorous duties. We sang the music of the various sonatas, symphonies, and concertos we knew—to the great delight of the patients.

How pitiful those people were! Most of them were chronically ill, either with palsy, diabetes, muscular dystrophy, or arteriosclerosis, and almost all were bedridden. For the first time in my life, I encountered the inevitable, incurable finality of life. There was so much work to be done to help ease the plight of the patients. To make matters worse, the news from home became even more depressing and the tragedies suffered by almost everyone I knew seemed endless. I threw myself into my work with all my heart and soul in order to bring some light into the dark and hopeless futures that these chronically ill faced.

Our social life in the hospital depended pretty much on what we ourselves could organize within its walls since we were not permitted to go to theaters, movies, cafes, restaurants, or to even appear on the streets.

I soon found myself part of a very congenial, intelligent, and fun-loving group—Marge, Ann, Suzanne, Sis, and myself. We slept near or above each other in the double-decker beds, and it happened more than once that one of us came crashing through the upper berth to become an unexpected visitor in the berth below amid hysterical hilarity and to the consternation of the other student nurses in the dormitory hall.

Dr. Buzaglo was an aristocratic-looking man, of Spanish and Portuguese origin, religious and considerate, who ran the hospital in a most competent manner. He and his wife, also a physician, organized a Friday night discussion group. The topics of discussion were very interesting and we always came away feeling stimulated.

On other evenings the dietician, Else Hartog, the wife of Alan Hartog, the building supervisor, gave us lectures on home economics, nutrition, and gracious living, which we thoroughly enjoyed. Alan Hartog introduced us to the world of ancient and modern architecture.

Jules Godefroi, the head of the technical staff, arranged recorded musical concerts and provided an appropriate commentary on the various selections.

All these well-appreciated activities were faithfully attended by the nurses, doctors, and technical staff of the hospital. We lived in a world of our own, on a veritable island that was isolated from the world outside, and, as a result, our friendships were strong and deep.

This new life suited me extremely well. I was busy every minute of the day and night and had little time to think about the war and its miserable consequences. The exertion of pure physical effort had a wonderful tiring and calming effect upon me.

I was excited about meeting so many new people and new challenges and I enjoyed and participated in the various classes and social gatherings. I felt compensated in no small measure for being away from my home and family.

But, unfortunately, I had no power to completely shut out the world outside. The latest Nazi decree was to put the stamp of Jew upon us outwardly as well.

As of May 1942 we were required to wear a yellow Jewish star, the size of the palm of one's hand, outlined in black, with the word *Jood* (Jew) printed in Hebrew type letters within the star.

Ann had already bought some stars and she had all the information: "We must wear it on the left side of each garment, even on our uniforms. You must never forget to put it on and if you are caught not wearing a yellow star, you can be punished or deported. That's the big news. How do you like it?"

"And we have to pay for this joke ourselves. The Nazis don't provide the stars for us," Sister Hartog remarked bitterly.

At visiting time in the hospital, it looked very strange, as people came in sporting the yellow star. To our great surprise most Jews were proud to wear it that day. Many Dutch citizens deeply resented this treatment of the Jews and expressed their sympathy by wearing yellow flowers on their lapels, too.

"You see, the Dutch people are really our good friends," one of the visitors said proudly. "They feel for us. Some of them even wear the yellow star. You should hear them curse the Nazis. They are so angry! I heard that in Rotterdam there are signs posted on the walls reminding the Dutch to show respect to the Jews, in the streets. They hate the Nazis just as we do!"

I remained quiet, but it was clear that the decree to wear a star did not spell out anything good or beneficial. Was it yet another step closer to the evil goal set by the scheming Nazis in their overall plan against the Jews? I shuddered with fear and premonition of what might lie ahead.

Almost everyone had additional supplies of food, since the diet in the hospital was not a well-balanced one. There was an acute shortage of proteins, but, by eating potatoes, soups, hot cereals, and puddings, we filled our stomachs and substituted quantity for quality.

I also received packages from home from time to time, which supplemented the hospital menus. Once, I undid a package and a piece of carboard fell out on which my mother had written in Hebrew: "*Mishloah Manot Lihvod Purim*" ("a gift of goodies in honor of Purim"). I looked at the package in my hands and I was amazed at the flood of emotion that these few words aroused in me. I felt I could not unpack it any further. Instead I wanted to keep it intact and preserve it as a permanent souvenir. Nevertheless, I took out a cookie, brought it to my mouth, and suddenly I burst into tears almost spilling the package on the floor. The longing for my father, mother, and brothers came over me in a sudden sweep of nostalgia.

The memory of happy festivals, such as Purim, when we would have a houseful of friends and guests for the traditional festive dinner, with song and laughter, aroused my deepest longing and homesickness. I recalled that as young children we would dress up in Purim costumes and visit the homes of friends. On such occasions I felt lonely and I missed my home and family so much. I had wanted to be independent, yet the separation from my family made me appreciate what I was missing. My ties to my family were very strong, now more than ever before.

That night after lights-out, Ann, Marge, Suzanne, and I pooled all our edibles and in stockinged feet and pajamas we sneaked out to the solarium next to our room. The moon lit up the scene with a silvery glow and we could see the rooftops of the entire neighborhood. It was an eerie still life, with not a soul stirring in the streets.

No sooner did we start the festivities, when the door opened and a small group of nurses came in to join us, each one contributing some refreshments to the get-together. We formed a circle and ate the food amid happy banter. We all had a particular story to tell about some incident that had happened that day in the hospital. We had to keep our voices down to a whisper but we could hardly control our laughter. This was the release from tension we all needed to relieve the unbelievable sorrow and misery we heard and saw in and out of the hospital during the day. When the party ended we were so exhausted that we, literally, fell into our beds. I swung into my upper berth and promptly dropped right through it onto the lower one. This was the hilarious event that capped the evening's festivities, for almost everyone on the floor had been awakened. The next day we were reprimanded by the head nurse, although we sensed she could not blame us too much for trying to forget the suffering around us. She knew that we all wanted so desperately to live and enjoy a normal young life.

Each day brought with it new realities that we had to face. Once, I entered the ward with a bright: "Good morning to everyone." My patients told me they enjoyed my friendly and cheerful countenance but I suddenly was hushed by Sister Hartog's announcement:

"Mrs. Freed has died. The doctor has been here already. Would you and Betty clean her up and make her ready to be taken away?"

I felt blood draining from my face. Sister Hartog must have seen my fright, but she went on briskly:

"There is always the first time. Go on. Betty knows how to go about it, you'll get over it soon. Maybe Mrs. Freed is better off now."

Mrs. Freed had been a cardiac patient in a very critical condition. As I approached the bed, I recalled her soft voice and easy manner. What I saw now was an impersonal, lifeless object, and I felt frightened and awed at the same time. I did not dare to touch her. Betty, who was a strong, husky girl, in her second year at the hospital, said in a no-nonsense manner:

"Come on, let's not waste any time."

I did whatever I was told to do without looking at Mrs. Freed's face until we had finished. Then I began to shiver and suddenly I ran out of the room to the bathroom and I began to vomit.

Periodically, by saving up my days off after working two or three weeks in a row, I was able to arrange for a weekend visit to my family in The Hague. Because of travel restrictions for Jews, I had to first apply for a travel permit from the Germans—a procedure that was administered by the *Joodse Raad.*

It was so comforting to come home and be part of the household again and I would not have minded working even harder for it, for it was worth all the effort.

Those were busy days when I came home on a visit. There was not enough time to talk to each other and to be with each other. I realized how much I missed them all and how much I felt myself part of them. My family was proud of my work at the hospital and very impressed with my experiences.

Kitty and I were so happy to see each other that we could not stop talking. We assured each other that distance and differing interests would not come between us ever. Our friendship would remain as strong and as deep as the ties that bind together the members of a family.

The latest Nazi decrees commanded us to hand over our bicycles, the only means of transportation left to us, and to deliver to the Germans all the jewelry and objets d'art we possessed.

That was a terrible blow, especially for Paul, since he needed his bicycle to go to school. We could not very well use it on the sly, and we were afraid some informers would betray us if we would dare to give the bicycle to a Gentile friend. The consequences would be tragic.

As for the jewelry, Father had a plan: "We will wrap it well, put it in jars and bury it in the garden. As Paul says, it is far better that the jewelry becomes corroded rather than add it to the German coffers. We will also hide mother's silver candlesticks and our ceremonial silver wine cups.''

We knew we were not the only people who tried to outsmart the Germans. Jewelry and other valuables were hidden in closets, doorposts, under wooden floors, and many other places by most Jewish families.

Then the axe fell! Jews were called for deportation to Germany as forced labor in the East—*"Arbeits Einsatz im Osten"*—and the German Nazis instructed the *Joodse Raad* to assign the Jews for transport.

The *Joodse Raad* notified four thousand Jews between the ages of sixteen and forty to come to an appointed place and to bring enough food and clothing for eight days, no more than they could carry.

Grief and hopelessness gripped our hearts. The sword of death that had been hovering above us had finally started coming down upon us. We had hoped against hope that the Nazi dragon would be satiated with our economic spoliation and social isolation and would be satisfied with the hardships engendered by the many decrees and commandments already unleashed upon us.

But, we were the enemy, they said; we first had to be robbed of all our possessions and then of our strength and ultimately deported. What else awaited us?

Most people did not respond to the call-up. We were afraid, yes, but we were also angry and indignant. The Nazis threatened us with transportation to the concentration camp at Mauthausen and many hostages were arrested. We were like mice caught in a trap!

As if to console us spiritually, we heard that the Christian churches were protesting vehemently against the deportation of Jews. Common distress brought all Christian denominations together, and the Roman Catholic church worked with the Protestant churches in planning a united front against the common enemy. A written protest was sent to the *Reichskommisar* Dr. Seyss-Inquart and special messages and pastoral letters were proclaimed and read from the pulpits.

How we appreciated their courage to protest on our behalf! But the grave physical danger remained with us.

10

People deployed various means in desperate attempts to avoid deportation, even though it proved later on to be only a short stay of execution.

Some attempted the hazardous escape route to Switzerland or Spain with the aid of smugglers, to whom they paid fortunes of money.

Many became aware of the possibility of going into hiding in the homes of Dutch Gentiles.

Others tried to register their names on lists that promised them exemption from transportation.

I implored my family to go into hiding with Gentiles. Father had already inquired about this possibility.

"I spoke to Mr. de Groot, my business associate, and he says it is too risky. He has no contact with anyone who would want to take the responsibility of helping us."

"Maybe I could inquire for you in Amsterdam," I replied, "Naturally you should not hide here in The Hague, where someone could recognize you. This whole concept of hiding with Gentiles is still very new. But, please, let's start working on it before it is too late."

"It would be a great imposition upon the Gentile family," Mother said thoughtfully. "Naturally we would pay them, for our upkeep but how would we react if we found ourselves with four more people in our house whose presence would have to be kept secret? Only brave and courageous individuals would take such a risk."

"O.K.," Father said to me. "See what you can accomplish in Amsterdam. In the meantime I will register the family on the 'Weinreb list'. We have to try every possible way to become exempted from deportation or at least to postpone or delay it. People are clamoring to get on the Weinreb list. It costs fl. 100 per person. Registration on that list is supposed to assure exemption from deportation and provide the official *Sperr* exemption stamp on the identity card.

"You should see the lines of people in front of Weinreb's house in Scheveningen! I was waiting for hours yesterday. Finally I got in and was promised to be placed on the list."

"It's amazing! How can Weinreb as a Jew have the privilege and power to *sperr* [exempt] and actually save Jews from deportation?" I was astounded.

"I heard that he helped a high-ranking German officer and in return he is allowed to save himself and his family circle from deportation. In the meantime the family has grown to fantastic dimensions."

Mother shook her head: "How can you be sure it is a safe and reliable way and not a swindle? Nevertheless, when drowning, one is ready to grasp even the weakest piece of straw. But I am still so worried! Maybe we should think of getting to Switzerland? What do you think, dear?"

Pointing at me, Father said: "You are safe as long as you remain working as a nurse at the Joodse Invalide Hospital, which is under the auspices of the *Joodse Raad* and thus you are exempted by the *Joose Raad* and you have a *Sperr* on your identity card." He sighed. "Paul, would you venture to go to Switzerland? Once you get there safely, we would follow. What do you say?"

Paul jumped up. Suddenly, the atmosphere changed from one of tragedy to one of excitement.

"Some of my friends went just a few days ago. Maybe I'll catch up with them. I'll go, sure I'll go!"

Father paced up and down the room. I could almost see his brain in action.

"I'll ask our friend Mr. Flinker to put me in touch with a

smuggler; he has already been scouting around, since he is trying to make the same arrangements for his own family. Listen, Paul. We'll have to equip you with warm clothing and you will hide some money on your person. I'll go now and see whether Lazer Flinker is home."

"Do you think I should change the color of my hair? Maybe to a dark reddish color. I cannot leave my own natural dark brown hair. It looks too Jewish," Paul said.

I looked at him. He had such a fine face. Did he look typically Jewish according to the Nazi stereotype?

His nose was not long and hooked, his hair was straight, his lips were not prominent. However it was still risky, since anyone who had dark brown hair and eyes was considered to be a Jewish type in Holland where the majority were blond and blue-eyed.

"How would red hair suit you? If you feel safer that way I think you should do it, because it will give you more confidence, Paul. I hope you'll succeed in getting safely to Switzerland. I wish you all the good luck in the world, just keep faith!" I loved him so much. We embraced tearfully.

Two weeks later when I came home for the weekend, to my great surprise, I found red-haired Paul at home. He was down-hearted and disappointed:

"Everything had already been arranged. The smuggler came, we traveled to the Belgian border, and there we waited in a trench for him to lead us safely across the border. After more than seven hours of nervous tension, danger of detection, and excruciating physical discomfort, we had to return home because the Germans had uncovered the illegal route into Belgium and had caught the man who was supposed to take me through the Belgian-French border. The whole chain of this operation has blown. It is a miracle that I did not fall into the German trap."

"God is with us, believe me. I am so grateful. So you'll try another time," Mother encouraged him.

"Oh, no, I am not going to Switzerland anymore. I'll have to find another way to escape. I can't stay here because of my red hair. People might get suspicious. One never knows how news gets around. Where shall I go?"

Through a friend of his, Paul found a safe address in the town of Gouda with Gentile people. Gradually he brought his belongings to his hiding place. He took off his yellow star, and always traveled in the evening. Under the cover of darkness he would stealthily approach our street and slip into the house. He did not as yet have a false identity card under an assumed name. If he were caught in a street raid or by the customary German identity control, it would mean his deportation. We were trying to make contact with a resistance movement, but it was a very delicate and dangerous undertaking, for it was still at the beginning of illegal activities.

By midsummer 1942 we understood what was involved from the moment deportation of the Jews to the east began. The deportations were not "resettlements in the east." They really meant slave labor and an even worse fate. People refused to respond to the summons of the *Joodse Raad* and the threats of the Germans to come voluntarily to the deportation center.

The relentless Nazi butchers changed their tactics and started rounding up thousands and thousands of Jews by encircling blocks of streets in nightly raids and loading them onto trucks and vans. Unfortunately there was practically no resistance, for the people were petrified with fear. They packed the few belongings they were allowed to carry with them and submitted to this degradation in order to avoid more brutal treatment at the hands of the Nazi soldiers.

Most nights, after the 8 o'clock curfew, we could hear the large German vans (*overval wagens*) packed with the unfortunate Jews who had been seized for deportation, racing through the empty streets. Their thundering echoes crashed back and forth against the walls between the houses. With baited breath we waited and listened, wondering before whose door they would screech to a halt. Often, we heard the heavily nailed boots of the Nazi stormtroopers as they jumped from the trucks; then the barking commands and the wailing, crying, and pleading voices of the helpless victims being rushed and clubbed into the vans.

"How many more? How long will this have to go on? When

will it be our turn to be shoved into those fearful death vans in order to be transported like cattle to a dread fate?

"God in heaven, help us! What did we do to deserve all this? We are God-abiding people who live as honorable decent human beings and bear neither malice nor evil thoughts toward any human being. Who has the right to snuff out lives at will without law and reason? What are we, that evil-minded people can murder, mutilate, and destroy us? Oh God, help us, because we cannot help ourselves—we are helpless against the vile German beasts."

Every day we heard stories about parents, relatives, neighbors, and friends being torn from their homes for deportation, leaving behind all their worldly possessions—all that they had worked and strived for during their productive lives. People of the highest standing—educators, artists, leaders in business, young and old, rich and poor—were being reduced to helpless creatures and treated like dirt. Young people, even children, who had not begun to taste life, whose future was still before them were being subjected with malicious sadism to the cruelest abuse and suffering. Before long the rounding up of people for deportation became the order of the day. We stopped asking why, we stopped crying, we tried to protect ourselves from the scenes of constant pain by simulating nonchalance.

We already knew the difference between the sounds of the *Messerschmitt* planes of the Germans and the bomber planes of the British. We shut off the lights and opened the blackout curtains to hear the ack-ack of the antiaircraft and watch the beams of the searchlights trying to focus on the planes or bombers.

We became so accustomed to the air battles above our heads that after a while the only reaction we had was: "Oh, they are here again." We just hoped for a dark night so that the Allied bombers would not be so easily detected on their way to bomb Germany.

Even in the hospital we were kept well informed by friends who listened to the B.B.C. broadcasts on their hidden short-wave radios and to the Radio-Oranje, the Dutch radio station broadcasting from London. In occupied Holland we were permitted to listen only to the broadcasts of the official station in Hilversum under the control of the German occupational forces, which gave the official Nazi interpretation of the news. News that was unfavorable to the Germans was held back. Only the bombastic miracles wrought by the mighty Hitler regime were announced over the air.

My parents wrote to me on several occasions that our friends, the Flinkers, had gone "on vacation." I understood they must have fled southward. I realized how much they, too, would have wanted to leave, but they did not want to take the risk of being caught.

Every day we heard about friends and acquaintances leaving Holland. It was a weird feeling, like people abandoning ship, without saying a word about it, in advance.

On one of my visits home, my friend Sophie asked me for permission to spend the night in our house before her departure to Switzerland. It would have evoked too much suspicion if she were to walk out of her house without wearing the yellow Jewish star, for the neighbors might see her. But on our street nobody would know her that well.

I said to her: "Sophie, you know how anxious and desperate we are to get hold of a safe and reliable contact to smuggle ourselves into Switzerland. Do you think you could tell us where to get in touch with your contact?"

She answered evasively: "I'll ask my parents and I'll tell you tonight when I come. I only know that the man is doing our family a favor. He doesn't want to take on too many people because it is too risky."

When she came that night, she was not alone. She brought with her another girl. "I hope you don't mind," she apologized, "I had to bring her here. She is a daughter of a business friend of my father's."

I froze up and said not another word to her. I prepared the extra bed for them, offered them refreshments, and muttered a quick goodnight. Sophie and I had been such good friends for many years. I was aghast, hurt, angry, and indignant!

She asked us to give her shelter and help her escape and instead of reciprocating by providing us with the right contact at no cost

84

or harm to her, she had the callous gall to impose a stranger upon us whom she was taking to safety, and to utterly disregard her dear friend's needs. I was good enough, in other words, to be used, but not to be saved!

Sophie must have felt my mood. She came out and thanked me: "We really appreciated your hospitality. I asked about the smuggler, but my parents said we were the last people he agreed to help. Isn't that too bad?"

I could not look her in the eyes. For the first time in my life I saw that one could only recognize character and integrity in times of emergency. Sophie obviously put her own selfish interests above everything else.

One day, my fellow nurse and friend Marge, told me that her parents and sisters had gone into hiding and swore me to absolute secrecy. I asked her: "With whom do you make contact to go into hiding? (In Dutch it is called *onderduiken*, literally, to dive under.)

Marge answered:

"One has to make connections with an illegal Resistance organization which is fighting against the Nazis in secret and underground ways. The members of this organization act and behave like normal citizens. One of their activities in their battle against the Germans is to bring Jewish people secretly to non-Jewish homes in different parts of Holland where they are hidden, and cared for so that they can avoid death in concentration camps. The Underground provides them with false identity cards stolen from the distribution offices with which they can provide food for the people in hiding. The underground workers act as contacts for the people in hiding. They lead very dangerous lives for if they are discovered in their illegal work, they are deported to the dreaded concentration camp in Mauthausen."

This was exactly the information I needed for my parents and my brothers. Marge promised to make contact for me with the Underground in order to have my family placed in hiding with Dutch Gentiles and provided with the necessary false identity papers.

"Do you think I could take a chance to hide?," I asked Marge,

"I have dark hair and eyes. The Dutch people are all so light-complexioned with blond hair and blue eyes. They will recognize me immediately as a Jewess. Besides, I heard that those who are in hiding are not allowed to be seen on the street and must remain inside constantly. I don't think I could ever subject myself to being closed up all the time. Going into hiding is not for me! I would rather stay right here in the hospital!"

Marge replied: "How long do you think the hospital will be able to hold out, before its patients and personnel will also be deported? Now we have a *Sperr* and we are exempt as long as the Joodse Invalide hospital is intact. Do you know that the *Joodse Raad* has warned Dr. Buzaglo on several occasions that there will be an evacuation of the Joodse Invalide?"

Indeed, shortly after my talk with Marge, almost every night when the bell rang after the 8:00 p.m. curfew, a wave of shock and foreboding went through the hospital. Our communication squad immediately stationed itself at the stairwell and then called to each floor up the spiral stairway, to inform us that the top representatives of the *Joodse Raad* and our Director-General were meeting with the murderous German Captain Aus der Fünten, in charge of the deportation of Jews from Amsterdam. For many months the director, Dr. Buzaglo, and the *Joodse Raad* representative had been able to persuade Aus der Fünten not to deport the patients of the Joodse Invalide hospital because of their weak physical condition. After the unwelcome visitors left, one could almost hear the sighs of relief throughout the hospital.

The tension mounted with each passing day.

11

My tightly knit family had begun to disintegrate. My brother Paul was hidden in Gouda and we prayed he would be safe there. My fate was linked with the Joodse Invalide Hospital and that depended on how long the Nazis would permit the hospitals in Amsterdam to remain operative.

Being very cautious, my father did not want to rely on the strength and safety of the "Weinreb *Sperr*" alone. The rumor was that as long as one of the heads of the family was hospitalized, the rest of the family would be allowed to wait and thus postpone deportation until the sick person came home. Many Jewish men took this way out in order to gain some time. My father, too, managed to get himself admitted to a private mental clinic. He accomplished this by judiciously furnishing an extra amount of money to the director of the clinic.

My strong, clever, learned, proud, and energetic father, the Rock of Gibraltar in our household, had obtained a certificate from a doctor that he had suicidal tendencies and would have to enter a mental clinic in order to receive psychiatric treatment!

The Jewish patients there would get together and study the Talmud in secret. However he could not eat the food there since it was not kosher and food had to be brought to him from home. By then, transportation by car or streetcar was forbidden to Jews and it took more than an hour of walking in all kinds of inclement weather in order to visit him.

I remember the last time I saw him at the clinic when I came on a visit from Amsterdam. We embraced and we kissed. I was crying. Somehow I had the feeling that this would be the last time that I would see him.

Sadly he said, "We Jewish people have never had it easy. I had such plans for you, my dear child, only God knows! What a world to be young in!"

I felt a closeness and a love for him as never before. I held on to him with my heart and soul, which I felt were being torn out of me.

On January 2, 1943, the clinic was "cleansed of all its Jewish patients," as the Nazis put it. It became *Juden-rein*. Now neither connections nor bribery helped. My father was sent by transport train, together with the other Jewish patients to the transit camp of Westerbork in the eastern part of Holland near the German border.

When I heard what had happened to father I felt crushed by grief and I cried all day and all night.

I had saved up two free days to be able to visit my mother in The Hague. I applied at the *Joodse Raad* for a two-day travel permit from the Germans. Without this special permit, Jews were not permitted to travel by public transportation. Luckily, I received the pass.

When I arrived home, I had to be very careful, since my family had received the call to register for deportation and officially we were not supposed to be in the house. My mother had not complied with the call for deportation for herself and Jackie.

As I entered the house my mother hugged me tightly to herself—she was so relieved to see me. We just stood there crying on each other's shoulders.

I urged her to go into hiding. I had all the necessary information and the contacts, but she refused. There had been many instances of people who had been caught by the Germans while hiding at Gentile's homes and they had been deported immediately. She found the risk too great and so she was afraid.

"At least you'll have a chance!," I argued. "You cannot stay here. The Nazis will surely come and get you, now that they see that people don't come to register voluntarily for deportation. They will raid every Jewish house. How long can you hold out?"

"Let me try one more thing," she replied. "Dr. Petersen, a gynecologist from the Zuidwal Hospital, does plastic surgery for patients who are willing to pay the price. He can be trusted. I heard that Mrs. de Fries had it done and she was allowed to stay in the hospital for two weeks. At least for two weeks I won't have to face deportation. Jackie will be able to stay in the Jewish orphan home during that time. I have already spoken to Mrs. de Fries and she promised to make contact with Dr. Petersen."

Mother made all the arrangements on her own, entered the hospital, and actually went through with the plastic surgery. I saw her at the hospital afterwards, weak and forlorn, as white as the sheets she was lying upon. She saw my struggle to keep my nerves steady, and how I was steeling myself not to display my innermost feelings. She said softly:

"It's worth it. At least I can sleep quietly for a few days without having to listen throughout the night for the Nazi van to stop at my house."

I promised her that from now on I would send extra food packages to father in Camp Westerbork. According to reports the food there was inedible and one had to supplement one's diet in order to survive. Father was permitted to receive food packages, but since all food was rationed and I had no extra ration cards for him, I had to buy everything at inflated prices on the black market. Mother told me that money was hidden with Mr. de Groot, my father's former associate, and that he would help me at any time I needed him.

Upon returning to the Joodse Invalide Hospital that evening I heard the tragic news that one of our doctors had committed suicide after being informed that his wife and children had been picked up from their hiding place and had been sent off to a concentration camp.

The indescribable sense of helplessness, depression, and terror in the face of the evil forces around us deepened with each successive day and crushed our souls with despair.

On January 21, 1943, the Apeldornse Bos, the Jewish mental hospital in Apeldoorn, was evacuated. The gruesome stories that were told of the deportation left us shaken and horrified.

With the help of one hundred Jewish orderlies from Wester-bork, appointed by the *Joodse Raad*, and a contingent of SS troopers, nine hundred mentally defective adults and children had been evacuated by trucks and then loaded onto cattle trains at the station. Most of the inmates wore only their nightshirts and some were taken without clothes. The fifty nursing personnel were placed in separate cars, too far away to care for their sick charges. The first group of patients was taken out on stretchers and loaded into vans. When Aus der Fünten, the German executioner who had come to inspect the evacuation, saw this he screamed at his subordinates:

"Are you all idiots? Have you caught it from these crazy people? Do you think we can afford to use more wagons? Everyone has to fit into the vans. The stretchers take up too much room, so get rid of them! And if there is no room for them next to each other, then put them on top of each other!"

The train departed for "destination unknown." Dead bodies were removed even before it had passed the German border. Then for four days the wagons, hermetically sealed, traveled on through Germany. When they finally reached Auschwitz, those who survived, including the personnel, were loaded into trucks and were never seen again. (This sordid act was confirmed at Aus der Fünten's trial in December 1949, by the least emotional witnesses in the world—the stolid Dutch railway men.)

With the ominous fate of deportation hanging over my head like a sword of Damocles, I tried to work even harder and to help and cheer up the patients more than ever before. While helping and feeding the patients, I told them stories, sang to them and tried to anticipate their every wish. The period just after visiting hour was a particularly difficult time for the patients. After bidding goodbye to their children or relatives they were never sure that they would be able to say "hello" to them the next visiting day. Very often we had to contend with and try to control hysterics, sobbing, and depression on the part of the patients.

Every day more patients and personnel were admitted into the hospital. The Joodse Invalide hospital was called "the human safe,'' which people tried through various connections to enter either as a patient or as personnel in order to delay deportation, even temporarily.

Everyone in the hospital was anxious and depressed about developments in the war. The daily deportations, the tearing apart of families, and most important, the fact that one could not plan one's own destiny, one's own future, made us feel trapped between the claws of the Nazi beast.

Jules Godefroi proved to be of immeasurable help to me during that trying time and we became friends for life. He was a very sensitive, friendly, and obliging man of about forty years of age, and his neat and trim appearance made him look much younger. At first, he did not seem to be very forceful and he rarely dominated any of our discussions. But after a while, one could feel his presence in a quiet, unassuming way. We had met casually many times during his activity as technical supervisor of the building. We had often seen each other at the Friday night cultural discussions with Dr. Buzaglo and the musical evenings that Jules had arranged.

He was easy to talk to and was always eager to listen, thus giving me a sense of comfort. A strong, personal feeling developed between us. It was a feeling of mutual appreciation mixed with his deep concern for my youth and inexperience. It was easy to relate to him without being aware of any sexual attraction, and this made our friendship so much deeper and freer both in expression and in intensity.

Between my off-duty interval from 6:30 P.M. until the 8:00 P.M. curfew, Jules and I often snatched a few moments to be together on a walk along the canals and small bridges of Amsterdam. These walks were the only diversion we had outside of the hospital. I gloried in the last rays of the day's sunshine filtering through the weeping willows into the water. I loved every flower, shrub, and piece of grass growing in the gardens along the streets. I admired the curve of every little bridge reaching from one side of the canal to the other. I was happy to be talking to the one person who was obviously concerned about my welfare. In a

91

world where everyone and everything seemed to be disintegrating, this relationship was a spiritual oasis that helped brighten the darkest days.

From time to time musical performances would take place in the hospital for the entertainment of the patients and personnel. A light operetta, *Im weissen Rössel* was due to be performed on February 28, 1943. That week I had the night shift from 11:00 P.M. until 7:00 A.M. and I could not sleep very much during the day because of the excitement, the noise, and the light shining into the room. I got up and watched the rehearsal together with some of the patients and other personnel. The singing, the acting, and the costumes enchanted me so. The yearning rose within me to be as carefree, as young and as happy as the young people portrayed on the stage.

And then the tragic news struck with the crashing force of a bombshell. The news we had feared for so long chilled our blood with the icy clutch of doom:

"The Joodse Invalide hospital will be evacuated on March first."

The news was made known to us through a leak via the *Joodse Raad*.

There had been so many previous rumors of deportations that one could never be sure whether this time, too, it would be a false alarm.

We lived in constant fear. But on the 28th of February, Dr. Buzaglo cancelled the performance of the operetta. The grapevine of information from the *Joodse Raad* confirmed the rumor that March 1st was to be deportation day. That morning I did not even go to bed after night duty. One by one the officials and personnel began to leave. The situation that I faced was a very crucial one, shared by all of the hospital staff.

First, will the deportation really take place?

Second, if so, then I must save myself, because it would be stupid to be caught waiting for the inevitable and knowing the fate that was in store for me.

Third, if I leave the hospital, now, before curfew, who would take care of all the poor, sick, crippled, and paralyzed patients during the night?

Fourth, if the deportation would not take place, how could I ever forgive myself for being such a coward to run away and leave the patients in a completely helpless state?

I was torn between these possibilities. My mother phoned from The Hague to a friend urging him to persuade me to leave. Ann and Marge and all my other friends made up their minds that they were leaving. However, they said, should everything be safe in the morning, they would return.

One nurse, Laura, had attached herself to me and decided to join me in whatever I planned on doing. I was terribly annoyed and feared the heavy responsibility.

"Laura," I said to her, "why don't you decide for yourself? Please don't ask me. I still don't know what I'll do."

But Laura persisted: "I don't care, whatever you do, I'll do. If you go, I'll go too. If you stay, I'll stay!"

"Laura, you make it terribly difficult for me. I can't take the responsibility for you. I want to decide for myself, but not for you!" I put it bluntly. "Supposing you stay on because of me, and the entire Joodse Invalide will be deported tomorrow including yourself. I will feel that I have been responsible for your deportation. This is a matter of life and death and you have to decide for yourself."

Jules, Marcia, and Alan caught up with me about one hour before curfew and begged me to leave. Jules really implored me and took me aside to point out to me that I owed it to myself to escape deportation.

By that time I had made up my mind and my heart was quiet with the conviction and the inner compulsion to remain in the hospital.

"Jules, I can't do it any other way. I can't leave the poor souls! Who will help them, the crippled and the paralyzed? They, too, have heard the rumors. Don't you think they are mortified with fear? I would never forgive myself if I were to leave them in their hour of need. I must stay. I cannot desert them. What are you and Alan doing?"

"Oh, we must stay. We have to take care of the building and all the technical machinery. I must stay."

"So you see? Why then do you insist that I leave, if you stay? Is your life not equally important?"

At the 8 o'clock curfew the doors were closed and I found that

I was a member of a skeleton nursing staff headed by Head Nurse Oppenheimer. Also remaining in the building were Dr. Buzaglo, his wife, and child; Mr. and Mrs. Alan Hartog; and Jules Godefroi.

That night of February 28, 1943 stands out in my mind with special clarity. I was alone, in charge of an entire department of fifty patients, and during the night I also had to help out on another floor. The sick were lying in bed, terrified, and hardly able to control their tears. Quietly and efficiently, I made the rounds, gave them their medications and attended to their needs. Suddenly an overwhelming feeling of love, warmth, and compassion for these people welled up within me. I went over to each one in turn, comforting this one, caressing that one and tucking them into their beds. The sight of the tears of gratefulness in their eyes and the sound of their words of blessing aroused in me the deepest instincts of love. When the head nurse came by, I sensed that our relationship had changed—we were like equals in our efforts. She complimented me upon my decision to stay and upon the way I was performing my duties.

During the night Jules functioned as the intermediary between floors. He brought me food, even though I was not very hungry. We talked about ourselves, about our hopes and aspirations as if tomorrow were just another day, and not a day of doom. A sweet tenderness developed between us, which served as a protective shield against the brutal reality we faced.

Alan and Jules had devised a hiding place in the cellar under the floor of the hospital synagogue. A little trap door covered by a rug led to the hiding place, which they supplied with blankets, mattresses, food, water, and candles. The plan was that, should the Germans come, all those who had stayed in the hospital that night would go quickly into the synagogue, lift up the rug, open the trapdoor and slip into the hiding place.

Jules made me promise to act quickly in case of danger. We could not be sure that the hiding place would not be discovered during the evacuation of the hospital. We could only hope and pray and sit tight there.

During the night, we held several consultations with the staff members who had remained. It was decided that if the Germans came we would first try to escape by way of the hospital's roof exit. From there we could jump onto the adjacent roof of the Municipal Health and Medical Building, enter through the roof opening and make our way down into the building and then out through the front door to safety. An alternative was to hide in the cellar of the synagogue.

When the darkness of the night gave way to the early morning light, we went up to the roof to investigate the escape route. Everything was so quiet and peaceful—beautiful Amsterdam was still slumbering.

I returned to my patients. I knew they needed me. They questioned me quietly whether I had heard anything new and whether there was any sign of the Germans. The 6:00 A.M. morning curfew passed and none of the hospital personnel returned. At 7:00 A.M. I began giving the patients breakfast. We were still hopeful and reasoned that if the Germans had not come by then, they would not come at all. To add to our feeling of security, Mr. Asscher, the head of the *Joodse Raad*, called the hospital at 8:30 A.M. to tell us not to worry and that the danger of deportation was over. A few minutes later Brother Hammelburg, the only male nurse to remain behind with us that night, ran down from the roof where he was on look-out and exclaimed:

"The Germans are beginning to surround the building!" Alan and Else Hartog, who were in the porter's lodge, gave the prearranged signal by dropping the telephone book on the buzzer to alert the director, Dr. Buzaglo.

As for myself, I felt a surge of fear going through me like a hot, searing knife, but instead of giving way to panic, my mind became very deliberate and alert. Six of us ran quickly to the roof as per our plan of escape. As we looked over the edge of the hospital we gasped incredulously. An endless row of trucks, wagons, and vans surrounded the entire block of the Weesperplein, Sarfatistraat, and the Nieuwe Achtergracht, including the adjacent Municipal Health and Medical Building. At various points soldiers of the Wehrmacht and the dreaded SS were standing on guard with drawn bayonets.

It was obvious that this planned route of escape was blocked and that we would have to put our alternate plan into effect. We retreated, running down the hospital stairs in order to hide in the cellar under the synagogue. But the Germans had already taken up positions at all doors and exits in the hospital to make sure that no one could escape. Our last hope, our last possibility for safety so close at hand, was lost to us. The frustration of dashed hopes was a bitter pill to swallow.

WE WERE TRAPPED!!

The German officers in charge of the deportation operation commanded us to go to our patients and prepare them for transportation. One of them drew his rifle and ordered me to walk in front of him to the wards. We were ordered to pair up in work teams. Betty and I worked together, trying as best as possible to comfort the patients and prepare them for their rendezvous with death.

The realization of what I was being forced to do almost broke my heart and made me so enraged that when one of the German soldiers handled the patients roughly while loading them onto the stretchers, I shouted at him:

"Don't you have any human feelings? The patient is in excruciating pain. How can you mishandle her like this?"

"Very soon she'll suffer no more," he replied.

We ignored the SS and tried to help the patients as much as possible. The operation went on in terrifying and accusing silence. By 3:00 in the afternoon the ghastly task was finished. Several hundred old, sick, blind, paralyzed, and senile patients had been hauled onto wagons either on stretchers or on foot. They were all so brave—there was no outcry, no hysterics.

Our small nursing staff was ordered to go downstairs in order to be distributed among the patients in the vans. In the lobby of the hospital we stood in a circle: Dr. Buzaglo, Head Nurse Oppenheimer, Jules, Betty, Laura, and myself. I noticed the absence of Alan and Else Hartog and Brother Hammelburg and I hoped they were safe in the synagogue cellar.

As Dr. Buzaglo shook our hands, I saw tears in the eyes of this composed and proud-looking man. He talked to us:

"I tried once again to stall Aus der Fünten, but this time I failed. How can I thank you for what you have done? You could have saved yourselves by staying away, but your consciences told you otherwise. Only strong people could have done what you have done, a deed of great charity — a *Mitzvah*. I thank you in behalf of our unfortunate patients. May God be with you!"

We shook hands and looked deeply into each other's eyes knowing that this might be the last time we would see each other.

THAT WAS IT!

The only thing to do now was to follow orders and join the patients on their journey to "destination unknown." I turned around, looked out on the square through the open doors of the hospital, and saw the crowded vans with the last patients being hauled into them.

At that moment something sparked in me. My heart started pounding and I felt that my determination to live was dictating my actions. With an audacity born of desperation, I set a plan in motion. I put down my rucksack near the wall, took out my wallet and identity card and then folded up my white nurse's apron so it would not stick out from under my coat. Laura followed my motions with intensity and almost moaned her question:

"What are you going to do? What are you up to?"

"Leave me alone. Don't talk to me or you will draw attention to me. Please, leave me!" She annoyed me terribly.

"No, I want to go with you. Let me join you, please?," she pleaded.

"I'm going to walk out of here. It's very risky, I may be shot and I don't want to be responsible for you. Please leave me to myself!"

I was very emphatic but she wouldn't let go of me.

"I'm coming with you, I don't care."

Time was of the essence. I saw I could not shake her off, so I told her to follow my instructions.

"Just keep quiet and follow my every move. Calmly!"

We walked to the door and turned left toward the Sarfatistraat. Every few feet a black-shirted soldier with drawn bayonet was standing on guard. Laura was always a half a step behind me.

"Make believe you are taking a stroll in the street on a sunny day. Just walk calmly," I said in a low voice hardly moving my lips. We walked past the lines of soldiers, past the trucks and vans, and past the motorcycle squads. We were almost near the corner at the Sarfatistraat when we heard one of the black-shirted soldiers call out:

"Hey, where are you going? Halt!"

Laura whimpered, my knees weakened. But I implored her, talking through my teeth:

"Walk calmly. Stop your moaning and don't turn around. Make believe you don't hear. Don't start running or they'll shoot us!"

We turned the corner and there were more blackshirts standing about three yards apart. Traffic in the Sarfatistraat was moving normally. When we came to the middle of the block, still walking calmly, I grabbed Laura's hand and we walked right into the traffic which to me, was less of a danger than the SS. When we reached the other side of the street we started walking a little faster. We turned into a side street past the Dutch breweries and by this time we were safely out of sight of the soldiers. We started running as if the devil himself was trying to catch us, our lungs almost bursting. I asked Laura:

"Where shall we go? Where can we be safe? They will try to hunt us down for sure!"

She suggested that we go to her cousin in the eastern part of Amsterdam. We kept on running for the next hour until finally we arrived at her cousin's, where it took us some time to calm down and recover from our excitement. I freshened up and went to bed where I slept for twelve hours straight. In the morning I decided to go to see my mother.

This time I did not even bother to apply for a travel permit. I simply took off my yellow star, got into the streetcar and went by train to The Hague.

It felt so good to see her again after my narrow escape. I was grateful and happy even though the threat of deportation was ever present.

We went to visit with Kitty and Iris, who lived across the

street. They could hardly believe the story I told of having dared to outwit the Germans. My mother was so overcome with emotion that she could not control herself. She cried and kissed and hugged me intermittently.

Together we listened to the news reports of the B.B.C. from London, which related rumors of people being gassed in the concentration camps. Places with the names of Theresienstadt, Bergen-Belsen, Dachau, Auschwitz, and Buchenwald did not sound strange to us anymore, even though they evoked the most frightening feelings of horror and terror.

The world was collapsing around us and we were on the verge of collapsing with it.

After discussing all the pros and cons, Mother and I came to the conclusion that it would be best if I return to Amsterdam, despite the risks, and try to join the staff of the Netherland Israelite Hospital, the N.I.Z. I was not legally registered in The Hague and I had no permit to travel. If I were caught here I might endanger my mother's safety.

Once again I tried to persuade Mother to go into hiding but she refused.

"Besides," she said confidently, "since father has started proceedings to be registered on the Palestine Exchange List, we will be able to remain in Westerbork until our exchange to Palestine will be effected and we won't be deported to concentration camp."

In order to qualify for this list, Father had to obtain an affidavit, via the International Red Cross, from our relatives in Palestine. These proceedings were handled by a Mr. E. A. P. Puttkammer, a German assistant manager of the Rotterdamse Bank in Amsterdam, for which we had to supply him with diamonds, money, or foreign currency and sometimes all three. I became the intermediary in Amsterdam in periodically delivering the diamonds and/or money to Puttkammer.

We embraced and stood together for a long while, not wanting to part from each other. I was so worried about her.

"O God", I prayed, "Please, don't disappoint her trust and confidence. Help us, Oh Lord. Please help us, in this fight for survival."

12

When I reached the Netherland Israelite Hospital (the N.I.Z. hospital) in Amsterdam, I met several of my friends who informed me that the director of the hospital, Dr. Kronenberg, had been accepting former nurses of the Joodse Invalide Hospital for work there. I went to his office, where he received me kindly and I told him the story of my escape. After meeting the head nurse, I was assigned to the old part of the hospital, where many of the former patients of the Apeldornse Bos mental hospital had been placed. They had been brought to Amsterdam by special permission prior to the evacuation of the institute.

The N.I.Z. hospital on the Nieuwe Keizersgracht was the largest and oldest Jewish hospital in Amsterdam. The various medical buildings surrounded a garden square with trees and benches where nurses, doctors, and patients could relax.

I enjoyed the hard work and the professional medical atmosphere immensely. There was a vast difference between the Joodse Invalide where we attended to the chronically ill and usually older patients and this general hospital, always buzzing with activity.

Soon I was transferred to the male division. I remember the shock I experienced the first time I had to wash a male patient. I learned quickly and adopted the required professional and efficient attitude.

The hospital was already full to capacity and yet every day more and more patients and personnel were admitted by special agreement and payment and "pull" emanating from the *Joodse Raad* or from someone of influence in the hospital. Healthy people came in to undergo appendectomies in order to stall deportation.

The hunt for Jews, or the *razzia* as it was called, was in full force. In April 1943, Hans Rauter, the SS German police leader, a man in love with violence, proclaimed that Amsterdam had to be "de-Jewed," quarter by quarter. We lived in constant fear.

One day I was assigned to bring a tray of food and medication to a patient under special police guard. The nurse in charge told me he had been shot through his chest while trying to escape. He must have been a man of importance to the Germans, for otherwise they would not have admitted him to be treated in the hospital.

As I entered the room I saw a young man, Peter, lying in bed, almost lifeless. I touched him and he opened his eyes. His gaze was so intent that I had the feeling he was looking into my soul. After a minute I realized he was whispering to me:

"You probably know why I am here under guard. They caught me this time and I feel I will not come out alive. I have to be quick because the guard checks every so often whether I have run away. I am in agony, not only about myself, but also about my unfinished work."

He stopped to catch his breath and noticing the questioning look on my face, he continued:

"Who will continue my work in the underground? Who will organize the hiding of children from the hospital and the children's home in Gentile homes to escape the iron claws of the Nazis? I can't get out and I am not allowed to have any visitors. The Resistance Underground Organization cannot reach me."

The guard looked in and I busied myself pretending to feed Peter. I consoled him:

"Peter, the doctors are doing all they can. You'll see in no time at all that you'll be well."

"Well for what? So that the Nazis can torture me in order to extract valuable information and then shoot me? No, my dear. For me there is no hope. But you could help me in a more vital and important way and if you agree, I'll have peace of mind.''

"I'll do anything to help you," I assured him with all my heart.

"Don't decide rashly. I want you to think about it for a few days. The task that I want you to perform is not an easy one and it will endanger your life. Now what do you say?''

I was thinking about my mother and my two brothers, all still free, and about my father in Westerbork transit concentration camp.

"Dear girl, I don't know you personally, but Hilda, the nurse in charge, told me about your escape from the Joodse Invalide. I can see in your face that you are a very determined young lady and from what I hear, a very resourceful one. My question is: Would you like to continue my fight against the Nazis by joining the Dutch Resistance movement, to rescue Jewish children and grownups so that they will not fall into the Nazi trap? There is so much to be done and time is running short. Don't give me your answer now. Think about it. Since I don't know whether I'll make it til tomorrow, just remember this address." He whispered it to me together with the password, "The tulips are red." "They'll know you were sent by me. Now please, leave and take the tray with you. *Je maintiendrai* and God bless you!''

I left him and went out of the room, past the guard. I was in great inner turmoil and felt as if I were plunging into a vast, unknown ocean. Should I join the Resistance movement? What will my mother say? Oh no, I could not tell anyone, not even my closest relatives or dearest friends. I would be endangering everyone in the Resistance movement by talking. Should I dare to endanger my life, as Peter said, by fighting against the Nazis? If caught, I knew what my fate would be.

But on the other hand, how safe was I now? They could pick me up on the street at any moment and send me to a concentration camp. The Germans could evacuate the hospital today and no one would have the power to fight against them. On the other hand, why should I submit meekly to this slaughter without offering resistance? I did not want to go on living in fear.

Suddenly from the far end of the corridor I saw Etty, my roommate, running toward me, motioning to me to come. She could hardly bring out the words:

"Your brother Paul just called from The Hague. Your mother and little Jackie were picked up from your home in The Hague and now they are at the central assembly place on the Paviljoensgracht, the former Zwaluwenrest, where they will be kept until their deportation to Westerbork tomorrow."

I hardly heard her last words. My brain and my heart began to race madly and I was plunged into a state of panic. My first and most immediate instinct was that I must go to The Hague to see them. I ran to find the head nurse and she granted me permission to go. But there was no time to apply for a travel permit from the *Joodse Raad* so I just took off my yellow Jewish star and made my way to the station. It was only when I sat down in the train that the meaning of my brother's message sank in. I turned my face toward the window panes for fear that someone would suspect me. I saw the landscape rushing by through a curtain of my tears.

When I arrived at the street where we lived, I walked up and down several times and kept passing our house. I did not know where my brother Paul was and whether our house had already been sealed off or "pulsed," which meant plundered by the big moving company Puls, appointed by the Germans to empty out all the Jewish houses after their inhabitants had been deported.

I heard steps behind me and someone called out my name. I turned and to my relief I saw our Gentile neighbor, who told me to come into his house. And there was Paul. We tried to console each other. He told me:

"When the Germans came to our street, Mother begged me to escape through the garden."

I asked Paul about our little brother Jackie. Mother had told him not to worry, since they were all registered on the Palestine exchange list, the so-called Puttkammer list. And in any case, she believed nothing would happen to small children.

Paul told me that when the Germans rang the doorbell, he had run out into our garden and jumped over the fence into the garden of our Gentile neighbors where he hid in the bushes until the *razzia* was over.

"I heard the Nazis inspect the garden several times. From inside the house I heard the banging of doors as they searched for people. I did not move the whole time."

So the German destruction machine had operated very efficiently and the vultures had swallowed their prey.

"Then it was quiet," Paul continued. "I waited a couple of hours before knocking on the back door of the neighbor's house. As soon as they saw who it was, they let me in. I can't begin to tell you how nice they are. They even let me call you at the hospital. It's so good to see you!"

I started to thank Mr. and Mrs. van Heeren, but they interrupted me:

"I'm sure you would have done the same thing. We have known you such a long time and we liked your parents very much. Now, let's see what we can do. I will go into your house through the gardens and see what's doing inside. Very soon the curfew starts and you cannot go outside."

Mr. van Heeren returned with the information that the front door was sealed by the Germans, but that everything was more or less intact.

"Stay in your house for the night. I'm sure they will not "puls" your house tonight. Be careful with the blackout and make no noise. We will leave our back door unlocked. If you suspect that the Germans may come back tonight, come over to us immediately, even in the middle of the night. Tomorrow morning you can leave through our house."

Paul and I thanked them profusely and then silently we made our way back into our house next door. Our formerly cozy, warm, and safe home looked forlorn now and strange. It was as if we had already parted with our own possessions. Our own furnishings seemed foreign and detached. Paul and I sat in the kitchen talking softly while we had some supper. We reminisced about times before the war, about our parents and Jackie, our sweet little brother. We had spoiled him terribly and had made him our family pet. Thinking about him was so painful.

We decided to sleep in our parents' bedroom and not in our separate rooms in case we had to flee in the middle of the night. I felt a tenderness and love for him as never before and we talked until late in the night, unable to sleep and to answer the questions on our minds:

"Why? How long will this suffering last? Will we have a future? Will each of us ever marry and have children and live like normal human beings?"

We wanted so much to enjoy being alive! Paul reached over and took my hand and this was how we finally fell asleep.

In the morning we assembled a few of our belongings. Paul had to return at once to Gouda, to his hiding place. It was too dangerous for him to be in The Hague. He had come knowing very well the risk he took of being caught by the Germans, because he had wanted so much to see Mother and Jackie.

It was very difficult for us to part. What wrong had he ever done to anyone, to be so persecuted? My handsome, learned, sensitive, and wonderful brother! We clung to each other and promised to keep in touch, but to be extremely careful.

Little did I know that this was the last time I would ever see him.

We left our house, thanked our neighbors, and told Mr. and Mrs. van Heeren they could help themselves to anything they wanted from our house. Better that they, rather than the Germans, should take our family possessions. We were sure they would return our belongings when the war would be over.

Because of my *Joodse Raad "Sperr"* —exemption as a nurse in a hospital as indicated on my identity card—I was allowed to visit my mother and Jackie at the deportation assembly place on the Paviljoensgracht. What feelings of pain and emotion we felt as we saw each other! Mother tried to calm me:

"My dear child, be strong. You'll see. We will be exempted and we will be able to stay in Westerbork until our turn will come to be exchanged to Palestine. God will surely help us! In the

105

meantime, be careful, darling! In the hospital you'll be safe. They will not disrupt the hospital, which is providing vital services!''

"What can I do for you?,'' I asked her. "I just can't let you go! I need you so!'' Mother held me close to her.

"I know, I know. But what can we do? You have to be brave. Take good care of yourself, dear child, and be a good Jewish daughter. When this will be over, with God's help, we'll be together again. You know where the money is. Please continue to send food packages to Westerbork. We will write to you. Please follow instructions concerning the delivery of money and valuables to Mr. Puttkammer, because we must continue to remain registered on the Palestine exchange list at all costs. It will save us from being deported.'' I promised.

Little Jackie ran in, he saw me and jumped all over me. I had brought chocolates and toys for him. He chatted excitedly about the nice friends he had met already, while I hugged and kissed him; I could hardly control myself. He gave me a blue label that they used to mark their belongings. On it he wrote in his first-grade handwriting:

"Jackie is allowed to remain here in The Hague.'' Despite the many dangerous situations I have been exposed to, I have kept that little label to this very day.

Finally we had to say goodbye because I had to be at the hospital before curfew time. On the way out I saw hundreds of Jews, including some of our good friends, crowding the assembly place. I could not tear myself away from Mother and Jackie. I never imagined that such pain, such sadness, and such unhappiness could exist. I felt as if a part of me was being torn away.

I still see Mother and Jackie, outlined in the entrance, waving at me. I looked at them as long as I could and then I turned the corner.

Coldness entered my heart. Bitter, powerless rage ran through my veins.

"How could we allow those Nazi murderers to so disrupt our lives, kill our beloved, and plunder our possessions? And why do we submit to it without offering any resistance? It made it so easy for them to perform their inhuman and evil deeds.''

My mind was resolute now. I was going to join the Underground Resistance movement.

I was determined that I would not permit myself to be destroyed and I would fight to the bitter end.

13

As soon as I returned to the N.I.Z. hospital in Amsterdam I hurried to Peter's room. I saw that there was a flurry of activity; doctors and nurses kept going in and out of his room and the German guard at the door was unable to keep track of all the personnel. So I took some sheets in my hand and walked into his room together with the doctor. Peter did not look well at all and was evidently in great pain.

I tried to catch his eye. He saw me and I nodded. The look of relief on his face told me that he understood that I had agreed to join the Underground Resistance movement. The room was still crowded when I slipped out unnoticed. I was glad that I had had the opportunity to communicate with Peter, for he passed away a few days later.

I went to the address Peter had given me where I was warmly received by a young man who introduced himself as Jan. We talked about Peter and his request that I join in the activities of the Resistance movement. Jan welcomed me and outlined how my cooperation would be utilized.

I thus became a link within the hospital to help hide patients with Gentiles. Whenever I heard someone who wanted to go into hiding, I would speak to him in secret. During visiting hours someone from the Resistance would come, ostensibly to visit a certain patient. Then at the conclusion of the visit, they would walk out together, unnoticed among the crowd of visitors. Sometimes I brought children to an appointed place and they would be met there by an underground contact and taken into hiding. It was dangerous but very gratifying work.

I had no time to indulge in self-pity. My work at the hospital, the shopping and sending of food packages to my parents in Westerbork concentration camp, and the tremendous efforts to assure that my parents remained on the Palestine exchange list kept me active all day long. As per father's instructions I periodically delivered money or valuables to Mr. Puttkammer at the Rotterdamse Bank in Amsterdam, to keep them on the list. I was so concerned with their safety that it left me no peace.

A new world opened up for me when I was assigned to the Obstetrics Department. I was permitted to attend and help with the delivery of a new-born baby. I had always been amazed and awed by the miracle of birth. But to see it actually happen and then to hear the first cries of life after the doctor held the baby by its feet and gave it a little pat was to witness the glorious miracle of creation.

More than once, I saw the parents looking at each other in happiness and then I heard the father say to the doctor:

"What shall I do with the baby now? How can I keep him safe and out of reach of the Nazis? Soon we may be called up for deportation and forcibly taken out of our house. Shall we go into hiding? But then the cries of the baby will give us away. Doctor, I feel guilty for having brought this new life into this miserable world!"

Here I could be of help. After consultation with my contact in the Resistance, the baby and the parents were hidden separately, somewhere in Holland.

On April 9, 1943, I was paged to come to the porter's loge of the hospital—there was a phone call for me from Rotterdam. As I hurried to receive the call, I wondered who could be calling me, since I knew no one in Rotterdam. Soon I found out. It was my brother Paul, who had been arrested in a German raid on the Gouda railway station platform. When the trained stopped all the passengers who were Jewish—or Gentiles who had falsified identity papers—were packed into vans and driven to the Rotterdam central assembly place for deportation to Westerbork. He was calling to say goodbye.

I became hysterical. God, will it never stop? One of the men sitting there, Mr. Wolf, who was the *Joodse Raad* liaison for the hospital, tried to calm me down. He talked to my brother and told him to call back later. In the meantime, he told me that he would use his influence to have him retained in Rotterdam. Mr. Wolf asked me to come to see him after he had contacted the *Joodse Raad*. He consoled me and said there might be a chance to save Paul.

When I came to my room, sad and distressed, my friends commiserated with me. But they warned me:

"This Mr. Wolf is a real wolf. Don't trust him when he promises to do something. He has a reputation, so don't go into his room. He likes young and pretty nurses and you fulfill the requirement."

However, my brother was more important to me than all the gossip, so I went to Mr. Wolf's office. Mr. Wolf treated me in a very businesslike fashion and informed me of his efforts on my brother's behalf. He served real coffee, which to me was a delicacy, since the only coffee available, then, was ersatz (substitute).

He said that he still expected to hear from the *Joodse Raad* and that I should come tomorrow to discuss it further. As I stood up he put his arm around me, as if in a friendly consoling gesture, and before I knew it he had me in a tight embrace, kissing me and trying to caress me. I did not know what happened, but in a flash I tore myself loose and I slapped his face. As I left I heard him say: "You'll be sorry for this."

When I tried to call my brother in Rotterdam, the watchmen at the assembly place told me that everyone had already been sent to Westerbork, including Paul. My friends were right; all the promises by Mr. Wolf to help me were simply maneuvers to lure me into his clutches. The situation was desperate, for now my entire family was in Westerbork.

I just hoped that Paul would be included with my family on the Palestine Exchange List, so he would also be exempt from further deportation.

People tried frantically to obtain exemptions from deportation even if only for a short period. Every Tuesday, trains left Westerbork eastward with destination unknown.

One day in June I had an unexpected visitor from The Hague. It was the son of friends of my parents, whose father was a famous cantor. He was on the run from the Germans and he had heard that I was in the N.I.Z. hospital. He asked me whether I could help him hide in the hospital for one night, since he did not know anyone else in Amsterdam. I talked it over with my roommates and we decided to double up with the nurses in the next room and give him our room. Within minutes everyone on the floor knew that we had a young man hidden in our room. We were fearful that the head nurse or the director might hear about it. But I could not refuse him. We brought him food and drink and we felt an atmosphere of conspiracy and nervous gaiety because of the chance we were taking. He left together with the visitors at the conclusion of visiting hours on the following day.

My walks with my friend Jules Godefroi provided me with the only moments of relaxation during that period. After my escape from the Joodse Invalide Hospital, we had become even closer friends. He had been desperately worried about me since he had not noticed what had happened to me when the Nazis ordered us into the vans. He also had saved himself by bluffing the Germans. When they had seen him standing in the hall, the head officer had asked him:

"What are you doing here?"

Jules could not very well tell him that he could not run away or that he could not get to the hiding place under the synagogue anymore, so he said very quickly:

"I stayed to help with the sick."

But the German insisted:

"Where are the others? Did they go into hiding? Did they run away? Why didn't you run away?" The Nazi was angry that they had not captured more personnel.

"I don't have to run away," Jules bragged. "I'm actually only a quarter Jew. My grandmother was a Gentile and my grandfather was a half-Jew. You can see. I have a special stamp on my identity card."

Until his employment at the Joodse Invalide Hospital, Jules had a special exemption because he had been a technical specialist at the Royal Merchant Marine, the K.P.M.

The German asked once more: "What is your name? Godefroi? It's not a Jewish name. Yes. I see your stamp. All right you can go.''

Jules lived on Amstel street with his technical assistant, Kurt. A week after the seizure of the hospital, the Germans contacted them, because they needed technical supervision of the Joodse Invalide Hospital. Dr. Mayer, who was to become the German head of activities in the hospital, promised that he would guarantee them exemption from deportation.

Jules told me about our mutual friends, Alan and Else Hartog, and how they and nursing-brother Hammelburg had remained hidden for two nights in the cellar hiding place under the synagogue. In the middle of the second night Alan crawled out on hands and knees. When he saw that everything was dark and quiet and that the German watchman was asleep, he quickly crawled back to get the others and they ventured out. They ducked under the watchman's window and escaped through the side entrance on to the Nieuwe Achtergracht.

The *razzias* went on at a furious pace. Policemen, soldiers, and SS men, uniformed and armed to the teeth, raided Jewish homes as if they were going into battle and dragged out the poor, helpless victims. The Undeground Resistance movement tried to save as many people as possible and to bring them to safe places where they could hide out of reach of the Nazis. On June 20, 1943 east and south Amsterdam were raided by the Germans in a round-the-clock operation that had netted 5,500 Jews.

There was talk that even the N.I.Z. hospital would soon be raided and that the patients and personnel would be evacuated to a concentration camp. We felt again as if we were caught in a trap from which there was no escape.

Toward the end of June, the raid we feared so much took place. When the Germans appeared, the director of the hospital, Dr. Kronenberg, begged the "executioner" Aus der Fünten to leave the acute cases in the hospital for the time being. After some bargaining Aus der Fünten agreed to deport only the patients in the mental ward, the old and the chronic cases and those who could walk.

The raid started early in the morning, and when we nurses

heard of it, we immediately went to our rooms and decided to hide somewhere in the hospital. The evacuation of the sick had already started. From the nurses' quarters we could see what was going on in front of the hospital and in the inside garden court. The Nazi police and soldiers were barking out their commands. Then we heard the voice of Mr. Wolf, the *Joodse Raad* liaison, call out on the megaphone:

"All nurses who have previously worked at the Joodse Invalide Hospital must report downstairs immediately! All nurses and brothers must accompany their patients on transport! That is an order!"

I hid in my clothes closet and arranged dresses and coats around me. I heard a voice calling and I thought I was dreaming:

"Hava Bornstein, Hasheeveynoo! Hasheeveynoo!"

It was Jules! How did he get there? He called out several times. (In Dutch-Jewish circles *hasheeveynoo* means "to disappear.") Where should I disappear to, there was nowhere to go! They could find me easily if they searched the place. Again the sound of the megaphone blasting away:

"This is an order! All personnel whose names I have mentioned must immediately report downstairs! If you don't come right away, we will be forced to take veteran nurses as hostages instead! Let me warn you, if you are caught, you will be dealt with severely!"

My conscience left me no peace—that another nurse should be sacrificed and be deported because of me! I would never forgive myself. Again the ear-splitting order! The weight of my responsibility was too heavy to bear and I called out to the other nurses:

"I'm going down. I can't stand this anymore!"

I picked up my bundle and walked downstairs, passed by the nauseating Wolf, went through the portals of the hospital, and climbed into one of the vans, already filled with patients. The Germans locked the doors after me.

When the vans arrived at the Borneokade, a secluded and well-patrolled area-quai, the trains were already waiting for us. The Germans commanded us to help the patients into the trains and to take care of them. We were grateful that we were on trains and not on cattle vans. At least we would be able to sit like human beings, and not be packed in on top of each other.

I was calm now, performing my duties and trying to console the patients. In my mind I had reconciled myself with the fact that I would see my mother and Jackie in Westerbork and maybe I could secretly see Father and Paul through the fence of the men's camp.

In the afternoon they brought out mashed potatoes and cucumber salad for all of us and we helped feed the patients. I looked around. The area in front of the train was full of Germans on guard. Along the other side of the train was a high wall. There was no possibility of escape.

It was 5:00 P.M. and the train engines began to warm up. Very soon we would be on our way.

"All personnel are to get into the train!" shouted the German guards. A unit of Nazi blackshirts marched in to the area and positioned themselves opposite us, standing shoulder to shoulder and carrying bayonets. It was a frightening sight!

Everyone was waiting for the chief of transports, SS Haupt Sturmführer Aus der Fünten. The shaking train with engine warming . . . the SS . . . the blackshirt police . . . the patients . . . and we. . . .

Suddenly we heard a roar and there was Aus der Fünten on his motorcycle, escorted on both sides by his many cohorts. He handed a paper to a soldier and then we heard him call out four names. I recognized them to be the names of four of our nurses and brothers who worked with patients in the communicable diseases department. Two nurses jumped down from the train and I saw them go back for their rucksacks. Again the soldier called out along the train:

"Brother de Leeuw! Lilly Bromet!" The full meaning of the situation struck me like a bolt of lightening. Brother de Leeuw and nurse Lilly Bromet must have escaped somehow! I quickly grabbed my rucksack, jumped down from the train and said to the soldier:

"I am Lilly Bromet." He motioned to me to stand with the two others and then I saw Etty Meyers, my friend and roommate, jump down, too, and join us. The train was almost ready to leave. Aus der Fünten stepped over—tall, overbearing, stiff, ramrod back, clean-shaven, trim in his SS uniform with skulls-head insignia, black leather jacket, and black shiny boots—a costume of death. He checked the list and then raised his voice and spoke sternly:

"Are you Lilly Bromet? Why didn't you come before? Are you Lilly Bromet?"

I said "Yes," and looked him straight in the eyes. My knees were shaking. "Next thing he will ask for my identity card," I thought, "and then he'll shoot me for having lied to him." I could hardly breathe.

He turned to Etty Meyers: "You are not Brother de Leeuw! That's a man! Who are you?"

Etty told him that she also had worked at the T.B. isolation ward. He said: "No such information was given to me. Get back into the train!" he shouted at her. Poor Etty boarded the train.

The three of us stood there not daring to look at each other. Had Aus der Fünten but checked my identity card, he would have seen that I was not Lilly Bromet. My knees were getting weaker. When the Germans turned their backs, I moaned:

"Is it possible?"

The other two girls and I communicated to each other with our eyes:

"Don't say a thing!"

We were told to get into one of the vans, which the Germans locked after us and we sat there numb and unbelieving, in the near darkness until we were returned to the N.I.Z. hospital.

When we entered through the porter's loge, trembling but relieved to see the German van pull away, we were greeted by none other than Mr. Wolf:

"What are you doing back here? There is no room for you here. The *Joodse Raad* has allocated only a certain number of exemptions for nurses to the hospital and you are not among them."

I was too overcome from the day's events to attempt to argue with him. But it was impossible for me to digest this expression of man's inhumanity to man. Instead of being happy for us that we had been fortunate enough to save our lives, this "agent of doom," Wolf, made us feel that we had no right to be among the living. By returning to the hospital we were interfering with the orderly procedures that he and the *Joodse Raad* had instituted. The more I thought about it, the more hurt, angry, and enraged I became. I went to see the director-general, Dr. Kronenberg.

I told him everything and how I had gone with the patients to be deported. I could have hidden somewhere in the hospital but another nurse would have had to go in my place. I didn't want somebody else to suffer on my account. Through my sheer daring I was able to outwit the Germans and escape deportation.

"Is it a sin to be back with the living? How can this Mr. Wolf tell me there is no place for me? I want to work here and this is where I belong."

Dr. Kronenberg listened to me with understanding and said:

"Calm down, my dear, calm down. Nobody is going to throw you out. It is true, the Nazis have limited the number of personnel exemptions. You came back under the name of Lilly Bromet, but your own name has been removed from the list. However, I give you permission to stay and to work here. We will take a chance since we are not at all sure how long any of us will be exempt from deportation."

When I finally fell asleep that night, it seemed as if I had crossed an eternity of time. I felt so alone and forlorn. My former roommates and all the nurses on the floor had left on the transport.

I began to think seriously of the possibility of going into hiding. Two very important factors prevented me from doing so. I still wanted to continue with Mr. Puttkammer. My father had received a Red Cross telegram from Palestine indicating that an affidavit would be forthcoming from our relatives. I had to deliver more money to Puttkammer and sign certain papers in his office at the bank. It was my fervent hope that the Palestine exchange exemption would be secured for my entire family in Westerbork, so that they could go to Palestine instead of a concentration camp.

My second consideration was that I wanted to help as many people as possible to go into hiding through the Underground Resistance movement.

I came to the conclusion that I could not as yet leave the hospital and that I would still continue to participate in the rescue work in the hospital.

The head nurse gave me a hearty welcome and assigned me to the gynecological department, which also serviced certain special cases. For the first time in my sheltered and innocent life, I learned the meaning of the diseases of syphilis and gonorrhea; I relieved nurses in the special T.B. isolation rooms and witnessed the painful suffering of a terminal cancer case.

The latter patient was a most remarkable young woman, whose beauty was still visible even though the dread disease had discolored and emaciated her body. She lay on her bed, her shining black hair spread over her pillow; she opened her deep black eyes and implored us again and again:

"Please, put an end to my suffering! Please, relieve me of my pain. What sense is there to live like this? If you would give me just one more drop of morphine I would be out of my misery. Please, be merciful. I beg you."

To see her in this state upset me terribly, especially when her adoring husband and little daughter came to visit her. Despite her pleading, the nurse in charge of the department forbade any of us to administer the morphine injections, and she suffered bitterly. I remember how she liked me to brush her hair softly.

I do not know where her life finally ended — in the hospital under constant sedation, or in the gas chambers of the concentration camp.

14

The Joodse Invalide Hospital was now under the German command of Dr. Mayer and had become a central storage place for all kinds of medical equipment, pharmaceutical and medical supplies that the Germans had confiscated from Jewish pharmacies, hospitals, institutes, and private doctors.

Alan Hartog, Jules Godefroi, and a technical staff took care of the building. A few nurses registered, kept inventory, and stored all the supplies. Jules claimed that the German Dr. Mayer behaved quite decently toward them. Soon after the takeover, Dr. Mayer called them to a meeting and said:

"I am the boss of the building and I am also your boss. You will keep the building in good order, clean and warm, and make sure that no supplies are lost or stolen. As long as you behave well and keep everything above-board, you will be able to stay here in safety, and for the time being you will not be sent away on transport."

Before very long the Joodse Invalide Hospital was assigned to treat girls with venereal diseases. They were Dutch prostitutes working in the service and for the pleasure of the Germans. A Jewish doctor and Jewish nurses had found temporary employment by providing medical aid to the girls.

On one of our now rare and risky walks along the beautiful canals, Jules impressed upon me not to take too many chances and that I should go into hiding now.

"In any case, if you have to run away suddenly from the

N.I.Z. hospital, come to the Joodse Invalide Hospital. We have a way to hide you for a short while."

"In the middle of the lion's den?," I asked.

"Yes, if there is no other alternative, then come to me as a last resort. I am deeply concerned about you, because you are very dear to me. Please, take care!"

His words were soft, soothing, and comforting. I had not realized I was so starved for a kind word and a loving gesture. We walked along the quaint bridges and canals, under the weeping willows, in the last rays of the setting sun, drinking in the sweet spring air, until curfew time.

July 10, 1943 and arrival of the day of doom. No amount of persuasion or reasoning by the director, Dr. Kronenberg, could keep the deadly efficient Nazis from performing their merciless task—the evacuation and deportation of the N.I.Z. hospital.

"O God," I prayed, "This is the third time I will have to witness the carting away of the helpless and sick. What did they do to deserve this fate? My mind cannot grasp the dreadfulness of this cruelty, my soul is in constant pain. Help me!"

Except for the dangerously ill and the postoperational patients, hundreds of sick men, women, and children were packed into vans together with the staff and nursing personnel, myself included, and were driven under heavy guard a few blocks away to the transit depot in the Hollandse Schouwburg. This delapidated building had come into use in 1941 as a specifically Jewish theater, when the Nazi occupation authorities forbade the Jewish inhabitants to take part in any form of public entertainment. The Hollandse Schouwburg became the center of Jewish cultural expression, where famous Jewish artists performed exclusively for Jewish audiences.

In 1942, with the onset of the "final solution" of the Jewish problem, the Hollandse Schouwburg began to be used as a concentration center and transit depot for the Jews of Amsterdam who had been dragged from their houses or from the streets. Here they stayed for a few days or longer until enough people to load up a transport had been collected for shipment to the Westerbork transit concentration camp.

In the Hollandse Schouwburg our sick people were packed into the already crowded hall. We looked around. It was unbelievable! So many disheveled, downtrodden, tired human beings. No daylight penetrated into the hall and the electric bulbs burned day and night. In the auditorium, folding chairs were stacked against the walls and straw mattresses had been laid on the floor in the center. On the stage were iron racks to accommodate the few belongings that the people had brought. The coffee room was fitted out as a sick bay and on the upper floor were rooms for infectious diseases. The galley was reserved for the so-called S penal cases, people who had been discovered hiding in the homes of Gentiles.

I helped out wherever I could. It was no easy task to calm the hysterical patients and make them comfortable in the deplorably unhygienic conditions to which they were subjected.

The behavior of the helpless victims was totally unreal. Some kept moving about aimlessly, talking loudly to each other as if to mask their fear, pain, and sorrow and afraid to reveal their inner feelings. They spoke loudly in order to subdue the shrieking pain that welled up in their throats, as if they wanted to deaden all other thoughts. Others did not speak at all. They huddled together in the worn-out plush seats and stared ahead with blank expressions on their faces.

The German soldiers were always there guarding the exit doors and the windows and telling us what to do. The *Joodse Raad* officials came every day to register us or to give us information. We, the young people, soon formed a group of our own, standing by to help those in need of physical or spiritual help. When we were not busy, we found comfort in being together and talking. We could not bear the close atmosphere inside the hall and asked permission from the Germans to go outside to get a breath of fresh air. Behind the Hollandse Schouwburg, there was a small courtyard, a few yards square, which was enclosed by high walls. Our request was granted and under armed guard, we were permitted to get some air for one hour a day. We young people liked it so much that we asked for an additional hour in the morning, which was also granted.

To us it seemed as if we were walking in the most fragrant of gardens. We walked around in circles, one small group after the other, and before long we started singing prayers, and songs of love for Palestine in Hebrew. It became our regular pattern of behavior, to clap hands and after a while to join in the dancing of the Horah, while the guard watched.

"Our hopes, our aspirations, our feelings, cannot be taken away from us!," I thought.

The next day, while we were singing and laughing in the courtyard, the German guard pointed to and said in German:

"You come to my room at 8:00 tonight."

When I heard his command my heart started pounding wildly. Later on, my friends and I began to speculate about what we should do.

"Do you think we laughed and sang too much and because of that he wants to punish me?"

"That's not the reason. We did that before. He just wants you."

At these words I became frightened and nauseous with fear and disgust. The men decided that, if after entering the German's room I would begin to scream, they would burst in. No matter how dangerous it might be, they would defend my innocence and fight for me.

At 8 o'clock in the evening, I knocked at the German's door. My friends were within earshot and I had a knife in my pocket. As I entered the room the German stood up:

"Ah, Fraulein, it was good of you to come. All I wanted to ask of you is to darn my socks. I am sorry I had to trouble you."

He put a bundle of socks and a spool of yarn and needle on the table and pointed to a chair for me to sit down. I was so relieved that I almost fell into it and without looking up I started to mend his socks. I was working away furiously with trembling hands in order to finish quickly, when I heard him say:

"You must hate me. Why don't you talk? I didn't do anything to you."

"Then why do you keep us here in prison? How would you like to be seized and loaded on a transport?," I asked.

"I'm just a soldier. I have to follow the commands and instructions of my superiors, otherwise I would be in trouble. I have a wife and children at home. We are also human beings—not all Germans are bad,'' he said.

I became more daring. I did not care about the consequences of my words.

''But if all Germans are not that bad, why don't all the good ones get together and refuse to implement the evil commands to harm innocent people. You see the people in the hall and the thousands and thousands who have already gone through here and other such places? How can you stand it? If you are not as bad as you say you are, then do something about it!''

''Fraulein, you are so young, you don't understand. It is not that easy to refuse any army order. There must be discipline. I can't do anything about it.''

I didn't say any more. When I had finished with his socks, he thanked me and left.

My friends surrounded me the moment I came out. I took out my knife and said:

''I didn't have to use it. Do you know what I did for him? I darned his socks!'' We laughed so much we became almost hysterical and I was afraid the German soldier would hear us and punish us. I also told them about my discussion with him and my exploit became the talk of the Schouwburg.

As the days passed we became more and more nervous and depressed. Each day we expected to be transported to Westerbork. There was constant tension in the air and all kinds of wild rumors about extermination camps. We were so frightened.

We also heard that hundreds of children from the Creche, the Jewish Children's Shelter opposite the Hollandse Schouwburg, were being brought to safe hiding places. They were being slipped out through the back doors, sometimes in garbage cans or rucksacks, in an organized effort by members of the Underground within the *Joodse Raad*. Apparently there was effective cooperation between the outside people and the people on the inside who were working hand in hand to rescue the children. Walter Susskind was the leader of the inside organization and Theo de Bruyn was the leader of the outside group.

SS Hauptsturmführer Aus der Fünten, accompanied by his cohorts, visited the deportation center almost every night, usually drunk and glorying in his power over the helpless victims. There were rumors that some people were being smuggled out of the Hollandse Schouwburg while the SS guards were sleeping in a drunken stupor from the liquor liberally supplied to them by the *Joodse Raad*.

On Thursday, the 15th of July, we were advised that on the next day we would leave by transport for Westerbork. It became almost impossible to calm the people. I proceeded from one person to the other in an effort to be of help to them.

In the evening a young man from the *Joodse Raad* approached me. After making sure that no one was within earshot, he said:

"You have been selected to be rescued, after which you'll be placed in hiding. Keep this strictly to yourself. Go through the motions of preparing for transport. Listen carefully! Be in the attic of the Hollandse Schouwburg tomorrow morning at 6:00 A.M. After the rescue you are to go to Alan Hartog and Jules Godefroi in the Joodse Invalide. Ring the bell at the side entrance on the Nieuwe Achtergracht." We shook hands and he left.

I was terribly excited at this new development. There was hope for life again! I wondered how the Underground Resistance could arrange such a dangerous act of escape. How could it be accomplished if every exit was controlled by armed guards?

That night the drunken Aus der Fünten came again to the Hollandse Schouwburg, proudly inspecting "his fruitful efforts."

I had not slept well that whole week, but that night I did not permit myself to even doze off for fear of oversleeping.

It was still dark when I noiselessly made my way to the attic. I could not see, but I felt that I was not alone and I kept absolutely still. A few minutes later I heard someone else come in and I was afraid that I had made a mistake.

Maybe it was a trap?!

Finally a flashlight pierced the dark, revealing the same young man from last night and, with him, I saw five of my friends. I was so happy that they also had a chance to escape, since I felt guilty that I was the only one chosen. The young man introduced himself as Ron and he gave us our instructions.

"Don't utter a word and follow me closely. You may have to take some extreme risks but this is your last chance. You can still back out if you want to. O.K. Let's go!"

He led us up a small ladder to the roof, opened the door, and one by one we climbed out. The air, the sun, and the wind hit me all at once and took my breath away. I had to get used to the light. We were on top of the roof of the three-story building of the Hollandse Schouwburg, which was detached on all sides.

It was impossible to jump to the next rooftop because the distance was too great. Armed soldiers were stationed around the building on the sidewalk halfway down the block, occupying positions in between the houses and the Hollandse Schouwburg. Ron motioned to us to go toward the back.

Looking down we saw an iron fire escape between the buildings. A partially protruding wall formed a niche hiding the fire escape from the street.

In the building opposite there was a side door situated not far from the sidewalk where an armed German walked on patrol. Ron explained to us:

"Climb down the fire escape and wait in the niche. When you see the German move away from the space between the buildings run to the door. It's open, go in and wait. This will take agility and nerves. Good luck!"

He left first. We laid down on the roof and watched. It took him almost a half hour until the German guard moved away and gave him the opportunity to cross to the door of the opposite building into which he disappeared.

The next one was a girl. She tied her skirt up so that it would not get caught while climbing down the fire escape. She had to wait more than an hour till she could cross to the door. She kept looking up desperately from the niche. Finally the German moved and she ran quickly to the door. The boy who was next in line was luckier. After a few minutes of waiting he disappeared into the next building.

When it came to my turn I almost became dizzy because I have a fear of high places. I grasped the sides of the fire escape and my body shook as I climbed down. I kept on saying, *Shma Yisrael*, "Hear, O Israel." I crossed, after what seemed to me an eternity, and entered the side door.

It took more than three hours until everybody managed to cross. We followed our guide, Ron, up the backstairs of the house, which seemed to be empty. When we reached the attic, he opened the small front window and he pointed to a narrow gutter ledge leading from the front to the side of the building. From there we would have to jump to the next rooftop and hide behind the chimney. The dangerous part was to make sure not to be seen by anyone.

I climbed out of the window and walked in the gutter along the front side of the roof. I steeled myself because I realized that it was either now or never. One by one we managed to land behind the chimney of the next building. The suspense of waiting for each other kept us tense, since we depended on each other's successful movements.

If one person were to make a mistake, we would all be caught and the consequences would be fatal. By now, the sun was beginning to warm us.

We climbed up to the next roof, which was covered with red tiles. There was hardly room for our feet to walk along the edge and we had to move sideways on our tiptoes with our backs against the roof.

We all managed to get to the next rooftop, which, Ron said, would be our last lap. He instructed us to enter through the roof window, go down into the building, and come out on the other side into a garden. From there we would be on our own.

He went to the window and tried to open it but...it did not move. The other men tried but still it would not budge. It would be too risky to break the glass and take the chance that someone might hear it. There was no other entry from the roof into the building.

What should we do?

Ron contemplated the space between the two buildings. There was a fire-escape on our side that extended halfway down. On the building opposite there was a small window level with the end of the fire-escape. We all watched as he climbed down the fire-escape. From the last rung he quickly swung himself over and grasped the ledge of the small window, which was one-story from the ground. He bounced off the wall with his feet and landed safely with catlike agility. He waved to us and beckoned us to follow him.

I shall never understand how I managed to get to the ground safely. I felt as if Satan were chasing me and that I had to escape his clutches. I landed on all fours and only scraped my hands, whereas one of the girls twisted her ankle.

We had to move cautiously one by one through a garden and a passage between two houses toward the street after which we were on our own.

I grasped the hand of our guide Ron, my eyes expressing my deep gratitude to him — and I left.

How sweet and thrilling this moment was! I stood on the Plantage Muidergracht, FREE!

I suppressed the urgency to run and swiftly crossed the bridge at the Plantage Muidergracht, shaded by weeping willow trees, leading to the Roeterstraat. Then I turned right into the Nieuwe Achtergracht toward my destination, the Joodse Invalide Hospital.

15

When I rang the bell at the side entrance of the Joodse Invalide Hospital, Alan Hartog opened the door and stood before me like a savior angel. After the ordeal I had just gone through he represented a haven of safety and refuge. Quickly he led me to a room on the fifth floor in the old part of the hospital that was not in use.

I collapsed on the cot. The tension, the feeling of being pursued and persecuted, together with the tremendous physical stress I had been subjected to had all taken a heavy toll of my resources.

Alan gave me a glass of water and wiped my face with a wet towel. When I came to myself I looked around the small room. It contained a cot, a small table and chair, a sink, a glass door leading out to a sundeck, and some hooks on the wall for clothes.

This tiny hospital room became my self-imposed prison for the next five weeks. There were no regular bathroom facilities and I was forbidden to switch on the light. Food was brought to me only at night by either Jules or Alan. I looked forward to these visits because the feeling of being closed up soon became unbearable. After a few days, it appeared to me as if the walls of my room were closing in on me. I had become a hunted person, forced to hide from the Nazis.

Since I had escaped from the Hollandse Schouwburg transit assembly point, I was now registered as having been deported. In case I was apprehended now, I would be sent away immediately to a concentration camp as an "S" case and would face severe punishment.

Jules explained to me:

"You'll have to lie low for a while until the heat is off. In the meantime we will get you a new identity card through the Underground Resistance movement, since the one that you have now with the "J" under your real name will have to be torn up. You don't exist under that identity anymore. But at this moment there are complications. The last batch of identity cards issued by the Underground was discovered by the Germans to be falsified and the people using them were arrested. We came to the conclusion that the only cards that are safe to use are those the Underground Resistance obtains by stealing from the official City Registry. Blank identity cards can be removed only a few at a time. We are in close touch with the Underground Resistance and you will soon get one under an assumed name."

Periodically, the Nazis came to inspect the hospital. But no one could predict when they would come and what they would inspect. Even though the old part of the hospital in which my little room was located was not in use, one never knew whether they might send a group of soldiers on a special search mission.

Jules and Alan informed me of the special precautions they had taken to protect me against surprise searches. When the alarm buzzer would sound it meant that the Germans were in the building and I would have to hurry into the service elevator in the rear and stay in it. By breaking the circuit cable of the power-motor on the roof, they had devised a way of having the elevator remain stuck between two floors. When the Nazis pushed the button they could not move the elevator. After the Nazis left they would fix the power-motor and the elevator would be in working order again.

The first time I had to escape into the elevator I found it to be a very frightening half-hour all by myself in the dark cabin. When the danger had past, I returned to my room where I found Alan waiting for me to see how I felt after the experience.

After he left, I opened the doors that led to the sundeck outside and breathed in the fresh air in relief. It was a beautiful day and the sunshine was like a wonderful tonic after the dark experience in the elevator.

Suddenly I saw a man approaching. I recognized Kurt, assistant to Jules. We looked at each other and he must have noticed the panic on my face. I moved my finger to my lips as if to tell him not to utter a word and he left quickly. The next thing I knew I was lying on the floor and my head ached. Evidently I had fainted and hit my head against the cot. The tension of my experiences that day had obviously been too much for me.

In the evening Jules put my mind at ease. He told me that Kurt was aware of the illegal underground activities, for he operated the freight elevator together with Jules.

Gradually more and more people were given a temporary haven within the walls of the Joodse Invalide Hospital. One did not know the identity of the other, even though we all met in the freight elevator in times of danger and panic. Sometimes the overloaded elevator would hang for hours in between the floors until the Germans left the hospital. We would not talk, whisper, move, or relieve ourselves. In sum, it meant going through an agonizing physical strain time after time.

Many on the hospital staff were engaging in illegal activities. One knew very little about the activities of the other and this had its advantages. If one of the staff were caught by the Germans, he could not tell on the others.

The two men from the Underground Resistance movement with whom Alan and Jules worked very closely were Dominee (Pastor) Ader and Jan Meilof Yver, both very active and brave leaders. Alan and Jules supplied them with blankets, sheets, medicines, and other items they needed for the *onderduikers*— the hidden Jews.

At the very beginning of the rescue operation, Jules did not know who they were. One day he saw two tall, rough and tough looking men, wearing black boots like those worn by the Nazis and the N.S.B. They were standing near the reception window in the downstairs lobby and Jules asked them: "Gentlemen, what are you doing here?"

"Are you Mr. Godefroi?" they asked. "Could we talk to you in private?" At first Jules was suspicious, but soon he found out that Alan had been dealing with them all along. As a matter of fact, Pastor Ader was the one to arrange my identity card.

On the evening of Friday, the 13th of August, 1943, Jules

129

rushed in and told me to follow him immediately. We left stealthily through the side exit on the Nieuwe Achtergracht and to my amazement he told me we were going to the N.I.Z. hospital. When we arrived there, Jules unlocked the front door and we entered. It was dark inside and as quiet as a tomb. Jules directed me into one of the rooms that had once been occupied by a doctor and then he explained:

"Today the Germans evacuated the last part of the N.I.Z. hospital. No one was allowed to remain; Alan and I have been left in charge of the hospital and all its equipment. We also got word from Dr. Mayer, the German head of the Joodse Invalide Hospital, that employees have been suspected of engaging in illegal activities within the hospital. Therefore, we decided that you should stay in the N.I.Z. hospital until the danger blows over."

I stayed there for two days and nights. Since I had not brought any food, I set about trying to find something to eat. I moved about very carefully and quietly. Roaming about all alone in the empty hospital building gave me a very eerie feeling. I even went to my previous room in the nurses' quarter to see if I might find some of my clothes that I had left behind, since I had escaped with only the clothes on my back. Sure enough, they were still there. So I packed my clothes into a suitcase and quickly went back to the room to which Jules had assigned me, and waited impatiently for further developments.

Finally on Sunday evening Jules returned and led me back to the Joodse Invalide Hospital.

"You should have seen with what thoroughness those Nazis went through the building. They checked every inch from top to bottom. It was good you were not there. Now Dr. Mayer has established a department of experimentation on the sterilization of mixed-marriage couples of Jews and Gentiles," he reported. "But I also have happy news for you. You'll be getting your identity card this week."

I was elated, for it seemed to me that I had waited an eternity. One morning, Jules brought the card and filled in all the required details. My picture was affixed to the middle panel, together with my fingerprints, the official stamp was pasted on, and I chose a new name, Elisabeth Bos, to be my official name. It was not long before everyone was calling me Leesha, short for Elisabeth, and my previous name, Hava Bornstein, was forgotten.

On Friday, August 20, 1943, Jules introduced me to Mr. Denencamp, the contact man of Jan Meilof Yver, who had been assigned to help me go to a new location in the underground. It was my first meeting with a Dutch Gentile working actively in the Underground Resistance and from the moment I saw him I felt confident. Soon I bade a tearful goodbye to Jules and Alan, whom I could not thank enough for all the concern and care they had lavished upon me.

It felt strange to walk away from the Joodse Invalide Hospital in the bright sunshine as a free person and to proceed along the same streets I had recently been driven in a Nazi van on my way to a concentration camp. At first I was hesitant and kept looking over my shoulder to see if someone was following me. But Mr. Denencamp took hold of my elbow and gently but firmly guided me along, while conversing with me about ordinary everyday topics, so that I gradually began to feel more comfortable. We were on our way to his home in Utrecht, where I would stay for a few days with his family and other "guests" until my next place of refuge would be cleared.

My first instructions began as we sat side by side on the express train rushing us to Utrecht.

"The most important thing for you to do at this point is to completely reorient yourself," Mr. Denencamp advised me. "You are Leesha Bos now. I don't even know your former name and I don't want to know it. You must construct for yourself a background of details about your home, family, education, and work. Memorize them well and stick to those facts at all times. Try to forget what happened during the last few years, shut out the past, and remember, never show fear or suspicion of being followed."

I listened to him intently. He must have sensed my concern and anxiety because he tried to put me at ease:

"Leesha, I don't know very much about you, but they did tell me that you are a girl with daring and courage. Your new way of

131

life will present problems and new challenges. While they will be difficult I am sure that if you'll adapt yourself, you'll be able to handle them.''

My future conduct was being outlined for me by this soft-spoken but determined gentleman, and I accepted his counsel with humility and grateful appreciation. Mr. Denencamp was a man in his thirties, of above medium height and of slight build. His blond and blue-eyed looks were typically Dutch, complete with a healthy, ruddy complexion.

From the first moment we met, I knew I could put all my trust in him. He encouraged me to discuss with him any difficulties I might encounter in the future.

"After this weekend we will know where you'll be placed. The Hague and Amsterdam are not safe for you. Too many people might recognize you. Ah, here we are in Utrecht," he announced.

The train came to a halt. Our exit led direct.y to a group of German soldiers on the platform. For one terrifying moment I hesitated, petrified with fear, but Mr. Denencamp put his hand on my shoulder and tenderly helped me to get off the train. He carried my valise to the baggage-check counter and left it there to be picked up later under the cover of darkness. It would be too conspicuous to arrive with a large suitcase that the neighbors might see and suspect. But it was all right to take the small grip, since it indicated a stay of only a few days.

As we approached his house we were greeted by the furious barking of a terrier dog, jumping excitedly on the window-sill inside. The thick, white curtains made it impossible to see within. When we entered through the hall into the family room, we were suddenly surrounded by about seven people with smiling faces who welcomed us warmly. The dog barked frantically until Mr. Denencamp picked him up. I was greeted by Mrs. Denencamp's pumping handshake and her jovial invitation to make myself at home with the rest of "our guests" in the attic and then to come down and help with the preparation of the vegetables for dinner.

I was prepared for everything, but such a welcome was so unexpectedly delightful that it made me feel comfortable, wanted, and at ease, immediately.

Mrs. Denencamp was a mousy-looking good soul. She was always busy with cleaning and cooking and talked almost constantly. She was the center of all activity in the house and everyone loved her because of her total lack of selfishness. Their teenage son, Jan, was the image of his father.

In the course of the five days I spent with the Denencamps, I learned to love the warmth of their crowded and informal household and its activities and chores in which everyone participated. In their home, responsibility for each other's safety was of the utmost concern. The "guests" were Jews either hiding there permanently or in transit like myself. We knew each other only by our first names—two teenage brothers, Hank and Tom; a former law student, Karel; and a mother, Marie, and her eleven-year-old son, Hugo.

A private alarm system had been instituted—friends and family of the Denencamps used a prearranged series of knocks on the door. But when a stranger rang the bell, especially someone in uniform, our excitable friend, the terrier, would growl and whine and warn us of the possibility of danger. In record time we, "the guests," would climb up to the attic, pull up the small ladder, lock the trap door from the inside and wait on our beds, hardly breathing. When it was all safe again, Mrs. Denencamp would call us down and we would continue where we had left off as if nothing had happened.

In the evenings when the curtains had been drawn for the blackout as well as for our protection, we sat around the family room, which also served as the dining room. We talked, played games, or studied. I learned to play chess from Jan and became quite fond of the game. This talented young man even taught me how to overcome my life-long fear of dogs, and before long the terrier and I had become close friends. I was completely integrated into the family, and when the time came for me to leave I felt a real sense of loss. I had barely become accustomed to my new surroundings and now I would have to break up the association and go somewhere else. I knew I would miss them all. When we said goodbye, Mrs. Denencamp invited me to come again on a weekend visit. Her warm invitation eased the unhappiness of my departure.

133

On the way to the train, Mr. Denencamp informed me that my next destination was the city of Leiden. He planned for us to leave in the afternoon, in order to arrive in Leiden after dark. He spoke to me like a father and a friend. I told him of my decision not to stay hidden inside all the time.

"I simply can't stand being locked up as if I were in a prison. Shouldn't I be able to go out of the house in which I'm hiding and live normally? Besides, I would very much like to continue to be active in the Underground Resistance movement. They probably told you what I have done in the hospital in Amsterdam. Perhaps I will be able to resume my work in the Resistance?"

Mr. Denencamp looked at me with new interest. He said:

"Leesha, you know the risks you would be taking by being above ground and not hiding? You don't look especially Jewish, although you have dark hair and eyes, but you might be suspected by those neighbors who are informers and N.S.B. — Nazis sympathizers. People are rewarded by the Nazis for offering incriminating information about Jews. You might be caught in an identity control check or in a street raid, when the Nazis are out to catch our boys for the work camps and factories in Germany. Think of the danger you'll be in every moment. As to your wish to resume underground work, which represents the ultimate in resistance, but poses the gravest danger to you, I have to give it some thought."

When he saw how unhappy I was about his hesitant manner, he added:

"I'll do my best. I'll propose your request at our next cell meeting."

I was most grateful.

"Mr. Denencamp, thank you for everything. How will I ever be able to repay you for all that you have done for me? Words are so inadequate."

"So don't try," he interrupted me. "I know how you feel, dear girl. I am part of the fight against barbarism and terror. We will not yield to the Nazi power. Our aim is to do everything possible to counteract and resist the brutal violence and inhumanity of the Nazi."

I had become so involved in our discussion that I did not realize that we had arrived in Leiden. We walked through town until we stopped in front of a large corner house on the Schelpen kade.

"Here we are," Mr. Denencamp said, "and here I'll leave you. I'll introduce you to Mr. and Mrs. de Koning and then you will be on your own."

It was already dark so he couldn't possibly have seen my apprehension. He went on:

"Leesha, take hold of yourself. It will work out better than you ever expected. In any case we have a date for you to spend a weekend with us in Utrecht in a few weeks. Time flies! I promise I'll pick you up from here and we'll travel together. O.K.?"

I nodded. This man was so good to me. He put his arm around my shoulders and pointed to the middle of the street:

"Look how beautifully the canal and the trees stand out in the moonlight! It's a clear night and perfect for the British bombers on their way to Germany."

I straightened up. "Mr. Denencamp, you have a deep understanding of human nature. I am ready now."

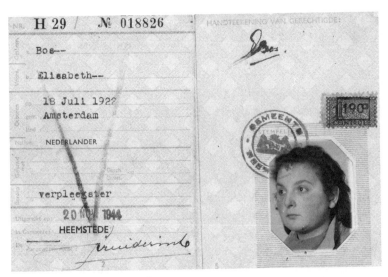

My illegal identity card.

The Hollandse Schouwburg, originally a concert hall, was used by the Nazis as a concentration center and transit depot. It is estimated that it was the last place of residence for 50,000 Amsterdam Jews. Their suffering was immense.

The entrance of the Jewish Invalid Hospital.

Letter K		VERZORGINGSRAAD VOOR LEIDEN	Nº 49033	
K 24	K 30	**EXTRA KAART** VOOR	K 12	K 6
K 23	K 29	**BIJZONDERE VERSTREKKINGEN**	K 11	K 5
K 22	K 28	t. b. v. de ingezeten n van Leiden K 1683	K 10	
K 21	K 27	De waarde der bonnen en de wijze van inlever ng zullen bij aankondiging worden bekend gemaakt Losse bonnen zijn ongeldig.	K 9	K 3
K 20		K 17 K 16		K 2
	K 25	K 15 K 14 K 13		

Food ration card.

Hiding place on the Boerhavelaan in Leiden.

Het Marishuis, convalescent home in Heemstede, where I worked as a nurse. It served as my base for illegal underground activities.

138

House of the Kruizingas on the Endegeesterstraatweg in Oegstgeest, hiding place for many and base for underground activities.

Reinier van Kampenhout, friend and mentor, who fought courageously while endangering his life in the performance of Underground rescue and Resistance operations. Five months before the end of World War II he was captured and tortured to death by the Nazis in the Amersfoort Prison.

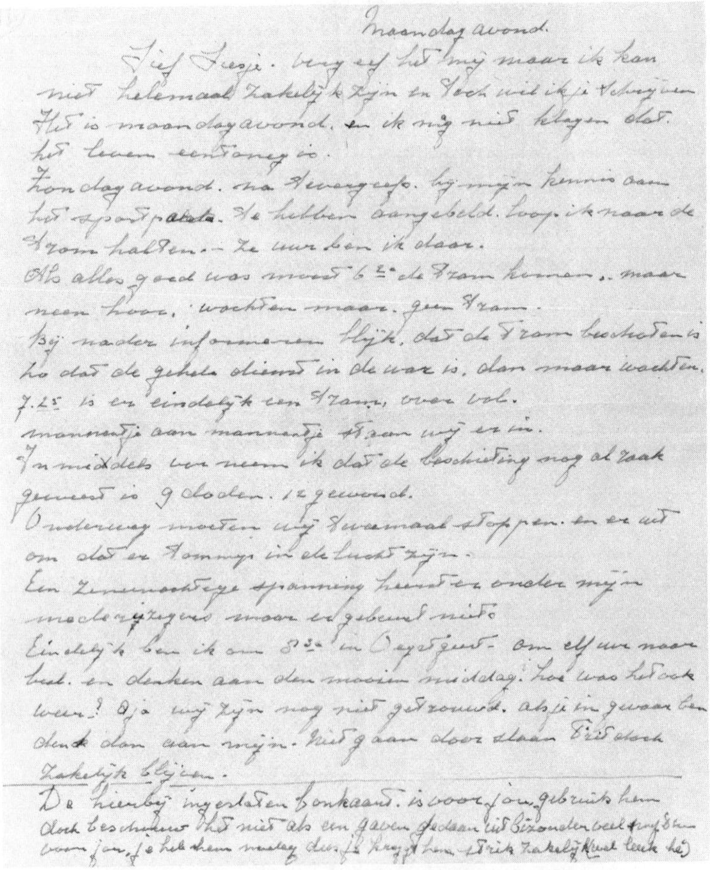

Maandag avond.

Lief [illegible]. [illegible] het mij maar ik kan niet helemaal zakelijk zijn en toch wil ik je schrijven
Het is maandagavond. en ik mag niet klagen dat het leven eentonig is.
Zondagavond. na [illegible]. bij mijn kennis aan het sportpark. We hebben aangebeld. loop ik naar de tram halten.- [illegible] uur ben ik daar.
Als alles goed was moest 6 [illegible] de tram komen.. maar neen hoor, wachten maar. geen tram.
Bij nader informeren blijk. dat de tram beschoten is zo dat de gehele dienst in de war is. dan maar wachten.
7.25 is er eindelijk een tram, over vol.
mannetje aan mannetje staan wij er in.
Inmiddels vernam ik dat de beschieting nog al [illegible] geweest is 9 doden. 12 gewond.
Onderweg moeten wij tweemaal stoppen. en er uit om dat er Tommys in de lucht zijn.
Een zenuwachtige spanning heerst er onder mijn medereizigers maar er gebeurt niets.
Eindelijk ben ik om 8 [illegible] in Oegstgeest- om elf uur naar bed. en denken aan den mooien middag. hoe was het ook weer! O ja wij zijn nog niet getrouwd. als je in [illegible] denk dan aan mijn. Niet gaan door [illegible] toch zakelijk blijven.

De hierbij ingesloten bonkaart. is voor jou, gebruik hem doch beschouw het niet als een gaven gedaan uit bizonder veel [illegible] van jou, je hebt hem nodig dus je krijgt hem. [illegible] zakelijk [illegible]

One of the many letters Reinier wrote to me in Dutch.

16

Living in the de Koning household was my first real introduction into the world of Gentiles. I had had a very cordial relationship with my Gentile friends in high school and later on at the School of Fashion Design. My father had had good experiences in his business dealing with non-Jews and many of our good neighbors had been Gentiles. I had enjoyed a wonderful weekend with the Denencamps. With all of them it was a natural and free association.

But I had never been intimately acquainted with Gentiles in their homes before. Mine had been a totally Jewish world until I left Amsterdam. And now, I, too, would become a Gentile, at least outwardly. The de Konings knew that I was Jewish but nothing else. Anyone who asked the reason for my being in the de Koning household would be told that I was to assist Mrs. de Koning, who was pregnant, with her many household duties.

Nel de Koning, who towered over me in height and size, was happy to welcome me. The combination of red cheeks, grey-blue eyes, and straight blond hair around her full face presented a picture of vibrant health. As she showed me into the living room, a little boy ran toward her and hid his face in her skirt.

"This is Joop," she said as she introduced me to a shy three-year-old boy. "He stays with us now. His Jewish parents are also hidden, separately. They had a hard time of it from the very beginning of the war. They lived in that part of Rotterdam that the Germans bombed so devastatingly. Everything they possessed was destroyed and they had to set up a new home. Last July they received the call for deportation. According to the Nazis, this little three-year-old Jewish boy is a danger to the German Reich. Well, to us he is not! We took him in, so the *Moffen* won't get him!'' She hugged Joop on her lap.

"You are now my little boy, isn't that right, Joopje?'' She cuddled him and called him by his diminutive name.

"Now let's get you set, Leesha. Your room is on the top floor in the back. There are two other couples living in this house and they are not Jewish. We don't know them too well. As far as we can judge they are not Nazi-sympathizers. Be careful. Act friendly to them but not too chummy. From the way you talk, I can hear you had a good education. Don't show it. Try to act like an average young Dutch girl. Tell them you are the daughter of a friend of mine in The Hague who came to help me, O.K.?'

"My husband will be home soon from work. His helper, Gerrit, who lives with us, is a young fellow hiding from the Germans in order to avoid work in Germany and he does not have to know about your being Jewish. He helps my husband with his truck gardening.''

"Come Leesha, do you want to help me set the table?''

Ari and Nel de Koning were thoroughly ingratiating in their honesty and simplicity. The risk they took in giving shelter to three human beings trying to escape the Nazi terror filled me with grateful humility. But Ari and Nel did not think it was something special. They helped because it was their conviction that this was the right thing to do. In their opinion a person who did not help another person in need and who did not resist the Nazis was a wrongdoer and certainly not a Christian.

At first I took Ari's reticence as being directed at me and it made me feel depressed and shy. But soon our friendship developed and I discovered within this balding, sinewy individual a wealth of thoughts and aspirations that rose way above his down-to-earth lifestyle. When we finally started talking I was amazed at the sensitivity and depth of understanding he displayed. A shy smile lit up his rugged, rough-hewn face when he read me a poem that he had written.

In the evenings, Nel knitted with her cat curled up on her lap.

142

Ari and I played chess, talked or studied Latin, for which we had registered in a correspondence course.

This routine represented a radical change in my life. I was no more the hunted object in full view of the sadistic Nazi persecutors who could strike out fatally at me at will. I no longer participated with the Underground in the exciting and tension-filled rescue of children and adults from the hospital. No longer did I witness my fellow Jews being beaten, robbed of their human dignity, dispossessed, imprisoned, and finally thrown into waiting trains to be deported to a "destination unknown."

The various dramatic events I had experienced and the hair-raising escapes from deportation only now began to take their toll on me. During the day I kept busy and was able to divert my thoughts from my deep inner anguish about my loved ones, but the nights were often pure torture for me.

What had happened to my parents and my brothers? Were they still in Westerbork transit camp in Holland? Did the "Puttkammer *Sperr*" still exempt them from deportation to a concentration camp? Would they be exchanged to Palestine?

I had delivered the requested amount of diamonds and cash to Puttkammer to keep them on the list. The International Red Cross had already confirmed the affidavit for my family from our relatives in Palestine to assure their exchange to Palestine. I prayed with all my heart for their safety. Were they suffering hunger, now that I was forbiden to send them food packages from my hiding place? I felt so helpless and frustrated. My family's faces appeared before me and the ache of longing to be with them and to feel their warmth and their love remained with me constantly. I tossed and turned on my small, hard cot, feeling cold and totally forsaken. In my loneliness the face of David lit up suddenly and a searing pain went through me. I had tried to push him out of my mind but my heart was not free of him yet.

In comparison with my immediate past, my present existence was quiet and uncomplicated on the surface. However, I was possessed of a constant fear of being found out as a *onderduiker*, a person in hiding, and thus of endangering my courageous hosts, Ari and Nel de Koning, and their other charges.

The German police was fully aware that Jews and young men disappeared into underground hiding places and that many of them were provided with illegal identity cards.

The German *Sicherheits Dienst*, the notorious *Gestapo*, offered a reward of fl. 25–40 head money for each Jew who was detected and a reward of fl. 1000 was given to anyone who reported offenses against the Germans.

The strictest precautions had to be taken to maintain a normal household situation. Anything exceptional could arouse suspicion and cause a Nazi sympathizer to inform on us. The consequences of a Gestapo investigation most often turned out to be either imprisonment, deportation, or death.

In the beginning of my stay at the de Konings I kept away from the windows. I did not open the front door, and I did not venture outside. But gradually I became freer and more daring.

Soon I went shopping, I traveled on the streetcar, and even by train to Utrecht to visit the Denencamps for the second time. Mr. Denencamp had kept his promise and had recommended me to the Underground Movement in Leiden.

I became a courier between Tom and Jan and traveled from an address on the Rijnsburger weg to the Oude Singel in Leiden. I never knew what I was carrying. Often, I was told, it was a very important package and I would hide it inside my bra. Now at least I felt I was doing something worthwhile. I was extremely careful that no one in the house, not even Ari and Nel, should suspect anything.

The most wonderful surprise came to me in the form of a letter from Jules Godefroi, telling me that he was coming to see me. He suggested that I meet him outside the Leiden station after dark. We were so happy to see each other and we had so much to talk about while we were walking through the blacked-out dark streets of Leiden, not even feeling the cold of winter.

Jules was still the head of the technical service in the Joodse Invalide Hospital, which was now used for sterilization of the Jewish partners in mixed marriages. Even these couples were unable to escape torment; they were forced to choose between sterilization or deportation. Those treated received certification from a German doctor, were exempt from wearing the yellow

Jewish star, and were allowed to work in limited areas.

Jules was worried about me, for he had heard about my renewed activities in the Underground Resistance and I had to reassure him that I was very careful. It was marvelous to hear about the many illegal feats he was accomplishing right under the noses of the Nazi doctors and the German soldiers in the hospital.

He missed his train and arrived in Amsterdam after curfew. I learned later, that he had walked stealthily, almost without making noise for one hour in the empty streets, from the station to the hospital, terribly frightened and knowing full well the consequences of being caught after curfew.

I skipped and ran all the way home. Not even the bombers overhead nor the shooting of the antiaircraft guns could dampen my high spirits. "Jules came to see me! He took off his Jewish star and endangered his life, just to talk to me," I mused happily. His very presence had consoled me; the warm and tender feeling of friendship and his concern for me had eased my loneliness for a while.

Ari and Nel were still up, waiting for me. The look on their faces alarmed me.

"Sit down, Leesha. We have something to discuss with you," Ari said looking anxious. "The Underground Resistance group in Oegstgeest, which is a suburb of Leiden, has successfully executed a raid on the distribution office and escaped with thousands of ration cards and identity cards that are so badly needed for the hidden people. The Nazis are furious and out for blood! They are cracking down on anyone who is even slightly suspect."

"Mrs. Kuyper, the nextdoor neighbor, told Nel that Mrs. de Graaf, who lives diagonally opposite our house, is known to be a N.S.B. Nazi and is suspicious about the many people in our house. Mrs. de Graaf also wanted to know about 'that' little boy."

I could see how upset Nel was, which was not good for her advanced pregnant condition. My happy mood began to evaporate.

"Do you recommend that I leave?," I asked directly. "I don't want to be any trouble to you. Please tell me!"

Nel sighed, but with great determination she said: "No,

Leesha. That's not the right thing to do. I told Mrs. Kuyper about Joopje, that he is a war orphan from Rotterdam and that his parents were killed when the Germans bombed their house. Now we are taking care of him. There was no talk about you. But in order to avoid any suspicion I want to suggest that next Sunday you come with us to church. Mrs. Kuyper and many other neighbors attend the services; the word will filter down to Mrs. de Graaf, that you are a Christian. Could you do this for us? Think about it, you still have a few days until Sunday.''

Ari sensed my consternation and added: "If you leave now, wouldn't that justify their suspicions? In my opinion we have to go on in our usual way, and show them that we have nothing to hide or fear. Leesha, if you come with us to church that would strengthen our case.''

The next few days and nights passed in agonizing soul-searching. What was I to do? Should I leave this house, rather than appear in a place of worship that was alien to me and that would make me feel as if I were betraying my faith? But then I had nowhere else to go! Any suspicious move could bring me straight into the hands of the Nazis, and would also place the de Konings in danger!

"Oh God, help me!,'' my heart and soul cried out. "Show me a way out of this dilemma!''

I was trying to think what advice my parents might have given me in such a situation. Wasn't one supposed to do everything in one's power in order to preserve life? I felt I was being torn apart and I couldn't find a peaceful moment for myself. Finally I decided that I really had no choice.

So on a crisp, cold, and sunny Sunday morning Ari and Nel de Koning, Joopje, Gerrit, and I went to church together. As we passed the house of Mrs. de Graaf we saw the curtains move.

"She saw us,'' Nel murmered, "good, that's exactly what we wanted.''

The Protestant church was a modern, clean-cut structure, and was bright and airy inside. After we sat down, I cautiously lifted my head and looked around. I saw no crosses, pictures, or Christian statues. The sun was streaming through the stained-glass windows, lighting up the church in soft geometric design. Members of the congregation were singing hymns. Nel had told me to follow her movements closely.

When the pastor started preaching I purposely shut him out of my mind by reciting Latin grammar to myself. Despite my efforts, my ears picked up words repeated by the pastor again and again. Unintentionally, I started to listen. The pastor was beseeching his congregation to remain faithful to God's commandments and to resist the temptations of Nazism. He spoke out openly and fearlessly against the Nazis, whom he accused of depriving people of their rights and liberties, and denounced the introduction of National Socialistic ideas in our press and schools and through vicious propaganda.

I saw the people in the crowded church listening with full attention, drinking in every word. The pastor continued:

"Those who deny liberty to the Jews fight against a people who may be called God's people—a people for whom God has certain plans. In the Holy Scriptures the people of Israel are represented as a chosen people. Therefore we should not despise them or consider them inferior. Moreover, from the viewpoint of charity and humanity, it is not permissible to segregate citizens of Jewish blood from the people as a whole. The Nazi's hatred of God is clearly revealed in their hatred of the people of Israel."

His words touched me to the very core of my being. The Jewishness that had caused so much hatred, persecution, deportation, and death of our people at the hands of the Nazis, that same Jewishness was now being ennobled, elevated and sanctified by this brave, outspoken, and honorable man of truth as he denounced the wickedness of the Nazis.

No wonder the people of his congregation came unfailingly to listen to his sermons. His influence upon them was obviously great. He strengthened their courage, clarified their understanding, sharpened their consciences, and steeled their resistance.

Then the pastor announced: "Let us pray." Whereupon the entire congregation bowed their heads and prayed silently. The services ended with the singing of the hymn "Rock of Ages."

The church experience left an indelible impression upon me.

More than acquiescing to their request, I was indebted to Ari and Nel for taking me to hear this courageous and fearless spiritual leader restore and cleanse the besmirched image of my own faith. Now I could give proper recognition to myself as a Jew and hold my head high. It made me even more determined to live through this dark and difficult period and to fight the evil forces that threatened to annihilate my people.

Nel and Ari reacted to my praise of the pastor with only one comment: "The pastor is a good Christian."

After the Christmas to New Year holiday season, which I spent in Utrecht with the Denencamps, in their ever-expanding household, we settled down to weather the cold winter and the approaching termination of Nel's pregnancy.

One afternoon, after lunch, Nel and I were discussing how to arrange the nursery when the front doorbell rang. As I opened the door a man quickly forced himself inside, locked the door, pulled out the key and pushed me into the living room, while simultaneously another man entered from the garden through the kitchen sidedoor, locked it, and took out the key. The whole thing took only a few seconds.

"We are from the *Gestapo*—security police—the *Sicherheitsdienst*," they announced in Dutch. "We heard you have a little Jew-boy here in the house. How many people live here? We want to see everyone's identity card. Nobody is to leave until we are through!"

These commands were barked out in staccato fashion and sounded like bullets fired from a gun. I looked at Nel, who at first blushed fiery red, but then the blood drained from her face.

For an instant I felt the room spinning around me and fear cut through me like a sharp knife. But the next moment I was acutely aware that the safe outcome of this encounter would depend on my acting as coolly and normally as possible.

One *Gestapo*-S.D. man remained with Nel, while the other followed me to my room to get my identity card. He ordered me to rejoin Nel while he examined the identity cards of the other couples and took his time to thoroughly search the house.

At any moment I expected to see the *Gestapo* man come tearing down the stairs, holding a bunch of incriminating ration cards that I had planned to deliver to Jan after dark. I had picked them up the night before from Tom and hidden them under a piece of linoleum floor-covering in a corner of my room. The suspense was terrifying. Finally he came down and nodded to his partner: "Everything is in order."

He settled down on the sofa and produced a couple of books containing lists of numbers of cancelled, lost, and suspicious identity cards. While he was examining my identity card and comparing the number against all those in his books, I forced myself to sit down so that I could hold on to my shaky knees, while trying to appear as casual as possible. At that critical moment I turned my face and a frightening scene flashed through my mind. I saw myself being forced onto a crowded cattle train on my way to a concentration camp. I prayed to God with all my heart.

"O.K., young lady," he said, holding the card against the light and studying the watermark, "Your card seems to be all right." Then he began to interrogate me, asking the same questions over and over again in an attempt to catch me in a lie. When he was through with me, he started the same procedure with Nel. It proved to be a good thing that we had synchronized our stories from the very beginning. Their main objective was to find out about little Joop, who, in the meantime, had awakened from his afternoon nap.

The *Gestapo* man insisted:

"We have it from reliable sources that he is Jewish. How did you get him? Where are his parents? You must tell us all you know!"

And each time Nel assured them:

"I can only tell you what I know. He is a war orphan from Rotterdam. His parents were killed during the bombing and he was brought to me through a war-orphan rescue committee. Believe me, that's all I know."

My own panic had subsided and gradually I began to feel more

149

self-assured. If these *Gestapo* men considered my identity card valid after their close scrutiny and did not suspect my outward appearance then I had nothing to fear.

Nel was holding Joopje close to her; I saw the pain and the agony on her face. The Nazis had been badgering her for two hours.

"Can I make her a cup of tea?," I asked the *Gestapo* man. "She is in her ninth month. Please, have some consideration for her. She is very upset."

One of them went with me into the kitchen—they were probably afraid that I would run away.

Nel served tea and biscuits to the *Gestapo* men, after which they became more talkative and gave us a lecture about the Jews.

"All of them have flat feet, prominent lips, and large hooked noses. They are despicable characters and they are cowards and weaklings. I could smell one a mile away," one of them boasted.

I looked him straight in the face and asked: "Really, are they that terrible?"

"Oh, young lady, you don't know the half of it! They don't behave normally like you. If you would see them talking and walking you would recognize them to be Jews and you would hate them as we do!"

It was getting dark outside and we drew the blackout curtains. Finally they decided to go, warning us that they would be back the day after to talk to Ari about Joopje. As they were leaving I realized that they had not returned my identity card to me. When I asked for it, they apologized, gave it back to me, and bid me a pleasant evening.

After I had closed the door behind them I leaned against it and hugged my identity card. Waves of shivers washed over me as I reacted to the tension and fear that I had experienced that afternoon.

Shortly afterwards Ari and Gerrit came back from work. When they heard of our ordeal at the hands of the *Gestapo*, we started moving fast. One could never trust the Nazis. They could come back that night and maybe they were even now watching our house.

It was decided that Gerrit would leave right away and go to his uncle in Leiderdorp. Ari would bring me to Nel's parents, the Rietvelds, on the Rijnsburger weg for the night. In the meantime, the Underground Resistance would arrange another address at which I could stay.

Nel was utterly exhausted and went straight to bed—the strain had been too much for her. Little Joop would stay in the house until the Underground would contact his parents and decide what to do with him.

I ran upstairs to pack my valise. When I hugged Nel, thanking her for all she and Ari had done for me and wishing her all the best, I felt an even stronger bond of friendship between us after the afternoon's experience.

Ari put my valise on his bicycle and together we walked through the dark streets in detour fashion. When we were sure that no one was following us we entered the house of the Rietvelds.

What fate was next awaiting me?

17

After the warm and friendly relationship I had had with Nel and Ari de Koning, it was a shock for me to be confronted by the almost Spartan quality of Tante Meta, in whose home the Resistance next placed me. Her lined, birdlike face, surrounded by wispy, dirty-blonde hair, had a stern and serious look. Nothing escaped her sharp eyes and very seldom did she utter a loving word or even make a friendly gesture. Although I knew that she cooperated with the Underground movement by hiding people in her house, her attitude of coldness made me feel unwelcome. The very piece of bread I ate was given as if it were an alm or a handout of which I was made aware with every bite.

The only devotion that I saw her display was toward her old and lame airdale terrier. Struggling under the weight of the large dog, she carried him in her arms and laid him tenderly on the sofa, which he occupied entirely. She spoke to him, fed him, and cleaned after the sick dog until her hands were rough and red from the scrubbing.

The Underground Resistance movement requested that I be confined to the house after the "unscheduled visit" of the *Gestapo* and their promise to come back for further investigation.

It was not clear whether Tante Meta actually owned the two large adjoining houses on the Boerhave laan opposite the Leiden University Hospital, but I soon found that each of the many rooms was occupied by a number of people—couples and singles, whose personal affairs were completely unknown to me.

Some of the people in the two houses opened their doors only for Tante Meta, for she provided them with all their necessities. During the day, the house was quiet, but on some nights I could hear male voices and movement below my room. I never asked questions or made any remarks. I had learned to make myself unnoticed and unobtrusive.

One day as I passed the large front room I almost let out a cry. Through a crack in the door I saw two large eyes staring at me. A little woman opened the door and asked me:

"Are you Leesha? I heard Tante Meta call you. Please come in and meet my husband. We are the Moppelchens, he is Mop and I am Pelchen."

We laughed and shook hands. The Moppelchens were so cute; both of them small, blond, and of German-Jewish extraction. They had been hidden for seven months in the front room of the house with the curtains and drapes always drawn. Sometimes in the dark of the night they went outside in turn to get some fresh air in the garden.

Their sense of humor and light-heartedness despite the war and the tragic situation in which we found ourselves was a welcome relief to Tante Meta's frigidity.

Whenever I could I slipped into their room after rapping on their door according to a prearranged signal. Mop, which means "a joke" in Dutch, kidded me a lot with his dry sense of humor and ready jokes. We drank cups of coffee substitute that tasted to me like nectar. We talked and dreamed about the future after the war.

"We have relatives in New York," Mop said. "Maybe they'll help us get to America."

I was amazed: "America? Why not Palestine? That's where the future lies for the Jewish people. Only in our country of origin will we be able to live as a free people and no one will dare throw us out. Oh, how I wish my whole family had gone there before the war!"

"Well," said Pelchen, "we are not young enough to work the land and to start the hard way. We will try our luck in America. Do you know there are millions of Jews living there?"

I mused thoughtfully: "It is hard to imagine that there are still free Jews in this world. Do you think the Jews in America and elsewhere know about our situation here in Europe?

"You know that in our religion we have a saying, 'All Jews are responsible one for the other.' Do you think their hearts bleed while our people here are treated with brutal violence? Do they cry out when we are beaten? Did they hear about the hell of the concentration camps? Does their life go on as usual? Do they love, do they marry and have children? Can they plan ahead for the future while one part of the Jewish people, like a vital limb from its body, is being ripped and butchered to pieces? Why don't we hear from them?

"A protesting word—even one outcry on our behalf—would mean so much and would console and strengthen us! What will become of us?"

"We can't think about the future yet," Mop said. "Everything looks so black! I don't even see the beginning of the end of this horrible war. In July when the Allies invaded Sicily and Italy we thought Hitler had already capitulated. But except for the Russian front, the Nazis are still going strong. The Allies are talking about a second front."

I exclaimed: "Let's hope it will be soon, maybe all the deported people will still be saved. Oh God, I have nightmares about it. There are so many wild rumors, I don't want to believe them. They are too terrible to imagine!" I was almost in tears.

"Shshsh," Pelchen put her finger to her lips. We heard something drop through the mailslot and someone outside running away. I went to the hall and brought in a crudely mimeographed sheet called *Het Dagelijkse Nieuws*, the *Daily News*, which was illegally and secretly printed by the Underground Resistance movement and distributed by courageous underground workers. Each day we looked forward with great anticipation to this news sheet and devoured its information, since it was the only means of hearing the truth about the war and news about the Resistance.

This time we read how the "Regional Actions group" (the L.K.P.) had liberated political prisoners; how the Dutch Nazi policemen "disappeared" and their uniforms and weapons put to

154

good use in the Underground. The Allies reported that the "great" German armies' withdrawal from the Russian front resembled a flight for life. The Germans were nervous about a Western coast invasion since Hitler had to defend the seventeen-thousand-mile-long coastline. The Germans ordered that the islands in the Dutch provinces of Zeeland and South Holland be evacuated and flooded and seventy-five thousand people were thus made homeless without a source of income. The Allies heavily bombarded Germany, especially in the Berlin area, which was almost completely destroyed. The paper gave us courage and lifted up our tired spirits.

That night I disobeyed the instructions of the Resistance to remain in the house and went out to see tall Jan. All along the way I was accompanied by dozens of R.A.F. bombers flying to their mission in Germany, a most reassuring sensation. After I passed the house on the Oude Singel several times and saw nothing unusual, I knocked on the window.

Jan and two unidentified young men took me to task for coming out of my hiding place. I was vehement in my justification:

"It is impossible for me to stay in the house anymore. I must do something. I feel I must participate in the fight against the Nazis. Send me anywhere you want. If it is not safe for me in Leiden, I can operate from another base. Believe me, this inactivity is killing me."

"Leesha, you have spent only a few months on the inside, that's not much. All right, we will come up with something," said Jan. "Give us some time to work it out. Until then, please be careful. You could get us into trouble. Now go home, my friend here will bring you to the corner."

I felt relieved. The anticipation of a change in my situation made it possible for me to endure the next period of impatient waiting.

I wanted to be involved body and soul in the activities of the Resistance movement, in order to blot out the steady flow of agonizing images about my parents, brothers, and friends that kept plaguing me without rest.

While my hands were busy with menial work, my mind was

free to take flight in the dark and fearful uncertainties that distressed me day and night.

"Where are they now? Do they suffer from hunger and cold? Have they survived the hard labor? Oh God," I prayed, "please help me to erase from my mind the horrible rumors that are being spread, that helpless people are being subjected to torture and to murder by gas. Don't forsake us! How is it possible that one human being has the power of bringing so much cruelty upon the world? God, You created all mankind as equals. We have the right to live in freedom like everyone else!"

Red-hot anger welled up within me against the Nazi perpetrators for bringing so much pain and suffering to innocent human beings. The depth and the extent of my hatred made me tremble. In its grip, I was capable of performing the most dangerous acts of revenge.

In our great hour of need, our only true saviors were the brave Dutch Christian people who cooperated with, and who were part of, the Underground Resistance movement. True to their democratic ideals and to their belief in the equality of mankind, regardless of race or social status, most Dutch citizens did not yield to Nazi threats but even intensified their resistance.

Knowing full well the consequences of being caught in an act of resistance or of concealing and harboring Jewish "hiders," the courageous Dutch were willing to take the risks. Their experiences in the reign of Nazi terror only toughened them and made them even more resourceful. They had to rely on their own human talents to hide those people who wanted to go underground—*onderduiken*.

Holland did not have thick forests, nor remote mountain areas capable of providing havens of escape. It was a flat, neat little country, without any safe exits, bordered on the east by Nazi Germany, on the south by Nazi-occupied Belgium, and by the North Sea to the west and north.

The least change or irregularity in the exterior of a Dutch home or a slight deviation in the normal way of life could arouse an informer's suspicion, complicate the work of the Resistance, and ultimately cause everyone involved to end up in a concentration camp. But the love of liberty inspired the heroic Dutch to acts of bravery; they could do nothing less.

A few days later Tante Meta received a visitor. To my great amazement I was called in and invited to participate in the meeting.

I could detect a definite change in Tante Meta's attitude toward me when Eddy informed me to be ready the next day. The Resistance had plans for me, and Eddy became my new link to the world of Resistance.

18

Situated in Heemstede, a lovely suburb of Haarlem, Het Marishuis was a large, sprawling thatched-roofed two-story house that served as a residential convalescent home for eight well-to-do elderly people.

When I first saw it, on my journey there with Eddy, I was enchanted with its setting in an area of tree-shaded winding streets, colorful and unique houses and gardens, relaxing parks, the canal opposite the house, and a windmill outlined against the horizon.

Heemstede was a fairy-tale village, untouched by time or war. Its well-kept houses were surrounded by shrubs and trees set back into the gardens. I immediately took note of this reassuring fact. It meant that one could not readily be noticed by prying eyes upon entering or leaving the house.

"Good morning, are you the new nurse we are expecting?," I heard a voice sing out to me from the entrance. I was so taken by the scene and so enjoyed its every detail that I was hardly aware of having opened the gate leading toward the house.

A pleasant-looking young woman in a nurse's uniform came down the path to meet me. My "Yes" was immediately countered with:

"Then you must be Leesha Bos. You have no idea how much I was looking forward to greeting you!"

She helped me with my suitcase, her words just pouring over me.

"I am Inneke and I am temporarily replacing Zuster Marie, who is recuperating from pleuritis. I struggle as best as I can. Can you cook?" she asked, leading the way.

The large kitchen was a sight to behold. Pots and pans, vegetables, and groceries covered all available space on the counters and on the center table. There was a smell of burnt milk that had boiled over on the gas stove. Inneke ran to turn the knob.

"You see what's happening? Be an angel and help me. It's eleven o'clock now and by twelve-thirty we have to serve lunch."

When Inneke stopped talking to take a deep breath I ventured to answer her:

"I have never cooked for so many people before, but I can try."

She showed me to a charming attic room under the eaves; the house had a slanted roof sloping toward the back of the house. I opened the small window set in the thatched roof and I could almost touch the lush, green trees that were interspersed between red and black roof tops. I could hardly tear myself away from the picture of sylvan beauty, but Inneke urged me to hurry since I had an important task to fulfill.

Within a few days I had become skilled in caring for the patients. I cooked their meals and attended to the various other tasks that I had undertaken. I performed them efficiently, quietly, and quickly.

No one in the house knew about my second level of activity—contact and cooperation with the Underground Resistance movement. During the train ride from Leiden to Heemstede, Eddy had informed me that I would be in charge of delivering and dispatching important items.

A "mailman" would bring me a package addressed to me. My name would be spelled "Elisabeth Boss," with two S's in red ink. I was to take off the outer wrapping, destroy it, and then repack the package. At times there was an extra message for me to meet someone at an appointed place. Then I was to deliver the package to an address that appeared as the sender on the original wrapping, after deducting ten numbers from the number of the house. All these precautions were of the utmost importance in

159

case someone should intercept the "mailman." It was my mission to dispatch the package quickly and unobtrusively, since finding it in my possession was equally dangerous.

This setup was arranged with the active Underground participation of a registered nurse, Zuster Johanna, who owned Het Marishuis and another convalescent home located fifteen minutes away from ours. This spirited and fearless elderly lady was the only one who knew my Jewish identity. After my placement at the home I heard through the Underground grapevine to what great extent Zuster Johanna was actively involved in helping to hide people in need of refuge.

Some weeks later, our head nurse, Zuster Marie, returned to her post after recuperating from sickness. She was pleased to note that the patients were well taken care of, that the household was running smoothly, and that the meals were being served on time. Zuster Inneke ascribed it all to me and praised my efficiency. Since we had set up a certain routine, Zuster Marie had no reason to notice my occasional slipping out of the house in the afternoons or evenings. I utilized my days off for arranging matters in places some distance away from Heemstede.

Growing tension could be felt throughout the country. Many people believed that the Allied invasion would take place at any moment. Each night the Allied bombers were heard flying overhead on their way to Germany.

The Dutch submarine base in Ijmuiden was bombed by the Allies in full daylight with thousands of people watching. The coast shook under the impact of the heavy explosions.

There were rumors that large armies were waiting in England and that eight-thousand ships were ready to move for a landing on the European coast. In Belgium and France, the railways and the station emplacements were under constant heavy Allied bombardments.

The food situation in Holland was grim and getting worse by the week. It was hardly possible to live exclusively on the rationed allotments. People had to supplement their meager supplies with food bought on the black market, at ever-increasing prices. We were all losing weight gradually and constantly feeling the hunger pangs gnawing at our insides.

How restless and unhappy the people were! Everyone was waiting impatiently to see the end of the miserable, long, and bloody war!

I was deeply worried at the fate that must have befallen my family and friends. Their absence left a cold emptiness in my heart. I feared particularly for the whereabouts and welfare of Jules Godefroi, with whom I had not communicated since the winter of 1943.

In order to sleep at night I drove myself physically to the utmost so that my body would be tired. In spite of this, I was plagued by frightening dreams and nightmares.

One night I woke up, my body shaking with sobs, tears streaming down my face. The utter loneliness I felt and my yearning for my parents filled me with despair. I felt compelled to put my feelings down on paper. I lit the little stump of a candle near my bed and poured out the words, which at times were blotted out by my tears.

My darling sweet mother,

How I long for your caring eyes, your words so sweet and tender. How can a person be so lonely? Do you know what it means to be all alone, when my heart almost bursts with loneliness and impatient waiting threatens to destroy me?

O my darling little mother, I yearn so for you, to put my heavy, tired head in your lap. Yes, sweet Mommy, I'm crying now. I cry so bitterly as only a lonely, longing, yearning soul can do. I can't stand it any longer. I don't know where to look for consolation.

I am looking at your picture, which I keep behind a plank in the closet. Darling Mother, will you ever be able to answer me?

And you, dear Father, my friend? Your penetrating, honest, yet tender glance is so true and confident. I miss your strong protective arms. I know, everyone of us was so self-reliant. But if we uttered just one word or gave a sign that we needed you, your always open hands were there. Will you ever be able to give me an answer? Ever? . . . I hurt so unspeakably much . . . You were both such good parents, so honestly good and intensely involved in all that we did, so self-effacing. Will this be the end? So bitterly and unexpectedly? I need you always, your love, your care, it is the most beautiful and

161

dearest feeling in the world, one cannot get another father and mother. We were so close!

Surely the strong love we have for each other will bring us together again? . . .

I blew out the candle, fell back on my bed, and pressed the pillow to my face so that Zuster Marie, on the other side of the partition, would not hear me in my misery.

The following day the "mailman" delivered his package. In it I found a note:

"Amice, our friend, Fritz van Dongen, and companion will visit you. Regards, Eddy."

When my visitors arrived I introduced "Uncle Fritz" and his teenage niece, Nora, to Zuster Marie and we retreated to my room. The nature of their mission was to place the sixteen-year-old Jewish girl, Nora, with me in the Marishuis as a helper.

While we were talking, various thoughts crossed my mind:

"Wouldn't it be taking too much of a chance, to have another dark-complexioned, dark-haired girl in the house? Her slightly aquiline nose might give her away. Why didn't she hide in a house, somewhere else? Would a sixteen-year-old know how to handle herself when confronted by inquisitive prying? Wouldn't she be endangering my Underground activities, if by chance she discovered what I was doing?"

I steered the conversation in such a way that it enabled me to evaluate Nora's thoughts on the war, the Jews, the dangers we shared, and our responsibilities. I remarked:

"We hear that Jews are being tortured and killed in the concentration camps. It is so important to help those who have escaped the Nazi clutches!"

Her immediate reaction persuaded me that she could be trusted: "That's the only thing that we, who are still left, can do for our persecuted race, to stay alive!"

Suddenly we all stopped talking, there was an embarrassing silence. Fritz and Nora looked at me intently. I turned my face, hoping that the golden-orange rays of the afternoon sun streaming through the window would not betray me. Had I given myself away? Had they guessed that I was Jewish?

162

I recovered quickly. "Well, I'll have to inform Zuster Johanna of your joining us. She will recommend to Zuster Marie that we need the extra help in the house."

Fritz got up. I saw him swallow hard and in his eyes there was an expression of powerless anger. Only later did I find out that he intuitively knew how Nora's words had affected me. He sensed that I was a member of the persecuted race and from that moment on he was determined to help me as much as possible.

I looked at him with renewed interest.

At first sight nothing betrayed the inner emotions lying behind the stern, penetrating grey eyes, the determined line of the lips and the ruddy, weather-beaten complexion of the face belonging to this thirty-five-year-old dark-haired man, Fritz. He was above-average in stature, lean and strong and seemed capable of great physical stress and endurance. He gave the impression of an average middle-class worker, with little hint of the great intelligence, resourcefulness, and perseverance that, I later learned, he possessed.

As we said goodbye, having agreed to get in touch with each other within a few days, we shook hands and he said to me:

"Fortunately, we have met a real human being!"

Nora's presence in the house brought added responsibilities and sometimes unexpected hardships to me. She was an only daughter, spoiled and indulged by her parents, who had not been able to stand up against her willfulness. Her total lack of knowledge of the most elementary household duties required me to spend extra time in teaching her or in correcting her mistakes, in order to shield her from Zuster Marie, who had already started to complain.

Following the advice of Fritz, I did not put up with Nora's attitude; I pointed out to her the dangers to which she subjected both of us and she soon began to apply herself seriously to her work.

But despite the extra trouble she caused me, it was nice to have a young person around, to laugh together and to recall good times before the war. She had long since discovered, in one of my purposely unguarded moments during a discussion, that I was Jewish.

She showed great interest in our heritage and a desire to live in the Jewish homeland of which she knew little.

I advised the Resistance to discontinue "deliveries" to me until further notice because I feared Nora's inquisitiveness. To my great surprise I was informed that from now on, Fritz van Dongen, my "Uncle Fritz" would bring "packages" personally to me on his visits. We would meet at a prearranged place and time and walk together part of the way and I would then make the final delivery.

Fritz van Dongen, whose real name was Reinier van Kampenhout, was an important underground leader in the Leiden-Oegstgeest-Leiderdorp region. He had participated in many dangerous and daring acts of sabotage with the L.K.P., *Landelijke Knokploegen*—the Regional Actions group. Its members raided police stations and distribution offices in order to seize ration cards and identity cards. They had liberated political prisoners, blown up bridges, attacked small German detachments, and performed the various missions that resistance to the Nazi tyranny required.

He was a building contractor by profession, but had given it up in order to devote all his energy and time to the rescue and care of Jews and other persons in peril.

He expressed his feelings most poignantly when he wrote to me in one of his many letters:

—No human being owes me anything! Whatever I do I consider to be a responsibility toward the persecuted race, for whom I feel great respect and love—

For five years we have read news of attacks, of defenses, of cities being bombed, of planes not returning to their bases, of hundreds of thousands of people being rounded up and sent to destination unknown, of people shot to death, of ships sunk, of the V-1 rockets directed at London, of Allied troops advancing.

The losses on both sides are great! Life goes on. But how much nameless suffering hides behind these short sentences, behind a few simple words? We live as if on top of a volcano! Oh, it is so difficult to live one's life with the full reality of everything around us. If we think of the millions of young and old on the battlefield and of those who are missing in action. If we think of those who were driven from their homes because of their religion and race, if we think of the prisoners in P.O.W. camps and concentration camps and those who perished there. And when we think especially of those who voluntarily resisted in order to help the oppressed and who were killed as a result.

Millions of people are roaming far from home and hearth. Did they not also dream of happiness and warmth?

Now everything is gone. And with all this mutual suffering we have personal emptiness and unhappiness . . .

But we, who want to live consciously, will not achieve it, if we close our eyes and fall asleep until this misery, cold and darkness will have passed.

If we want real light, it is our task to nourish whatever light there is now, so that it will not be extinguished by the misery that surrounds us. When this storm is over, it will be our task to make sure that this small light will grow larger and become a flame—a flame that radiates ever more light and warmth. Perhaps our suffering now will strengthen us for the future. Let us consider this as an experience from which we learn. In the meantime we have to help and support each other in these difficult days—

His courageous personality and strong belief in the future became indispensible to me in a world in which misery seemed to continue without end. It was hard to imagine that we would ever survive the fear of discovery, the reign of Nazi terror, the bombings and the killings.

I looked forward to my meetings with Fritz as a thirsty man to a spring of fresh, life-giving water. Our conversations at first were concerned with illegal activities, his responsibilities, and difficult problems concerning the Jewish people he had hidden.

Although he had little academic education, he was recognized and esteemed for his natural political talents and had been appointed to serve on the local *Oegstgeest* governing council as a representative of the Social Democratic party.

On one of his visits Fritz informed me with glee that the R.A.F., at the request of the Dutch Resistance, had bombed a building in The Hague in which the personal records of all citizens were kept. He said with relish:

165

"This will prevent the Nazis from verifying personal information on the identity cards. The raid is a tremendous help to the Underground, for they will no longer have to worry about the legality of the information on the cards. The people in hiding can relax in the knowledge that even if they are caught, the Nazis will not be able to check their identities with the records, because now there are none."

The cities and railways of Holland were being bombed constantly. In Italy, Cassino was captured by the Allies and was followed by the battle for Rome. In Belgium and France not only factories, trains, and railways were being destroyed by the Allies, but even sections of towns, resulting in many dead and wounded. At the Amsterdam railway station there was a notice to avoid travel as much as possible.

Fritz was very punctual for our appointments. When he did not show up one day at our prearranged place, I became terribly worried, since he always carried incriminating evidence. But I received a letter in which he reported:

I can't complain that life is monotonous. After having unsuccessfully tried to get in touch with Henk, I walked to the intercity tram stop on my way to Heemstede. From the waiting crowd, I found out that the railway train from Amsterdam had been hit by the Allies and that the entire service had been disrupted, with a total of nine dead and twelve wounded. Finally the intercity tram arrived full to capacity, because the train from Leiden to Haarlem had been derailed as a result of bombing and all its passengers had been transferred to the intercity tram. We had to stop twice and had to get out because the British planes, the Tommies, were overhead. A nervous tension prevailed among the passengers. I got to my destination and quickly finished my business. My friends warned me not to get on the tram at the Sportpark stop, because the Germans were rounding up the men on the streets to send them to workcamps.

I took my monthly allotment of ration cards for my "patients" (which was quite a bundle), went to the "Iron Bridge" stop, and there boarded the tram. After a few minutes the tram stopped and fifteen German soldiers ordered all the men off the tram . . . .

A panic started! . . . I thought of my dangerous package of illegal ration cards as I was leaving the tram . . .

Suddenly, I made a quick, smart move. I got off on the other side of the tram and stood dead still against the tram. Some other men got off on the same side, but they started running in order to escape the claws of the *Moffen*.

Unfortunately, the minute they started running the *Moffen* started shooting. The men gave up their efforts to escape and came back.

I used this period of panic to sneak back into the tram and stretched myself out on the floor in the passageway. At once I was surrounded by the women who had remained in the tram asking me if I was wounded. I told them I was a heart patient and that my heart could not take all this excitement and tension. At the same time I had to be careful that they should not become too solicitous in rearranging my clothes and thus betray my dangerous package.

One of the Germans came in to inspect whether there were men still hiding inside. He ordered me to stand up, but the women succeeded in pleading for me and he disappeared. Now I had to simulate a heart attack because even among these women there could have been an informer who could have betrayed me.

Outside, the men were required to show their identity cards and their papers for inspection. Those between the ages of 18–50 years of age had to go with the *Moffen* with the exception of the men belonging to the N.S.B.—the Dutch Nazi Party.

Unfortunately for me, two N.S.B.-ers got into the same compartment, where I was. They came right up to me and asked me what was the matter. After I told them, they advised me to sit up. I agreed and they made room for me. You can well imagine how during the whole trip the eyes of all the passengers were upon me. They were constantly inquiring about my condition and I continued pretending. After the tram was well on its way and the danger of being caught by the Nazis had subsided, my nerves really began jumping. I tried to get a hold on myself and even this made a good impression on the passengers.

Some of the passengers commiserated with me and said to me: "Sir, in the future you should be more careful. Your heart could have stopped and then you would have been dead."

It seemed that everyone in the tram had a friend or a relative to whom the same thing had happened. Well, now they will be able to tell one more story when they get home. And if the listener won't believe it, they will say: "I saw it with my own eyes!"

As you see Leesha, I came through once again . . .

JUNE 6th, 1944, INVASION!

The long-awaited day had finally arrived! We were drunk with the exhilarating news about the Allied landings in Normandy.

A fleet of four-thousand warships, including aircraft carriers and thousands of smaller landing craft, unloaded thirty divisions of fighting men, tanks, and equipment while another fifty divisions were standing by in England.

Overhead, eleven-thousand aircraft had dropped paratroopers, strafed the enemy troops, bombed airports, bridges, and railways, and dropped ammunition and military supplies.

The Germans were now fighting on three fronts. In Russia they were retreating. In Italy, Rome had been taken by the Allies, and now they were facing invasion in France!

The battle in Normandy raged with fury despite the stormy weather that made the landings more difficult. It spoke for the power and self-confidence of the Allies that they had chosen this strongly defended part of Normandy for the invasion.

From the illegally printed newsletters—*De Waarheid (The Truth), Het Parool (The Word),* and *Ons Vrije Nederland (Our Free Netherland)*—we heard about the progress of the fighting.

Winston Churchill made a speech in which he promised great things to come. It was not improbable to expect that peace would come this year!

In the official daily papers the Germans announced their new weapon. They called it the *Wuwa* (miracle weapon)—an unmanned projectile rocket with a speed of five-hundred km that exploded at a set time with devastating results and caused a sea of flames to land on the target. The rockets were directed to land on the southwestern coast of England and London, and according to German reports there was great panic in England, as a result.

We began to carefully watch the moves of the Germans in Holland. People were apprehensive about their reactions. "A cat performs strange leaps when driven into a corner,'' they said. The Germans were still brazen and still believed in their invincibility. They never reported their own losses. The Dutch had a joke about this:

''The English won the battles on the seas; the Americans in the air, the Russians on land, and the Germans in the newspapers.''

Did the Germans still have the armaments, manpower, and strength to withstand all these offensives?

Would the invasion be the decisive battle? We talked about it constantly. Our hopes were high and we all prayed for its success and the speedy end of this unendurable waiting for peace.

19

For my birthday on the 18th of July, Fritz sent me an authentic delft-blue tile, which he had beautifully framed by hand.

I was very touched by his gesture. On opening the enclosed letter I found a few food coupons. He wrote:

Dear Leesha, (Forgive me if I'm not allowed to use these endearing words . . .)

How are you after the stormy Friday? [Referring to a German street-control-raid, while I delivered a "package".] Despite this unpleasantness, I loved to visit with you. It is difficult for me to write to you yet I wanted to do so. How was it again? Oh, yes. "In four days it will be my birthday"; that's what you said. Well, Leesha, my heartfelt congratulations on the occasion. May the next birthday be in peace. With the enclosed coupons, please buy something to celebrate.

I was very busy on Sunday, just like last week. But instead of seven there were four guests [people he had placed in hiding].

I wish I had a place for my aunt. She had a nervous breakdown [which meant the present place was not safe anymore] and she should get away for a few weeks. Do you know of a place for her?

What a dry letter! But what I want to write, what wants to flow out of my pen, I have to control with all my might . . .

Please write to me if you need anything for yourself. Oh no, I remember. You don't need anything!

Leesha, do you know what I wanted to do on Friday when we said goodbye? No, I won't write, you would only get angry with me.

I'm closing now. It's a short letter but it took me a long time to write it.

Heartfelt regards,
Your Uncle Fritz.

The present was dear to me beyond words, especially the fact that he had taken the time and trouble to personally frame the precious tile.

I read the letter over and over again, trying to understand the insinuations, which puzzled me deeply.

What I felt for this selfless, noble, and dedicated human being was respect and admiration, based on the love of one human-being recognizing the wonderful attributes of the other. To work with him meant to learn from a master who knew and understood all the ramifications and dangers that our work entailed. I needed his strength and his guidance to avoid the inevitable pitfalls of my underground work. At the same time I dreaded any development that might trouble or interfere with our straightforward relationship. I did not react to his letter.

Two days later there was some unexpected excitement. In the Underground press newsletter we read of an attempt on the life of Adolf Hitler in Germany by a group of his military officers. Unfortunately, it had not succeeded. But it was reported that unrest was brewing in Germany.

Was it a revolt or civil war? In the Nazi papers the incident was reported: "The bomb intended to kill Hitler was imported from England at the orders of the Jews in Moscow and planted by a criminal reactionary."

The Dutch people were incensed. Did the Nazis really think that we would swallow such ridiculous fabrications?

We followed the battle in Normandy with impatient eagerness. The Allies fought bravely and furiously. Our fervent hope and prayer was that they would quickly advance northward and liberate us, too.

The German front in Russia was crumbling and in Italy the Germans were retreating in advance of the pursuing Allied armies.

But tragically, the more losses the Germans sustained in the war, the worse the situation became in Holland. No male between eighteen and fifty years of age was safe from deportation for work in Germany.

There were raids in the streets and in public buildings. Houses were searched, people arrested and, at the least provocation and suspicion, sent to concentration camp.

Without any given reason, death sentences were pronounced and hostages were executed in public. This terror was aimed at showing the presence of the still unrelenting Nazi power and to make the Dutch people nervous and submissive. But it did not succeed!

The Resistance fought back against the hated Nazis and the Dutch N.S.B. with a determination born out of desperation and became progressively more daring.

The Allied air-raids in Germany continued at an ever-increasing pace. In Holland the R.A.F. bombed locomotives, trains, and railway tracks; travel became limited and extremely hazardous.

Fritz came every week with new instructions. We made deliveries of food cards and money to hidden people. We met, consulted, and planned raids of resistance with our colleagues in Heemstede, nearby Aerdenhout, and Haarlem. Often, I was sent to Amsterdam to deliver important papers of information.

Afterwards Fritz and I would walk in a beautiful park, called Het Hout. Our talks, which at first had stimulated me intellectually and had become indispensable to me for my spiritual well-being, gradually began to revolve around the personal and emotional attraction that Fritz had developed for me.

From the beginning I tried to discourage his hopeless involvement. I liked him and admired him so much as a person and it hurt me deeply to see him suffer because of his unrequited love for me.

His letters touched me to tears and left me frustrated because I could not reciprocate his feelings of love for me. Even on the days after we saw each other, he would write letters expressing his feelings and his doubts. He wrote his reflections with a sensitivity that was short of poetry:

He had had a busy day and in order to get some fresh air he went for a walk. Feeling tired he sought rest on a park bench and looked around at the scenery.

How beautiful the weather was! The large clouds floated slowly in the sky—sometimes one passed in front of the sun, then suddenly everything looked much darker. But no sooner had the cloud disappeared than the sun began to shine again through the trees richly decorated with green foliage.

It was as if the woods were covered with gold. Around him it seemed the birds had decided to give a concert in his honor. How small he felt in this setting of nature!

In front of him stood two beautiful oak trees. One was taller and older than the other. Straight and proud, each held a crown of branches. They swayed in rhythm with the wind, occasionally bending toward each other as if to whisper to each other.

He was absorbed by this interplay, he had eyes only for these two trees.

Was it a dream? Did he hear the taller oak talk to itself? Although he could not follow every word, it seemed that the tall oak was very envious of its neighbor.

This was understandable; the younger one was much more beautiful than the older one. It was not only a question of age. The younger tree stood on much better soil, so that it absorbed more nourishment from mother earth. This was evident by looking at the tree. Its branches were better developed and its trunk was much more stately. Although they were both oak trees one could see that the younger one was superior by far.

The old oak had never before noticed any other trees near it. And now that it did, it wished it had never seen the younger oak. But still, it was irresistably drawn to the younger tree.

When a strong wind blew, he took great pleasure that his branches touched hers. He liked her presence. Sometimes he tried to engage her in talk, but being a real oak tree—she did not open up eagerly.

And while the tall oak was contemplating the smaller one, she stood in all her glory. It was not necessary for her to impress any one. She knew that many were attracted to her and she did not particularly care for the old tree. He was nice to her, especially in stormy weather when he caught most of the wind. Then she appreciated him, she looked at him in a friendly way, and she allowed her branches to touch his—

Suddenly a tram came by and woke him up to reality. He checked his watch and stood up quickly. His work was waiting for him.

Leaving the park he thought of how much trees were like real people. But he wanted to be a realist and he should not think about sentimental things.

Leesha, if I have courage, I'll mail this nonsense. Also Uncle Fritz will help you in your work and your difficulties. But in reality I'm not your uncle; think of something else. Fritz.

I could understand the intensity of this wonderful man's inner conflicts, but I was powerless to do anything to help him. In another letter he questioned his own emotions, which had taken hold of him:

My thoughts go back to our meeting today and they are all mixed up. It was so beautiful and wonderful to see you. I ask myself: Is all this a dream? Do I have the right to be so busy with myself?

Judging this question with my head, I say no. If one wants to live consciously one must sacrifice and give, one must even suffer. Let me consider all the facts:

I am married to a woman who is good to me. Yes, I know she loves me and I appreciate her work and care for me. But to like her, to love her? No! The reverse is sometimes the case. Yet I was always true to her. There has never been another woman who could attract me, whom I yearned to see. I accepted it and I arranged my life and made my peace with it. It is not good, I thought, to think about oneself. And when one spoke of love, I laughed about it.

But now? Now something has awakened in me. It is as if I am no longer myself. How did this come about? Is it your voice, your expressive eyes? Is it your intellect that attracts me so much? I don't know! I know no answer to this!

But all this places an ominous question before my conscience. Do I have a right to steer it toward the direction which I would like it to go? With my reason I say, No!

You are so young, so accomplished, you are so good! I feel so small in comparison with you. What can I offer you?

To claim you for myself would be a crime. No, I have no right to it.

Some day you will be happy with the man who will belong to you. Then you too will speak about great "LOVE." And I will think back to this time and all that has happened and I will be glad that all will be well with you and feel happy to witness your happiness.

174

All this is sober talk and the logical thing to do is to break the friendship, because I don't start something without finishing it. For me the friendship between us is more than mere friendship.

But then my feelings speak up; to break with you? What nonsense! How could I break with you who occupies all my thoughts? To break voluntarily, just like that, no longer to yearn for you, not to hear you talk any more, not to walk with you in quiet thought? . . .

No, no. A thousand times no! I won't do it voluntarily. I will control myself and I will not expect anything from it. I will stay sober and I will consider it to be an ordinary friendship.

I know that sometime we will have to part and perhaps never see each other again, but let it always remain beautiful—a friendship that we will never forget . . .

Leesha, if you have time, write to me. Even if it is a businesslike letter. I need to hear from you so much.

Bye, sweet darling,

Fritz.

P.S. The latest news item.
This morning the Nazis requisitioned my bicycle. A terrible disappointment! Tough luck!

I could neither deny nor end our relationship. It was an unbreakable bond of pure friendship in which the one filled certain specific needs of the other. Those needs were not necessarily similar. Fritz accepted the fact that I did not love him the way he would have wanted it to be.

In a world of war and hatred, in a time of killings and raids, insecurity, hunger, and loneliness he was the only human being who cared about me, who restored my ties with humanity, and who unreservedly offered me warmth and love on my terms.

I loved him as a close friend, as a generous benefactor, and above all, as my mentor. He understood me so well. He wrote to me on another occasion:

Leesha, tell me what bothered you last Wednesday afternoon. I only want to be good to you and show you some consideration in your dark life and in your loneliness and to bring you light. Oh, I myself know what loneliness is!

175

Darling, I have thought about you so much and I understand fully that you, who have dreamed of love; you, with your broken heart always thinking about your family; you, with your youth and wonderful background; you, who still have to conquer the whole world, you could not be for me what you perhaps would like to be.

Leesha, I can well imagine what goes on in your mind; I appreciate your honesty and therefore I don't blame you.

Dear, it is so wonderful to think about you! Sometimes I see you vividly standing before me with your cute dark head and your dark eyes, then I hear your voice like music to my ears. Before I knew you I felt so lonely, but now no more. You have given my life meaning, something for which I will always be grateful to you. How wonderful it is to have a friend like yourself!

I know that my feeling for you is entirely different from your feeling for me. But do not feel guilty about it. I love you the way you are, I can't expect more. I prefer something small given from the heart than something large that is pretended. I cannot demand that you love me!

I also love the white water lily [referring to a poem by Frederick van Eede I had sent him] and because of my great love for this lily I am prevented from plucking it. Therefore, as long as I am able to observe the lily I hope to continue to do so, and if my eyes can touch her, then I will stay here until the end. I dare not wish for more . . .

Your devoted Fritz.

Ever since the Allied invasion in Normandy in June it was expected that the war would be over before the winter.

The Allied forces made another landing in the south of France between Toulon and Cannes. After the fall of Paris into Allied hands the German forces began to disintegrate and what was left of them retreated behind the river Seine.

The Underground illegal newsletter reported that Dutch soldiers from England were fighting in Normandy in the Princess Irene Brigade, the Dutch fighting unit. This was encouraging news, and our sagging spirits lifted a little.

Rumors began to spread that the Americans were advancing so quickly that they would be in Holland in fourteen days.

Germans and N.S.B.-ers were packing and retreating

176

eastbound to Germany, stealing cars and bicycles in order to get away quickly. People were afraid that Holland might become a battlefield between the Allies and the Germans and that the country might suffer heavy destruction. There was talk that the Germans would use poison gas as a last resort.

But we felt that deliverance was in sight!

The Dutch government-in-exile named Prince Bernhard as the commander of the *Nederlandse Binnenlandse Strijdkrachten*— the B.S. for short—the Netherlands Forces of the Interior.

On September third the Allies crossed into Belgium, driving the retreating Germans before them. By late afternoon they had freed Brussels, and its citizens ecstatically welcomed the liberators. But in our local German-controlled newspaper we read only about the executions of Dutchmen accused of treason. Oh, how we hated the Nazis now more than ever!

September fourth. With every hour there was more and better news. Prince Bernhard was now with the approaching troops! Everyone was as tense as in 1940 but this time we were optimistic and happy.

Antwerp had been liberated! Our excitement began to mount with each item of good news.

September fifth. All schools, shops, restaurants, and cafes were closed. The "Green Police" had mysteriously left.

Streetcars were no longer operating. Posters announcing martial law and signed by Dr. Seyss-Inquart were displayed; the decree made the death penalty mandatory for anyone acting against the occupying German power. And the most amazing fact of all— there were no Germans around.

It was unreal! Was it finally over? By midday, rumors were flying that Rotterdam had been freed! The Allies were rolling toward The Hague and Leiden and at mid-afternoon they would be here in Heemstede!

This was too much! Nora and I started to practice our high school English. Together with hundreds of grownups and children we rushed to the main highway to wait for the approaching Allied army.

Children were singing Dutch national songs, some people were waving the Dutch flags, others came prepared with flowers to welcome the Allies.

We were standing there unafraid, waiting impatiently, talking freely, full of enthusiasm and drunk with anticipation.

It was within reach . . .

We waited and waited, a long time . . . But our Allied friends did not come to liberate us on that *Dolle Dinsdag*, on that mad, crazy Tuesday.

Soon the Green Police appeared and dispersed the waiting crowds. Our disappointment and downheartedness were indescribable! We had rejoiced too early. Quickly we ran home, in fear again of the deadly threats of the Nazis.

We knew that we had to have patience and that we would be freed eventually. We knew also that unless the war would end soon, we would face a long, hard, and bitter winter.

20

One night, while trying to fall asleep after an exceptionally difficult day, a sudden insight came to me like a ray of light.

"It must be Rosh Hashana, the Jewish New Year," I almost cried out, remembering the festive celebration of the holiday at home with my family and the solemn prayers in the synagogue.

I felt so far removed from that time as if it all had happened on another planet.

How could I celebrate the holiday now? What prayers could I possibly add to the ones that were constantly on my lips and in my heart? My whole being was calling to God:

"Please, help us! Oh, Lord, help our people! Have mercy and don't forsake us!"

I called out for my parents and my brothers, I felt a stabbing pain going through me. I missed them so.

Not having a Jewish calendar I decided to arbitrarily set a date for Yom Kippur, the Day of Atonement, for fasting and introspection, ten days from that night.

A poem, expressing my thoughts and feelings, began forming in my mind. By the light of a little candle I worked on it at night whenever the spirit moved me, sometimes even waking up from sleep to jot down a word or a few lines in the dark.

Overpeinzingen

En als ik denk aan de tijd van voorheen
Met z'n zoete veilige herinneringen
Een tijd vol gelach en ook geween
Momenten afwiss'lend in al heur schakeringen.

Zij staan weer op en leven weer verblijd
Trachten verlijdelijk de realiteit te verkleden
En het gelukt ze na pijnlijke strijd
Dan werp ik mij in de stroom van 't zalig weemedig verleden.

Een vage geur, een bepaalde kleur
Als een herinnering van heel ver
Een weerschijn van poetische fleur
Een herkenning van jaren her.

Als een straal, die zachtkens in 't lover begint
Steeds heviger toeneemt in kracht
En straalt en goudt en verblindt
Ons ontroert in al heur pracht.

Doch plots'ling! Welk noodlot heeft 't zo beschikt?
Welk duivel breekt de banden
Wie de snode woesteling, die ons zo schrikt?
En voert ons naar verre, vreemde landen?

Als een dief in de nacht, door niemand gezien
Plundert en raast en verscheurt
Door een woesteling in dolle dronkenschap gebien
En . . . door de goden goed gekeurt?

Als een dol, dronken uitgelaten beest
Trekt hij van stad tot land
Niemand ontzien, moorden een feest!
Een geweer, een granaat in de hand.

Is dit rechtvaardigheid, is dit recht?
Is dit de uitkomst van een eerlijk gevecht?
Zijn dit mensen of zijn dit dieren?
Mogen zij moorden en plunderen en tieren?

Wee ons in dit vreemde land
Niet eens een mens, niet eens een gast
Weer de bedelstaf in de hand
En velen, velen tot last.

Als een vogel in de kooi gevangen
Springend, vechtend, verplett'rend tegen d'muur

Geklemd tussen ijzerhete smarte-tangen
Gejaagd, gehitst, gedreven naar het hellevuur.

Geknakt, gebroken, gekrenkt
Geen krachten meer, zo eenzaam en moe
Geen mens, geen vriend die ons denkt
En opstaan?... Niet weten hoe...

Dan in waze, nevelige gedachte
Zien we vaag onze zoete, veilige herinneringen
't Ons verbeelden zijn we niet bij machte
Zien slechts gekleurde kralen, schitt'rende ringen

Kralen aaneengeregen zo wonderlijk van kleur
Ringen beschenen door millioenen van stralen
Een verre klank... een vage geur
Altijd maar weer, steeds weer herhalen.

Zal de hoop eens herrijzen?
Zal er nog durf in ons lichaam, geest in ons'ziel?
Zal iemand de weg ons eens wijzen?
Vanuit dit smartelijke asyl?...

Reflections
(from the Dutch)

And then I think of times passed
With memories free, without fear,
Times of laughter, also tears,
Moments so sweet and so dear.

They revive and live once again.
Forgotten, they surface at last
And after painful struggle they succeed
To submerge me in the nostalgic past.

A fragrance vague, a color soft,
Recalls promises we made,
Reflects a poetry of senses
Which years did not fade.

Like sunlight starting 'tween trees,
Slowly growing in starts,

181

It shines so golden, it blinds,
Its brilliance warming our hearts.

Behold! What fate has befallen us?
What devils break our ties?
What heartless tyrants overwhelm us so?
Deport us and treat us as spies?

Like thieves in the night, by nobody seen,
They plunder and raid and destroy,
Commanded by sadists and drunks to amuse,
And this . . . in accordance with God's ploy?

Like uncontrolled, bloodthirsty beasts
They tear through towns and lands,
No one spared; To murder—a feast;
With a gun and a grenade in their hands.

Is this justice? Where is truth?
Are they human, have they no soul?
Is this a result of honest strife?
Will they be sentenced for killing us all?

Woe to us, in this beleaguered land!
No right to be man, no right "to be" . . .
Again we beg for a helping hand
So indebted to many are we.

Like birds caught in a cage,
Jumping, fighting in vain to be free,
Thrown into the pits of hell's fire,
Driven, tormented, cursed are we.

We are broken, abandoned and crushed,
So tired and lonely in our despair,
No kin, no friend to call our own.
Will we ever arise? . . . Will our spirit be there?

Our far-away thoughts so misty, afloat,
Play tricks with our innermost needs.
Sweet memories recede, remote
Shimm'ring like diamonds, like colorful beads.

Beads linked together in such wondrous array
Precious stones reflecting myriads of lights.
A faraway sound, a fragrance so soft,
We want to relive, again to delight.

Will life-giving hopes rejoin us again?
Will our bodies be strong, our souls ablaze?
Will someone ever light up the path
Out of this sorrowful maze?

After completing the poem I felt empty and drained. It was the first time since the war had started that I had indulged in expressing my feelings and doubts about the fate and future of the Jewish people, and a wave of sorrow and utter hopelessness shook my body.

I closed my notebook and went to wash my face. Looking up at the mirror I saw my reflection and I was shocked.

"Come now, that's not you, Leesha! That's exactly how the Nazis want you to be: frightened, weak, submitting to despair. They will never get you down, not you! You'll fight and resist until your last breath! You are proud of what you are! You are not inferior to anyone! Your main purpose is to accomplish what you set out to do. And now your goal is to stay alive, to keep others alive, and to do everything possible to prevent the Nazis from doing more damage.

"It has to be over soon! The final stretch is always the most difficult." My soliloquy produced its effect.

I straightened up, feeling my self-assurance returning to me. I decided I could not afford to indulge in weak sentiments and doubts. It was my determination and strength of action that would make me or break me.

I saw my task clearly; I had to carry on with my responsibilities no matter what risks were involved.

The news reports in the Underground press kept us informed about the Allied progress into Belgium, Luxemburg, and Germany.

It soon became apparent that, despite the valiant and daring all-out Allied attack on Arnhem in Holland, the English would not get the upper hand. The bad weather was against them and seriously interfered with their attempts to establish a bridgehead in eastern Holland. It obstructed their landings in force at their main objective and prevented reinforcements and supplies from arriving. The heavy losses they incurred at the battle of Arnhem destroyed any chance of a swift victory in Holland.

The Allies were fighting hard and steadily on all fronts according to their master plan, but the Allied advance northward into Holland had come to a standstill.

Trains, trams, and buses were constantly being fired at by the Allies. Gas and electricity were rationed and could be used only for a few hours a day.

The Germans launched the new rocket, the V-2, to attack England. Because of Allied air-attacks and because of the danger of firing mishaps, thousands of people had to be evacuated from Wassenaar, near The Hague, within a day. The Germans made no provisions for the people, nor did they care whether they found new housing.

Radio Oranje from England reported that Maastricht, in the southern province of Limburg, was the first Dutch city liberated by the Allies. We were so very happy but it was so far away from us.

The Resistance movement became more aggressive and more dangerous to the Germans with each day. The Nazis were able to keep themselves well informed of the many activities of the Resistance and about its Underground news setup and distribution of papers by using informers and quislings. They learned about the care of "hidden" people, financed by the Dutch government-in-exile. They were painfully aware of Underground acts of sabotage, of the infiltration of German-controlled government and municipal offices, of the Allied droppings of arms and equipment for the Underground Resistance and the B.S.—the Netherlands Forces of the Interior.

The Germans feared the Underground Resistance groups and did everything in their power to crush them. They extracted whatever information they could by torturing and eventually killing captured members of the illegal Underground Resistance movement.

The most spectacular act of resistance was executed when the Dutch government-in-exile, in a broadcast from London, ordered all railroad personnel to go on strike in order to hinder movements of the German army. On the following day all railway traffic came to a halt. This strike was an extraordinary and sensational act of moral defiance on the part of the Dutch railroad men and it gained the admiration of each Dutch citizen.

The underground took care of the strikers financially and arranged for their leaders to go into hiding. The Germans were furious at the strike and threatened to starve the population by seizing all trucks and barges and placing an embargo on food transportation from east to west in the Netherlands. Nevertheless the strike of the railroad men continued.

Then the Germans started to systematically seize railroad equipment—locomotives, cars, electrical wiring—and to ship them to Germany. Special railroad men from Germany were brought into Holland for that purpose.

In addition the Germans began to bomb and blast port installations, cranes, and warehouses in Rotterdam and Amsterdam harbors. All docks, machine factories, dry docks, and electrical installations were either stolen or destroyed by the Nazis. When workmen tried to put out the fires they were driven away under the threat of German machine guns.

Traffic in Holland came to a near standstill and the remaining tram transport was very limited.

The Germans made good on their promise, and the food embargo began to have tragic effects on the population. Meat and sugar were no longer distributed, and all other rations, including potatoes and vegetables, were once again in short supply. Since delivery was no longer possible, Nora and I had to personally carry the weekly provisions, which were needed to feed the patients of our convalescent home, Het Marishuis.

On one such errand, while struggling with a heavy sack of potatoes, we passed a bakery store. The smell of baking bread that struck us was headier than the finest perfume in the world.

Our ever-hungry stomachs reacted strongly and we stood there drooling, looking at the loaves of bread coming out of the oven.

With a happy start I remembered the extra bread coupon I had received from Fritz. I rushed into the bakery and bought a small, warm, heavenly smelling bread. I broke off some pieces and we devoured the delicious chunks with ravenous eagerness. We so enjoyed the luxury of stuffing our mouths to capacity and not being limited to just one rationed slice of bread, twice a day.

We continued on our way, taking turns in carrying the sack and in holding on to our pocketbooks. After we had finished eating the loaf of bread, Nora remarked:

"I'm still hungry. I could eat a dozen breads. Do you have any more coupons?" She proceeded to examine my pocketbook while I protested strenuously. The more I implored her to stop, the more brazen she became and began to run ahead of me. I could not move quickly enough with the sack of potatoes, nor could I leave the sack unattended, because someone would be only too happy to pick it up.

Laughingly she took everything out and not having found any coupons, she picked out my identity card and said teasingly:

"If I don't get more bread I'll destroy your *persoonsbewijs* [identity card]!"

Now I really become angry: "Nora, stop it! Don't be stupid! You know how essential the card is. You can't do this to me!"

"Oh, no?," she asked. I didn't understand what had gotten into her, but right there in front of my unbelieving eyes, she tore up my identity card and threw the pieces into the gutter.

My identity card that had passed the scrutiny of the notorious S.D. *Sicherheitsdients,* the intelligence army of the Nazi *Gestapo*—my passport to security—was floating down the Heemstede sewers.

Furiously, I tore my pocketbook out of her hands and controlled my passionate, strong urge to slap her face. I said icily:

"You are a despicable creature!," and I turned to go. Now I was almost running while carrying the heavy load. I could not forgive myself for having agreed to keep her in Het Marishuis. At the same time I was terribly frightened, for at any moment I could expect a Nazi street-raid check of identity cards and I knew only too well what would happen to me for not presenting a valid identity card.

My only thought was Fritz. I had to get word to him, he was the only one who could help me.

Nora was running after me, crying. She realized now what she had done and she begged for forgiveness. She didn't want me to hate her and to be angry with her.

I was crying, too, more out of sadness than anger. How could one person hurt another to such a degree? Even more shocking, how could one Jew do this to another Jew, knowing full well the consequences of such an irresponsible and dangerous deed?

For several days I did not talk to Nora, even though she knocked every night on my door begging me to forgive her.

Upon hearing of this incident, Fritz immediately set the machinery of his Underground connections into motion. To my utter astonishment he directed me to go to the Heemstede police station to report the loss of my identity card. I was to appear there at an appointed hour and ask for Mr. de Veen, whose description I had received from Fritz.

Although I was reassured that Mr. de Veen was a member of the Resistance movement, I died a thousand deaths before I mustered up enough courage to enter the Heemstede police station.

"What if he was not there? What if someone else, a N.S.B.-Nazi, would take care of my case and begin asking questions? Would they become suspicious when I hesitated or did not know the answers?"

But my fears proved groundless, for my visit turned out to be a quick and impersonal transaction and I blessed Fritz for making this arrangement. However, it was only the first step; now a new legal identity card had to be processed. I could even detect concern on the part of Fritz when he wrote:

"Leesha, I hope that it will be O.K. with your identity card. In the meantime, use the police identity paper, but be careful with it. If you don't mind, let me know your real name. It is not nosiness, that I am asking, but it is in your own interest. If something would happen to you and I would not know your real name, I would not be able to help you. I cannot afford to lose you."

Even going to a photographer for new photos for the identity card meant taking a chance on being discovered or betrayed. I did so anyway and to my great surprise I was soon instructed to go to Mr. Geruiderink at the local Heemstede municipality office, to receive a new, legal identity card.

This was almost unbelievable! It meant that the Underground Resistance movement had penetrated into the official government offices and that their workers were performing their illegal activities under the very eyes of the N.S.B.-Nazis and the Germans. I marveled at the daring and ingenuity of the Resistance and I was eternally grateful to Fritz for his swift action, his reliability, and above all, his loving care.

I very seldom wrote to him, because of the danger that the letter might be intercepted and used against him as incriminating evidence by the *Gestapo*. But I simply had to express my thankfulness to him right away. So I enclosed a letter to Fritz in a bundle of messages that was taken to Leiden by an Underground courier and thanked him for all he had done for me:

I owe you so much. You give and give and keep on giving. All your beautiful, warm thoughts and care you send to me. I feel them; all your best and innermost wishes are reserved for me. Oh dear Fritz, I wish I could reciprocate fully with everything in my power. It would be like heaven on earth. I have an inexhaustible capacity to give with a complete effacement of my ego.

But fate or predestination wills things to happen differently than we humans would wish, Fritz. We have already discussed this. One cannot force nor pretend love. It is everything or nothing.

It is so cold here; cold, somber, frightful, and black! I can't explain it exactly. There is no safe and warm haven, nothing to console a lost soul that yearns for peace. Everything becomes more difficult and more miserable.

Fritz, no one knows about these feelings. I hide them behind a mask of even-tempered efficiency and politeness.

My dear God, when will all this be over? When can we be ourselves, without chains in our own world, unafraid?

Wouldn't it be wonderful to lie down and sleep through days and nights for months and years until all terror, bloodshed, evil, and ugliness would leave this world? To sleep an unconscious, drunken sleep, until . . . .

I would wake up warming myself in the light of a trusted and familiar atmosphere; until my heart would find fulfillment for whatever it was yearning; an atmosphere of purity, warmth, and music; a home filled with my own belongings; a place filled with people, honest and good, whom I love deeply . . . .

Do you understand me? I am not used to expressing my fears and doubts to anyone. So you see, Fritz, even proud, self-assured oak trees feel cold and lonely inside, though others may not notice it . . . .

The latest news about Nora is that she has been sleeping in my room for the last few days. The storm broke the window in her room and it is a frozen icehouse at present. She wants to use this opportunity to the fullest to learn from me and wonders if there is any possible chance of making her life more worthwhile. She came to me out of her own free will without any pressure on my part and she begs and insists that I am the person to help her.

Dear Fritz, you can imagine how overcome I was, though I did not show it to her. You understand, even if it will involve me completely, here is a chance to help a human being that I cannot refuse.

God help me with it! I hope to succeed, especially now that she has put herself so completely and defenselessly into my hands. Fritz, that is something so unbelievable after what she has done to me!

Maybe this unfortunate incident will be the beginning of a constructive education for Nora.

With heartfelt thanks and the very best to you, Leesha.

Despite the fact that we had a working meeting in four days time, I received a reply from him even before that. He explained later that he hoped that his letters would help me to feel less lonely.

Dear little Leesha,

Your letter was like a wonderful piece of music in my ears, played by a mighty orchestra and conducted by a steady hand. The violins were supported by the mellow tones of the cellos. Suddenly the percussion section took over with a double forte and it overwhelmed all the other parts. The whole piece was played in a crescendo with a fortissimo in the climax.

It is wonderful to hear such music, it brought me into a state of mind as if I had stepped into a new life. Everything was so

189

perfect, it sounded so lovely and honest, despite some expressions of mystery. One wished to hear it over and over again.

The sounds of this music will always be with me and I will eternally admire those who can write such music for me and can interpret it in such a manner.

You write that you owe me a lot, but that is nonsense. I am even more grateful to you for the friendship that you give me.

You have ignited something within me, a small flame that keeps on growing stronger and stronger. Yes, even to such an extent that I feel it burning all day long. Why all this? Why couldn't I have remained sleeping? I ask myself sometimes.

And then I realize how beautiful it is to have loved someone. I would not want to have missed out on it!

How beautiful it would be if I could devote myself to you with all my power. But indeed, just this great love of mine for you holds me back. How I have to fight with myself! As you said, it is everything or nothing.

If I would want everything, you would have to make a great sacrifice and it is my great love for you and my reasoning that holds me back. If someone has to sacrifice, I'll do it.

Even if I were not to see you anymore, I'll always think of you with love and tenderness. I ask myself: what is it that draws me so to you? How mysterious is love. Dear Leesha, it is wonderful to know that you like me and that you think of me sometimes.

Later on you'll probably leave and I hope you'll think of me once in a while. You'll marry a man of your own age and standing and you'll be happy.

And I? I will spend a lonely hour in a quiet park and think back to this time.

Leesha dear, I'll end now, perhaps everything is a little mixed up. But it is so difficult to stand at the crossroads of emotion and reason. Let us preserve this beautiful friendship in the meantime. Bye, sweet. In my thoughts I am always with you, Fr. v. D.

Dear Leesha,

I still can't take leave of you. It makes me happy to communicate with you on paper for a few hours. I have never done that before with anyone.

I also had many hopes and I still have. But hopes remain hopes until we put our will behind them. With good hopes and a strong will we can achieve more, but if we want to achieve more then we have to dare to live.

And do you dare to live? If you dare to live, then you'll be free and you will achieve more.

Darling, you are still so young and life has already disappointed you. Nobody can feel it more than I. You will still have to go through a lot, and many disappointments will follow.

Be courageous, fight if necessary! But be careful not to become an ordinary Jansen or Pietersen! Dare to live! I know so little about you, dear; you are like nails in this respect. I only know that I love you. I know that you cannot love me and it does not matter. I don't wish for more. I want to wish, but I dare not.

Come to me with your sorrow and I will try to console you. Come to me with your worries and I will try to solve them. For years I was so alone, that was after my mother's death. Now I can look after you and be happy.

Live your own life and do what you think you have to do. Be happy; I will stand by you in all your difficulties. And I will try as much as possible to stay sober. Maybe our paths will cross sometimes, although we may not take the same roads. Mountains and valleys don't meet, but people do. I'll leave this to the uncertain future.

Darling, I will put myself in your circumstances. I will not make it more difficult for you than it is already.

In these two letters I am standing before you naked and I am not ashamed. How happy I am to have a friend! I will not bother you anymore with expressions of love. Forgive me this time, it just escaped from me. Accept from me much tenderness and if you feel so inclined and you have time, please answer. I have such need to hear from you. From your devoted Fritz.

The beauty and the strength of his character struck me with full force. The selflessness of his love was like a most precious gift to me. It humbled me and made me feel even more indebted to him.

Was I meeting the challenge?

Was I daring to live?

I was searching within my depths. The most important criterion in my life was honesty toward myself in all its ramifications.

This honesty controlled my conscience and all my actions. It gave an equilibrium to my life and I could not accept anything less.

Hypocrisy, pretense, or half-truth would be detrimental to any satisfying and lasting relationship or situation.

Did I dare to live?

If daring to live meant to resist the injustice, the terror, and persecution of innocent victims, if daring to live meant defiance of the evil Nazi murderers, then I was meeting the challenge.

I could not live any other way. I could not appease my conscience by remaining quiet and inactive.

I had to account to myself and I demanded of myself the utmost.

To what extent my daring and determination would be challenged until the war would end, I had no way of knowing.

21

"Soon we'll have to make a decision," Zuster Mary said one morning; "I don't think we will be able to continue taking care of our patients in Het Marishuis. The rations are diminishing to nothing, we have no provisions in stock, and we cannot afford to pay the astronomical prices of the black market. How can we sustain them without meat, chicken, fat, butter, sugar, milk, and eggs? We can only offer them two slices of bread a day, which tastes like clay, a few potatoes, some vegetables, and a drop of oil. There is not even a good cup of coffee or tea available. Nearly everything we eat is substitute!

"It's already getting cold and after we burn up the little coal we still have for the stove in the diningroom, it will be freezing here. The gas is rationed to a few hours a day. If, God forbid, the Germans stop it altogether, what will we do then? Zuster Johanna and I have discussed it. There is no other way out. I'll have to get in touch with the families of our patients and tell them that we are forced to close the convalescent home.

"Leesha, you and Nora will have to find your way home. I am so sorry! It had all worked out so well. You have been indispensable to our people here and they love you."

"Wait, Zuster Mary. In the meantime we could try to get by with the food from the public soup kitchen," I suggested. "There is a place of distribution right here at the Royal Yacht and Sailing Club. People who tried it say the food is not that bad. Sometimes they have mashed potatoes with vegetables and gravy—*stamppot*—and sometimes it is porridge. You get one portion for

193

each ration coupon. This way we can use the gas we save to cook other things and boil water for the hot-water bottles, which the patients need in this cold weather.''

Zuster Mary agreed to my suggestion and we tried in every possible way to keep going. Nora and I dragged big, heavy pots of *stamppot* from the soup kitchen every day. However, the "gourmet" cooking left a lot to be desired.

I encouraged Zuster Mary and helped her to keep the convalescent home in operation, mostly because of the cover it provided for my underground activities. It was most important that our work continue despite the latest calamity that the enemy had brought upon us.

In a surprise raid the Germans began rounding up all men between the ages of seventeen and fifty and deporting them for work in Germany. Heavily armed sound-trucks drove through the streets ordering males to pack essential provisions and clothes and to assemble at special centers or outside their homes. They were promised good food, cigarettes, and pay.

Homes were searched at random in order to find men for deportation. The Germans threatened to kill anyone who tried to hide or escape. In street raids the Germans fired into the crowds. Between eighty to ninety thousand men obeyed the German orders, to the great scorn of the Resistance, who tried in the illegal press to persuade them not to report to the Germans.

To avoid the roundup, young men in the Resistance went into hiding for a while, and key illegal underground communications were carried out by female messengers. Our work became even more difficult and complicated.

Periodically I met with my colleague, Betty, from Haarlem, at the St. Bavo Cathederal, where we exchanged packages of ration cards, illegal identity cards, or other messages to be delivered to various addresses in Leiden, The Hague, or Amsterdam. Many times while waiting for Betty, I heard parts of organ concerts performed in the ancient cathedral.

An intense need for music, harmony, and serenity overwhelmed me. The sonorous tones of the organ seemed to flow through my every fiber, leaving me trembling and vulnerable. Silently, I cried out inside:

194

"When there is so much beauty to be enjoyed, Oh God, why do we have to suffer war, terror, and death?"

It appeared as if the elements were conspiring against us. The weather was cold, stormy, and rainy. Because of their weakened condition and the poor food situation, many people became sick. In an open letter, the Dutch doctors accused Dr. Seyss-Inquart of starving the entire nation still under German occupation. They warned of epidemics and an unprecedented number of deaths.

There was now a lull in the Allies' efforts to free occupied Holland. We knew that Allied actions were undertaken according to an overall plan, but we were impatient and we wished the war's end would come faster.

We lived in constant fear of German street-raids, of Allied air-raids and most of all, of hunger. In the cities where stocks of food were depleted, the people suffered most. In rural sections the farmers still had stored-up food from their farms.

The lack of electricity and coal forced most factories to close down and more and more people became unemployed. The cities all looked lifeless. Houses were dark inside and were lit only with oil lamps. Most people went to bed early. We could no longer use our electrical appliances. By now, there were no means of transportation, neither train, tram, nor bus. Some individuals were fortunate enough to have a bicycle with one or two wooden bands instead of tires, but most people had to walk.

The constant bombing caused damage to homes and businesses that could not be repaired because of the lack of glass. The boarded-up windows and the store-fronts nailed down with triplex or beaverboard gave me the eerie impression of being lost in a ghost town. Everything appeared black, sombre, cold, and hopeless as if it were the end of the world.

We heard rumors that Sweden, Switzerland, Spain, and Portugal were ready to send food to us through the Red Cross, but that the Germans refused to give permission.

After much soul-searching and discussion Zuster Mary decided to close down the Het Marishuis the week after New Year 1945 and to give the patients a few weeks time to make arrangements with their families.

The decisive factor was the added danger to our safety from the close proximity of the V-1 and V-2 launching areas, which the Germans had moved from Wassenaar, near the Hague, to Heemstede. The noise of the rocket firing was deafening and frightening; windows rattled and often shattered in pieces; houses shook to their foundations, and we lived in constant agony lest the V-2's backfire and drop in the periphery of Heemstede causing death and damage to us.

So Nora and I were faced with the difficult problem of finding new quarters. It would be no easy task to find a place of refuge now that so many people—young men, railroad strikers, Jewish "hiders"—needed a hiding place.

Who would want to take in additional mouths to feed at this time or to accommodate more people in this cold and dark period? Who would take the risk of being betrayed by N.S.B.-Nazis at a time when the nervous Germans were executing sabotage and resistance suspects at the least provocation?

We looked forward eagerly to seeing Fritz. No matter how difficult the problem, we were sure Fritz would find the right solution. And he surely came!

Despite the danger of raids, despite the driving rains and stormy weather, he rode the entire distance of 30 kilometres between Leiden and Heemstede on his bicycle, getting wet through and through.

Zuster Mary informed Nora's "Uncle Fritz" about the fate of Het Marishuis. Fritz assured her that he would take care of Nora and he would also help me move. If she guessed our Underground involvement she did not let on.

I felt reassured and comforted by his presence. Suddenly everything was not so black. When Zuster Mary left the room, Nora and I asked him what he had in mind. For Nora he had a secure place in mind. However, he had to discuss my situation with the Leiden Resistance leaders as to whether I would continue to stay here in Heemstede or work in Leiden. No problem!

How relieved I was! The responsibility of deciding what to do was taken from my shoulders. He was the one who made things easy for me to bear! I could always rely on him!

Afterwards Fritz and I went out in the rain to attend to our responsibilities. Coming to one address I suddenly noticed the curtains slightly opened on both windows. It alarmed me because I knew Jews were hidden there and the draperies were always drawn, even during the day. I walked past the house and returned to Fritz around the block, whistling our danger song: *"Daar by die molen"*—"There near the windmill." He got on his bicycle and drove off.

I continued in the direction of Het Marishuis, proceeding cautiously and looking back to see if some one was following me, turning into streets, backtracking, until I came to our street near the canal, where I stood under a tree waiting opposite the windmill.

When Fritz came by, I jumped on the backseat of his bicycle and holding on to him, we made our way to Haarlem. On the way I explained to Fritz about my suspicions. His praise was like a tonic to me:

"That was good thinking and fast acting. I am proud of you. Who knows what could have happened, had you gone in. We'll go to Betty. Maybe she knows more about it. In any case we'll have to find some other contact to whom we can give the ration cards, for the people need them badly."

Betty told us the tragic story: "One night last week the Germans came and raided the house. Kees, his wife, and three children, together with two Jewish ladies, were taken prisoners. His oldest girl was sleeping at a friend's so she was saved. The Nazis found underground newspapers, a crystal radio receiver, weapons, and illegal identity cards. It's a good thing you did not ring the bell. The house is being watched. We are terrified because someone must have betrayed him."

"The L.K.P.-actions group is planning a rescue raid. They will not tell me until their Underground action is accomplished successfully. Kees is such a fantastic worker, we miss him so much!"

"To be caught now, so near the end of the war, is a catastrophe." Fritz was furious; I could see his face turn grim. "What a reward for all the unselfish deeds Kees performed, for all the risks he took. I want to participate in whatever the actions group is planning. Please tell them, Betty, that I must be part of the rescue raid.''

Betty took the ration cards and we waited at a café-house while she went to contact her Underground source. In less than ten minutes we saw her pass the window with an elderly gentleman. Fritz paid for the tasteless substitute coffee and we followed in the direction Betty and her escort had taken.

In the shelter of a covered-up empty store entrance, we exchanged a few brief words. The gentleman's name was Dirk and he would be my contact instead of Kees at Het Marishuis for the duration of my stay there.

I would have to watch for him on the street opposite the kitchen window and go out to meet him. The most important slogan was now, ''Be careful!''

As we were leaving I heard Fritz talk to him about ''up north.'' Dirk said something I could not catch and then we parted company. The rain had stopped and now Fritz and I were walking back to Heemstede. As if he could read my thoughts and feel the subdued mood I was in, he said:

''Leesha, I am grateful to the Great Lord for saving you. Just imagine if you had gone into that house. I couldn't have guaranteed the consequences of my actions. I shudder to think that I could have lost you now. Don't look at me like that. I know I promised not to talk about love anymore. I won't, but I can't help feeling it.''

Then, as if to break the sensitive mood, he added: ''Oh, I almost forgot. Here is a candle for you. You will never believe what I had to go through in order to get it. But you deserve it!''

The tension before he came, the uncertainty of my future place, the tragedy about Kees, and now again Fritz's wonderful expression of concern, his desire to fulfill my every possible need, all these emotions overwhelmed me. Holding the small candle protected in my hands, I put my head on his shoulder and let my tears flow freely. I could feel him shiver with the force of his controlled emotions, but he did not touch me. We just stood there, knowing the goodness and understanding of human love.

"Leesha, how would you like to come with us on a bicycle trip up to North Holland?," he asked. "We will go after New Year's, and upon your return you'll go to your new place of operation. Most probably Dirk and Betty or some other underground workers will join us. The food situation is grave and we need to investigate some unconventional possibilities of supply."

I was overcome with joy. To be invited to be part of such a team was indeed an honor. Naturally I wanted to go! What a question!

"But I don't have a bicycle!," I cried out in dismay. "How can I get one now?"

"Don't worry. Heemstede will arrange it," he said confidently. "It's still a few weeks off. Let's hope things don't get worse. I'll still see you before we go."

The inevitability of our parting hung sorrowfully over the household of Het Marishuis, its patients, Zuster Mary, Nora, and myself. Knowing that they would not see each other again, the patients lost their usual inhibitions and began commiserating with each other, forgiving and forgetting their petty quarrels, jealousies, and irritabilities.

A few days before Christmas, Mrs. Flory, a patient, came into the kitchen with a tiny bag half-filled with real cocoa and a few nice napkins. She said tremulously:

"Here children. That's all I have. Maybe you can use it to prepare something for our Christmas dinner."

Her gesture set off a chain reaction and nearly everyone of the patients offered something they had saved up: a few tablespoons of sugar, a can of peas, some peppermint candies, paper flowers, and two chocolate squares.

We were gratified at the outpouring of sentiments and the precious gifts. Suddenly we were a loving family, feeling the tragedy of imminent separation. For as long as time would permit we would stay together.

That Christmas dinner was one that everyone present vowed never to forget. With the little we had in provisions we managed to create a semblance of sumptuousness and elegance the likes of which we had not experienced for a long time. The prevailing mood of friendship and goodwill mixed with sadness enhanced and deepened the festive occasion.

Observing the animated faces around the table, I couldn't help wondering: "Will we survive this war and this hunger?"

Fritz did not come to Heemstede before our trip up north; instead I received a letter via Dirk in which he wrote:

31.12.1944

Dearest girl,

How much I would have liked to be with you on this last day of the year. A lot of beauty 1944 did not bring us. How much we looked forward to peace! The war is still raging with consequences so frightening we cannot imagine even in our greatest fantasies.

Thousands, no millions of people, are far from home and hearth either as soldiers, prisoners or fugitives. Death and decay are rampant all over this earth. Those staying home carry on a difficult fight for their very existence. Everything that could make life pleasant has fallen by the wayside. The basic instincts left are to eat and live.

Life is difficult with so many storms and so little sunshine. The will to live will triumph ultimately and we will overcome all difficulties.

Though I can't be with you, my thoughts go out to what is so dear and beloved to me, to you, Leesha. I think of our walks in Het Hout and our long talks. I remember how happy I was when I could smooth over your difficulties and how I almost skipped and jumped as if the papers were for me. Darling, so much has changed in me. You are the one who has awakened me, just like the prince in the fairytale story of Sleeping Beauty. For this, I'll forever be thankful to you. It is as if I'm no longer myself. My businesslike and sober behavior has disappeared. I am living a beautiful dream. Reality will wake me up soon enough when you'll be gone.

In all my activities my thoughts are with you, Leesha. I am writing whatever comes into my mind. I have so much in me to say about you, I gasp for air. We have no light now but when I sit in the dark of the night, the small light in me lights up and that light is you. You are within me.

The Germans are picking up people in the streets. I will be careful; not because I am afraid—Oh no, but because I want to stay alive to look after you and your people.

I would like to write to you about everything in detail, but for this I will need a lifetime.

Dear Leesha, receive much devotion, strength, and daring, willpower, and perseverance in the coming year. My greatest wish is that our friendship will grow to even greater and more beautiful closeness than before.

I take leave of you reluctantly and I shall see you next Monday. Be ready for North Holland, Fr. v.D.

A few days later, I saw Dirk through the kitchen window, walking across the street. I quickly ran out and met him around the corner. His instructions were for me to be ready on Monday. Betty would be waiting at the Iron Bridge with a bicycle for me. I should ask permission for a leave of four days to a week and dress for the worst kind of weather.

Zuster Mary agreed to my urgent request when I told her that I had to attend to my best girlfriend who was terribly ill and lived all alone. I promised to be back in time to help our patients to pack and close up the house.

We couldn't have picked worse weather than the freezing rain, snow, and wind that greeted us on Monday. Except for my few toilet articles and some other small necessities, I was wearing all the sweaters and blouses I had intended to take along. Betty was also hardly recognizable, since she was all bundled up. With her was a young boy holding a bicycle, which he handed over to me and then left.

Betty and I got on the bicycles and started out for Haarlem, where we would be joined by Fritz and Dirk. I was so intent on my peddling against the wind and storm, it took me some time to realize that the back wheel was equipped with a wooden band instead of the usual rubber tire. Every time I hit a stone or a hole, I could feel my bones and insides jump, but I felt fortunate to have a bicycle. After a while I became quite adept at avoiding bumps in the road and it was still better than riding on two wooden tires.

In Haarlem we stopped at a café-house where Fritz and Dirk were waiting. While trying to warm up with a cup of substitute coffee the men outlined their plans for the trip.

Because of the near-starvation conditions of the western part of the Netherlands and the responsibility of the Resistance to provide for all the people in hiding, we were embarking upon a fact-finding trip to the northern part of the province of North Holland to try and find new sources of food among the farmers of the area.

Dirk said: "It will be a tough job and if we do not succeed with the farmers in North Holland we'll try to get into the province of Friesland, where we have good connections. There is more food available in the northern and eastern provinces that the Germans purposely do not transport to the west in retaliation for the railway strike."

Fritz showed us a small map. "From here we will go straight up north to Alkmaar and on the way we'll stop at the farms. If we are lucky we won't have to go further and we will make our way eastwards to Hoorn. I hear we can cross to Friesland on a boat. We can't possibly consider taking the Afsluitdijk [the enclosing dam], which connects North Holland with Friesland. The Germans are constantly patrolling, and now with this storm, it would be too dangerous. Well, let's button up and leave! Dirk and I will ride in front of you. Let's hope we won't encounter any *Moffen* surprises."

This well-planned and highly necessary trip turned out to be a most frustrating and tragic nightmare. The snow, which intermittently changed into freezing rain, and the lashing wind hit us with full force as we traveled on the totally flat and unprotected road. With the greatest of efforts, we mustered up enough energy to scout out all the farmers on the way, with uniformly negative results. The farmers claimed they had no potatoes or other vegetables, let alone meats or fats, and to get rid of us they sometimes used their barking dogs to chase us off their land. Fritz made careful note of the reputation of the farmers who were Nazi sympathizers. This information would be very valuable to the L.K.P.—the Actions group of which he was a member. Later they would raid those farmers and in the name of "The Free Netherlands" they would confiscate their hoarded stocks of meats, fats, potatoes, and wheat for distribution to the needy people in hiding.

In Alkmaar we found no hotel to accommodate us. The bad weather had detained us and we had to be off the streets by curfew time. Fortunately some good citizens took us in; Betty and I in one house and the men in another.

Despite our frustration and misfortunes of the previous day, we set out on our way to Hoorn, fighting the elements. We arrived exhausted, and upon inquiring we heard that there was not the slightest chance of crossing over to Friesland. There were no boats sailing in such stormy weather. The seaman advised us to go up to the most northern point, Den Helder. Perhaps there, we would find a boat.

We stayed over in Hoorn, sitting up in the soup kitchen all night, since no other place was available. Despite the difficulties we did not give up hope. We were determined to reach Friesland. But Betty and I, already numb from tiredness, could not conceal our disappointment when we found out halfway to Den Helder that the Germans had closed off the entire port. There was nothing left for us to do except to turn back.

Never in my life will I forget the sight of hundreds upon hundreds of Dutch citizens walking along the highways and roads in search of food. They were freezing in the stormy winter weather and pushing little carts or baby carriages in front of them. They begged the farmers for food and offered them their finest linens, silver, furs, and clothes in exchange for potatoes, wheat, or vegetables. No one dared to ask for meat or cheese. For many, unfortunately, the "hunger march" was too great a physical effort. They died in misery, on the side of the road.

Betty crossed herself, calling out: *"Oh Gottegot!"* I almost screamed out my still unanswered question: "Why, Oh God? How long is this still going to last?" My hot and angry tears mingled with the driving rain on my face. Fritz took one look at me and understood. He stopped and ordered me to sit on the back of his bicycle. He drove with one hand and with the other, he held on to my bike. I leaned against his back, totally spent in misery. When I looked up to verify his assuring presence, I saw his determined face, his hard line of lips, and I met his compassionate loving eyes. That's how we returned from our hunger trip.

Het Marishuis gave me the security of a beautiful haven, and my hard and narrow bed felt like a downy nest. How I wished I could remain here and not have to move away to adjust again to new surroundings and confront new dangers!

The patients of our convalescent home began to leave; we had no food for them beyond the meager rations and we had no coal for heating. I was busy packing their belongings when Nora called me and said there was someone to see me. I went to the door and to my great astonishment there was Dirk. He said:

"I tried several times to get your attention from the kitchen window. This is an emergency! Leesha, our friend has gone on vacation! Drop everything you are doing and go to Tante Meta today. They need you. Go quickly with Godspeed! *Tot ziens.* Till we meet again!"

I saw him disappear around the corner. I stood there frozen with fear. Dirk's words still sounded in my ears. My brain refused to absorb their meaning:

"Our friend . . . on vacation? Go quickly. They need you . . . . Tante Meta in Leiden . . . . Our friend Fritz did not go on vacation! . . . Fritz is gone! . . . The Nazis have caught him! Oh my God, how is it possible? They need you. Go quickly . . . . I must go to Leiden . . . with Godspeed . . . go!

22

I saw Nora moving her lips but I did not hear a word she said. She must have seen the terror on my face for she led me to the kitchen and made me sit down.

"Fritz is gone," I whispered; "They took him. My dear friend, as strong as the rock of Gibraltar, is no more. The Nazis have captured him. God, how could it happen?"

Then the full impact of the terrible news struck me with violent force. But although I wanted to scream in order to give vent to my agony and raw pain, I did not. I had learned to channel my emotions with the utmost control. Clear reasoning and efficient and swift action took over.

"I must go to Leiden without a moment's delay. Where is Zuster Mary? I must tell her that I am going now."

"Leesha, take me with you." Nora implored me. "I don't want to stay here without you. Everyone is leaving anyway."

"Where will you stay, Nora? First I must see whether it is possible to arrange a safe place for you. Fritz was so careful. Who knows what the consequences will be and how many people were taken with him. I am not sure whether it is safe enough to approach our contacts in the Underground. Stay here until tomorrow and in the meantime I'll scout out the possibilities."

But she insisted: "I'll go to my parents. Don't worry about me. I want to leave with you now."

There was no time for arguing, so I packed all my possessions into one bag and secured it together with Nora's on the back of my bicycle. There was no other means of transportation. We would have to walk the distance from Heemstede to Leiden, some 25 to 30 km. Nora and I alternated, riding the bicycle and walking next to it while holding on to the bags. The road seemed endless in the pouring rain. Often, we had to ask for directions, since we were making our way through the smaller towns and avoiding the main highway, where we might risk being noticed by the Germans, who still traveled in their cars and vans. Only once did we encounter a Dutch policeman, who asked where we were going. I answered that Nora's mother was very ill and that we were on our way to see her. Nora appropriately went into an act of crying and put on a good show. After the policeman left us I complimented her. She answered:

"You know, it was not too difficult to cry. I was so afraid that the tears came by themselves."

We arrived in Leiden, drenched, exhausted, frozen, and hungry. It was already dark and I brought Nora to her parents' hiding place. I went to Tante Meta, where I had been previous to my stay in Heemstede at Het Marishuis. No sooner did I knock on the door than Tante Meta opened it and quickly let me inside. She had been waiting for me impatiently. She said:

"Eddy sent for you and it is most important that you see him right away. Something has happened; the situation is very critical."

After a few moments of rest and some food, I revived a bit. I was not sure whether she knew what had happened, so I did not tell her what I had surmised from Dirk's message.

The safest way to carry on Underground Resistance activities was to reveal information only when it was necessary. In this way each Resistance member knew only the most basic facts concerning the immediate task and the necessary contacts. Even this information could be sufficiently incriminating, if one was caught and forced to talk. We tried as much as possible to give only the most pressing information to each other. Naturally, a worker involved in caring for a large number of people in hiding was known by many and had a large number of contacts. To safeguard oneself, one had to take extra precautions, such as not making lists of names and addresses, not keeping diaries, nor keeping an account of one's actions. Everything had to be remembered. One had to avoid holding meetings in the same place and going and coming through the same entrance. Each outsider, neighbor, and even co-worker had to be looked upon as a potential spy or traitor. Before one was admitted to membership in the Resistance movement one had to be recommended.

Tante Meta told me that Julie, whom I knew as a courier for the Resistance, would wait for me at the entrance to the Academic Hospital on the Rijnsburger weg opposite the Boerhave laan where Tante Meta lived.

When Julie and I came to Eddy's place, a meeting of five people was already in progress. Of the group, who were all in their early twenties, I recognized only Eddy, since he had been my contact before I had met Fritz.

Eddy stood up and introduced me: "I sent for Leesha Bos to come here immediately. I had originally put her in Heemstede where she has been our contact in the region and where she has fulfilled her duties fearlessly and effectively. She worked closely with Fritz and knew him very well. Now, Leesha, Victor will tell you what we have in mind for you."

It was obvious that Victor was the leader of the group. Subsequently I learned that he was called *Zwarte* (Black) Vic, since he was dark-complexioned and he always wore black boots and a black leather jacket. He stood up, began pacing up and down the room, and then spoke to me in a direct, authoritarian manner:

"Fritz, and now we will call him by his real name, Reinier van Kampenhout, and his wife, were picked up yesterday when the Germans raided his home. They found stolen ration cards, underground news bulletins, short-wave radios, and many guns. It was a stroke of bad luck for him and devastating for all of us. We will find out where the Nazis are keeping him and then we will try to get him out to freedom. I am sure of one thing. They will not get any information out of him. He is strong; Leesha, you know that.

"He was responsible for the needs of nearly two hundred hidden Jews and non-Jews. He provided them with food, ration cards, payments for their lodgings, and even supplementary food rations. His capture is a lamentable loss for us.

"Leesha, we asked you to come here to fill the void left by Reinier. We know your abilities, you must take his place. We will help you and give you full cooperation, but we must tell you that there is no existing list of people he took care of. He was so concerned not to carry incriminating information with him that he kept everything in his head. We have only a few names that we know for sure. You will have the difficult task of proceeding very carefully to find the other hidden people and to reconstruct the list.

"We don't know the contacts yet; you cannot trust anyone. But, somehow the people who take care of the 'hidden' will find you, since they cannot exist without your help. It will be very dangerous work on your part and we wish you good luck. Here are the six names we have. Look up these people tomorrow. I'm sure more will follow in no time at all."

I sat there, listening to him, overwhelmed. How could I possibly do all that Reinier had done? How will I ever discover the names and addresses of the hidden people and get food and money to them in time?

Vic said: "Don't worry, you'll do all right. You'll start right away in the morning. Do you have a bicycle?"

When he heard that my bike had one wooden tire he promised to get me one with rubber tires. Then he informed me that he might need me for special activities in his L.K.P.—Underground Actions group. Also, I was advised not to stay with Tante Meta, because of her inquisitiveness. He asked me to come with him.

Everything had happened so fast. So much had occurred since the long and trying trip from Heemstede, and now a new and heavy responsibility was suddenly resting on my shoulders. I was nervous and perturbed.

Vic waited for me at the corner while I got my suitcase and bicycle and we left for my next base of operations: the house of the Kruizingas on the Endegeesterstraat weg in Oegstgeest, a little suburb town and an extension of Leiden.

It was a little house almost at the end of a street that connected with the highway. Tom Kruizinga was a psychiatric orderly in the mental hospital down the road. Ada, his wife, who was much younger than her husband, took care of their small daughter,

Miep, and a number of people hidden in their house, which was also used as a meeting place for some of the Resistance workers. In the attic, six people were hidden and more could be brought in an emergency.

From the moment I met Ada I felt so much more at ease. She was a sweet and friendly person, tall and blond with a ready smile on her face. Nothing bothered her and she took everything in stride. After Vic left, Ada showed me to a small, studylike room in the front that faced the street.

"This is where you'll sleep, on the couch. You can use part of the closet. Please join us now in the family room. You have time to unpack."

The large table in the center of the family room was used for meals, for preparing food, for work, and for conferences. It was the only room that had a heating stove and where an oil lamp burned at night. The house itself usually buzzed with activity, with young people coming and going through the back door. I was introduced to everyone but no one revealed anything about his Underground activities. We belonged to the same group, each one had a different task to perform, and it was far wiser for everyone not to know too much.

When Tom Kruizinga came home from work at the mental hospital we went to my room and talked about the mission that lay before me. He had the greatest admiration for Reinier, and he, too, was apprehensive about the consequences of his capture:

"The Nazis had known exactly where to look and they found a lot of incriminating evidence. It could have been a betrayal from close by—Leesha, I have my suspicions. Please, be careful! Reinier was very popular as a leader. It could have been some rival who betrayed him. It is a tightrope we are walking on, working in the Resistance and exposing ourselves to danger every minute of the day and night. We are deeply involved and we have to wait and watch for the next move. Let's hope it was not a traitor from within our organization, because then nobody will be safe. In the meantime we have to go on with our tasks."

After listening to my doubts about the delicate detective work ahead of me, he assured me:

"Look, you can only do your very best. Go easy, that way you will not arouse suspicion. I am sure that within a few weeks you will have added even more *onderduikers* [hidden people] to your care than Reinier had. I will help you with information and in every possible way. Leesha, I am glad you are here. Welcome to our house."

I felt so much better. Tom and Ada Kruizinga were exactly the kind of people I needed at that moment: trustworthy, strong, and friendly. They had no way of knowing the impact and depth of my friendship with Reinier. I felt lost without him, as if a safe protective membrane had been brutally torn away from me and I had been left raw and exposed. But there was no time for such thoughts now.

We joined the others in the family room just as Black Vic came in with Hans and Phil. They were all so excited. They had just executed a daring mission. Under the cover of darkness they had broken into Reinier's house and rescued from the hidden part of the cellar a small transmitter, more weapons, and radios. This was a terrific coup and they had already brought the items to various hiding places.

"That's a good sign, Leesha," he said. "At least the *Moffen*-Nazis won't get their dirty hands on these treasures."

Later that night in my bed, all alone and half-frozen with cold, I listened to the howling wind outside. Each little noise startled me but I did not move, trying to preserve the little warmth generated by my body. I forced myself to sleep, I needed it so badly. But in front of my burning eyelids I saw a kaleidoscope of moving faces: my father, my mother, Paul, Jackie, Jules, Kitty, Reinier, and David. I felt a stream of hot tears rolling down the sides of my face.

Tom Kruizinga was right. It did not take three weeks and I had recovered the names of about one hundred and fifty hidden Jewish and Gentile people whom I took under my care. It started very slowly with the six names I got from Vic. I went to visit them right away and when they realized who I was their gratefulness and relief were so intense that I was almost embarrassed by their expressions of thanks. They had been petrified lest they be forgotten and unattended. All the Gentile people who were hiding Jews in their homes knew someone else who was also hiding Jews or knew someone who could lead me to the right person.

I could not find a moment's rest for myself, as I worked at my job relentlessly. The idea that someone might be in need and I could not reach him drove me on to increasing activity. It weighed heavily on my conscience and left me no peace of mind. I started talking to shopkeepers, grocers or bakers and the florists about Reinier. My questions about what had actually happened there, whether anyone had ever heard from him since he was imprisoned, brought forth various reactions. Very often the shopkeeper would tell me that many people were suffering because of his capture. That was a sign for me and the following day I would go to him when he was alone and very delicately persuade him to reveal where I could find the hidden people in need of help.

My *onderduikers*—the hidden people I took care of—were eagerly looking forward to seeing me. Very often I was the only outside person whom they saw in their isolation. I brought them news and stories from the outside. I supplied them with food ration cards, by special arrangements with Vic. Sometimes I brought them extra food that the Resistance requisitioned by raiding farmers or other storage areas, to supplement their meager rations.

I was shocked to see the pitiful condition of most of the people in hiding. The starvation diet of less than five-hundred calories a day had left them skinny, weak, and without resistance to sickness. They looked grey and waxen from being shut in and shabby in their old torn clothes, and they smelled unwashed as a result of their lack of soap and laundry detergent.

People started eating strange dishes never intended for human consumption: sugar beets, fodder beets, tulip bulbs, spinach, and other vegetable seeds. None of these foods satisfied the pangs of hunger, whereas they caused terrible gas pains. Small babies and the very old suffered most from hunger and underfeeding. The icy and freezing winter weather intensified their suffering. The death toll rose at an alarming rate. Wood for coffins was scarce and the dead were often buried in cardboard boxes or blankets.

One morning I was confronted with a tragic problem. When I came to see an aged couple, the grocer in whose attic they were hidden informed me that the old man had died during the night. The interment had to be done clandestinely after curfew. The grocer was distressed:

"What shall I do? He cannot be buried at the Christian cemetery; one must have a plot. It's also too dangerous. People know me and they will ask questions. I'm so glad you came today, Leesha. What do you advise me to do?"

"First, let's talk to his wife. She has to be informed of whatever we intend to do," I said.

The little old Jewish lady was grief-stricken. I tried to calm her, and together with the grocer we decided that there was really no other way but to bury him temporarily somewhere on the outskirts of Oegstgeest. After the war she could reinter him wherever she wished. She cried bitterly:

"Even in death the Nazis rob us of our dignity!"

I promised to be present that night at the burial, even though it meant breaking curfew and being subject to search by the German nightly patrol.

A storm was raging in full force as I walked by myself to the appointed place on the edge of a meadow. I had to cross a narrow moat in order to join the grocer and his two sons at the tree that marked the place of burial. They took turns digging the grave, working quietly but with great speed. The rain turned the fertile Dutch soil into a clinging paste, making their labor doubly difficult. Finally the hole was large enough to slide in the body, wrapped in a sack. They had carried the dead man from the house, since there was no wagon available for transportation.

That nightmare, my first burial, became symbolic of our deteriorating and hopeless situation.

Would we survive this blackness that was gradually choking off our last breath of life?

While the men quickly covered the grave and raked around to avoid detection, I silently said the *"Shma Yisrael"* prayer, "Hear, O Israel."

It was so dark I could hardly make out the contours of the men as they left. I followed them guided by the sound of their steps. Suddenly I felt no ground under me. Panic went through me as I was sinking up to my shoulders in the icy water of the moat. The men heard my cry and reached down to pull me out. For my protection the grocer wrapped around me the same blanket that had been used for the dead man. Nevertheless the rain and the freezing wind were biting through me and by the time I got home, a half hour later, my body was shaking, my teeth chattering, and my clothes were frozen wet around me.

To judge from Ada Kruizinga's reaction I must have looked like a ghost. I wanted to say something, but I could not coordinate my words. She put me to bed right away and everything went blank. Afterwards I recollected feeling fiery heat that alternated with shivering iciness while I battled frightening images.

When I opened my eyes, I saw Ada. "Hi, sleepyhead," she greeted me. "Did you have a good rest for two days? You have had a serious attack of the flu and we called Dr. Hogenholz to see you. What a nice man he is, he didn't even want to charge anything for his visit. He is known to be very helpful to the Underground Resistance."

I was so grateful to Ada for taking care of me. When I started to thank her she made me stop. But something bothered me and I had to ask her.

"Ada, when I was delirious, did I give away all my secrets?," I joked with her. She answered lightly:

"You mumbled nonsense. I couldn't make any sense out of it. Don't worry about it!" She avoided my eyes.

Did she find out I was Jewish? I was sure it was safe with her for she said I should not worry about it. As soon as I could stand on my feet I got back to my work, still shaky and coughing, but I had to help my people—they were counting on me.

Gradually I became accepted as an integral part of the Resistance group located at the Kruizingas and led by Black Vic. I kept him informed of my progress and shared all my problems with him. He was obviously relieved that I felt so responsible about detecting all the hidden people and providing them with the necessary care.

"Leesha, I told you that you would succeed because you have

the right personality to do this kind of work. I have other important things to do," he added impatiently.

While he was stating that I had "the right personality" I asked myself with a start, "Does he know that I am Jewish?" Since I had become Elisabeth Bos, very few people knew that I was Jewish and no one alluded to it. I lived like everyone else around me. I had to, in order to safeguard the people I took care of as well as myself. If there was one ounce of suspicion, I could be found out. Only a few key people, including Reinier, had known that I was Jewish, but since I came back to Leiden none of my co-workers knew my real identity and I didn't know theirs. If the betrayal and finally the imprisonment of Reinier was caused by an inside source wouldn't it be dangerous for me if someone found out that I was Jewish?

Vic saw that I was disturbed because he assured me: "I mean, I have no patience to take care of the *onderduikers*. The hidden Jews are not my cup of tea."

He continued:

"The L.K.P.—the National Actions group work—is more important to me now. Three weeks ago we blew up the railway tracks at Warmond when a convoy of V-1 missile weapons was being transported. That was something! The raids on the distribution offices have to be executed regularly to keep you and the other workers supplied with food ration cards for your hidden people. And then the raids we carried out on farms of the N.S.B.-Nazi sympathizers who still have meats, fats, potatoes, and vegetables, for distribution to the hidden people. Do you know, now that the railway men are unemployed, we must feed them too? We have enough problems, believe me—and the end of the war is still not in sight."

"Vic, you never told me about it, but did you ever find out anything about the whereabouts of Reinier? You mentioned on that first night that we met about raiding the police station or the prison."

He got up and started his usual nervous pacing: "That's a sad story and I didn't want to make you feel worse than you do already; I know how closely you worked together. Unfortunately,

214

we can't track him down. The Nazis transported him from one prison to another in quick succession. The Germans know they caught an important Resistance leader and the security around him has been very tight. But I am still trying.''

He looked at me more intently and asked: ''Would you like to assist us in some 'event' soon? I need you. Your face is not known around Leiden. It will be right to use you.'' I agreed and he said he would let me know.

A few nights later, Vic, Hans, and Phil came into the house and talked around the table long after everyone had retired. I heard the rustling of papers through the sliding doors that partitioned off my small front room from the living room.

I heard instructions being given. I caught words like guard, door, window, vault; names of people and street names. The men sounded very excited. I wondered whether they were preparing the action in which I would be involved, too. Would Vic call on me? I knew that any raid the L.K.P. performed would be dangerous. It could mean that any or all of us could be caught if something went wrong.

But I felt as if something beyond my control was driving me to become part of every action that would mean resistance to the long years of oppression. This, in spite of the demoralizing hunger and the increasing danger of betrayal. For the Germans encouraged the N.S.B.-Dutch Nazis to report any suspicious persons in return for money or extra rations. I did not fear exposing myself to serious danger. My firm intention of defying the enemy drove me to take any risk, a feeling that increased even after what I had heard about the atrocities in the concentration camps.

I had closed my mind to thinking about my family, but I could not block out my subconscious. Many nights I woke up crying and my body shook with feelings of anguish, longing, and love for my family. My heart cried out:

''Oh God, hear me, help me. Please . . . I am ready to bring any sacrifice but let them live. Please let them all return . . . I beg You . . . let them return . . . ,'' and I would cry myself to sleep.

The following day Vic was very nervous. He paced back and forth and did not eat a thing. When Tom Kruizinga pointed out to

215

him that it was a pity and a sin not to eat the food, Vic said:

"Tomorrow something big is coming up. I won't sleep here tonight." On the way out he said to me:

"Stay here tomorrow morning. You'll hear from me."

At about 9:00 A.M. Hans brought a message from Vic and we went together to yet another meeting place of Black Vic and the L.K.P. group. There were about twelve young men plus Julie and myself in the room.

The foul-smelling ersatz "black grass" cigarettes made it difficult to breathe in the room. Vic had just finished explaining something to the others. He turned to me:

"Leesha, it's good that you are here. The news is that we are going to raid the Rotterdamse Bank on the Rapenburg at around twelve noon. By that time the people in charge of the soup kitchen will have deposited their day's receipts in the bank. We need that money desperately for our unemployed railway men.

"You and Julie will stand across the street from the bank and be on the lookout for either the police or the Nazis. Our action won't take more than ten minutes. We have it all figured out and very well organized and coordinated with the help of an employee of the bank. Hans will stand at the entrance, outside the bank. You and Julie will make-believe that you are talking to each other. If you see either a policeman or a Nazi, wave your hand and call out: 'Yoohoo,' as if you see someone and you want to say hello.

"Hans will give the alarm sign to us, inside. That's all you two girls will have to do. When the raid is over and you see us come out, leave the scene as fast as you can and head for a safe place. Understand?"

We waited until everyone had left one by one on their bikes, which had been leaning against the wall of the house. Finally, Julie and I left separately.

It was a cold but clear day and I peddled against the wind until I got to the Rapenburg, right across from the Rotterdamse Bank. Julie arrived and we positioned ourselves facing each other, making believe we were talking and holding on to our bikes while we scrutinized the street. Soon we saw our men going in, one by one, with Hans remaining outside the entrance.

Julie and I were nervously talking to each other: "No, nobody. I see no one. I see no *Moffen*. I see no sign of police. I hope everything will go alright. Vic is O.K. He researched everything meticulously. Oh God, let no Nazi come now! I hope the boys make out alright, so that no one will get hurt!"

After what seemed like ages, but in reality, was only minutes, the boys came out two and three at a time, some of them with briefcases. Everything had gone O.K.!

Julie and I jumped on our bicycles and raced away in opposite directions. As I came to the Oude Singel, I saw two big green German vans standing on either side of the canal. The soldiers had cordoned off the street and everyone passing on foot or on bicycle was asked to show identity papers and was frisked for weapons or black market food.

Oh, I was in trouble! I had a small gun in my belt, about fifty ration cards rolled up in my bra, and two blank identity cards. Such evidence of illegality would incriminate me without a question.

I spotted the danger but I saw no way out, not even an alleyway I could turn into. I quickly made a complete U-turn and started to race against the traffic. One of the German soldiers saw me and started yelling: "Halt! Halt!" He grabbed a bicycle and raced after me.

I was desperate. If he caught up with me it would be the end of me. Who could help me now? Like a flash I got an idea and began to whistle the first four notes of Beethoven's *Fifth Symphony* in C minor. This was a whistle we used in the Underground; if there was a friend nearby he would answer me with the second part of the phrase: "bum bum bum bum."

As if from heaven I heard a whistle answering me and then a crash of bicycles, shouting angry voices and cursing in German:

"*Verfluchte leute!* Damned people!"

The oncoming cyclists kept to the right of the road leaving me a path. I raced against traffic and as I turned the corner I looked behind and saw a pile-up of bicycles with the pursuing German caught in the middle.

I ducked in and out of side streets til I reached the home of the Kruizingas. When I finally caught my breath again I related my adventure of the day to Ada. I could not get over my miraculous escape. Ada was so happy:

"You see, Leesha, there are some wonderful people in this world. You have to keep on believing."

That night, Vic was the hero of the hour, as he told the story of the raid on the branch of the Rotterdamse Bank on the Rapenburg and how he had planned the whole procedure:

"When our twelve L.K.P. men entered the bank, one by one, I went over to a little man guarding the vault and I said to him: 'In the name of the Prince of Orange raise your hands' and I stuck a gun in his ribs. The frightened little man put up his hands and started singing: *"Oranje boven"*—"The House of Orange I hold high."

"When the cashier saw two of us approaching his window, he threw everything down and fled. Then, we confronted the bank director with two guns under his nose and he had to hand over the money. We pushed all the people in the bank including the employees, into the vault, while we quickly packed away fl. 95,000 into our briefcases. After we finished, we let the director and the rest of the people out of the vault. We assembled them against the wall and I said to them:

"Gentlemen, this is not a theft or a burglary. This is a raid executed by the Underground Resistance movement. This money, instead of going to the Nazis, will be given to people in hiding, whose lives we are saving and to the railway people who are now unemployed. Long live the Queen."

We could not stop discussing the exciting events. We were making so much noise that Tom Kruizinga sent one of our group to be on guard around the house, for he was afraid we might attract unwelcome visitors. Then he took out a bottle and we each drank a glass of wine. He said:

"Boys and girls, I am still saving a bottle of real Dutch 'Bols' gin to celebrate the end of the war and the end of the Nazi occupation and persecution."

We fell quiet, each one filled with his own thoughts. We almost heard the unspoken question: "When?"

23

Despite the hunger, misery, and suffering inflicted upon our region by the Nazis, wherever I went people were talking hopefully about the end of the war.

Our main source of information, the Underground illegal newsletter, kept us up to date about the latest military developments on all the fronts:

"The Russian winter offensive resembles a Blitzkrieg. Inhabitants of East Prussia and Silesia are fleeing from the approaching Russians.

"Berlin is in a panic, full of refugees and transients, and is being bombed constantly, especially at night.

"The southern Dutch province of Limburg has been freed by American and British troops.

"American armoured cars are rolling toward the Rhine in Germany.

"In Italy the German defenses are collapsing.

"Budapest has fallen after heavy fighting."

The German position became hopeless, yet Hitler in a speech on the occasion of the twelfth anniversary of his taking power in the German Reich was overbearingly confident:

"Every German will defend his country as long as possible, either to conquer or to go under."

Hitler called on Almighty God: "You cannot forsake the wonderful hardworking German nation in favor of Jewish-Asian bolshevism."

We read and discussed the Allied successes but it all seemed so far removed from our own reality. We were painfully struggling to maintain our daily hour-to-hour existence.

Germany was being bombed and destroyed, but in Holland the Nazis continued to operate the firing squads and conduct street raids and reprisals with the greatest efficiency, leaving the dead on the streets as a visible testimony to their ruthless powers.

The Germans had plundered all our food and confiscated the boats and trucks that could transport food from the north and help save thousands from death by hunger.

The workers of the Resistance were in constant fear of being caught, imprisoned, shot, or deported. Indeed we kept losing many of the most valuable and dedicated members of the Resistance.

The memory of Reinier's courage and strength drove me to work unceasingly. I was unable to rest as I tried to emulate his example by giving of myself to the utmost in every situation. This almost relentless drive, assuaged my burning desire to help those in need and gave me an avenue for expressing my pent-up hatred for the Nazis.

I found solace in attending to the needs of the people who were now in my charge. It was a source of deep pride and satisfaction to make a difficult decision and then to execute the daring deed that the situation required. Above all I loved to visit my *onderduikers*, the hidden people, to talk to them, to advise them, to bring them ration cards, extra food, financial aid, and even coal for heating.

With some of the younger people I developed very warm friendships. One such couple was Terry and Johnny Naber, who are my friends to this very day. I was immediately attracted to them by their warmth and friendliness. I couldn't take my eyes off Terry's face, the black hair falling softly around it in dramatic contrast to her white complexion and her melancholy eyes lighting up whenever she smiled. Johnny adored her; that was obvious. He was a descendant of a long line of Spanish-Portuguese Jews with proud and aristocratic traditions. He was of medium stature, lithe, and quick of movement. One had but to look into his kind blue eyes and feel his understanding and outgoing personality.

They told me of their two-year-old little daughter who had been hidden since her birth with a family of farmers in Vaasen, outside of Apeldoorn. I shared their concern and their heartache, they missed her so!

The minute I stepped into their house on the Emmalaan in Oegstgeest I felt at home. It was as if we were kindred souls, talking and feeling with a depth that came straight from the heart and in words that were honest and uncluttered. We talked about every possible subject. We discussed books, philosophy, and music, but we never brought up the topic of my being Jewish.

One night we were so involved in our discussion, I forgot the curfew hour, and I stayed the night. We drank substitute coffee and Johnny rolled terrible-smelling imitation tobacco into loosely packed cigarettes that he secured by twisting the paper on both ends. This represented a proud accomplishment even though when he lit one up, the cigarette burned-halfway and he had to be careful not to burn his nose or hair.

We discussed the Yalta meeting attended by the Big Three: Roosevelt, Churchill, and Stalin.

"The decision is not to destroy the German nation, but the Allies in victory would impose certain conditions upon her. They would occupy Germany, demilitarize and disband the German forces and the German General Staff. The Allies would destroy the German forces, the Nazi parties, and Nazi institutions. There would be trials and punishments for all the war criminals. Germany would be occupied by the four Allied powers—the United States, England, Russia, and France. Germany would have to provide restitution for goods that they had plundered. A Polish State and a Yugoslavian State would be established."

We weighed and disputed each point. Terry argued vehemently:

"After their barbaric behavior, their persecution and destruction of innocent people, the agony, slavery, and plunder they inflicted upon the countries they occupied, the Germans deserve to be totally destroyed!"

"Germany is destroyed already," Johnny answered. "Most of the cities and especially Berlin have been bombed into ruins. They will have a hard time to rebuild them again."

Something bothered me and I said at last:

"This sounds like a final accounting with the enemy. The Big Three have outlined Germany's punishment and promised the re-establishment of a Polish State and a Yugoslav State. However, the Germans deported and persecuted another people, whom they considered to be their enemy. Was there any mention by the Big Three of the rehabilitation of the Jews at the Yalta Conference?"

We fell quiet. Terry and Johnny looked at me quizzically, and then at each other, but did not say a word. I continued:

"The Jews have a long history of being persecuted, of becoming the sacrificial lamb. I wonder what will be the outcome of these deportations after all this is over. I fear . . . ."

Johnny broke in: "Leesha, let's not go into it now. So far Terry and I have consciously avoided speaking about this unknown—the concentration camp. How can we imagine what the rumors mean: massacres, gassing of humans, and burning in ovens? Let's hope to God that the people will all come back; probably undernourished from lack of food, weary and exhausted from the hard labor to which they were sent by the Nazis.

"In the meantime we have to be doubly careful now not to be caught by the Nazis. By now they are desperate, they shoot hostages in cold blood. Certainly any suspected Jew would be easy prey for their ever-ready death-tools."

We talked until very late, huddled in blankets to protect us from the cold. To save the carbide lamp fuel, Terry had opened the blackout curtains and we looked out onto the empty moonlit street. The houses, the trees, and shrubs were sharply outlined. Suddenly we heard a droning noise that reached us with ever-increasing loudness. Squadrons of Allied planes were flying eastward on their nightly mission to bomb targets in Germany.

"How long will this senseless destruction go on? This waste of young lives snuffed out before they started living, the suffering and starvation and, most important of all, the suppression of our personal freedom?" I must have said it out loud, because Terry answered:

"Leesha, I have the feeling it won't be long. I wonder how it will feel . . . after the war . . . I don't dare think about it."

The number of my "hidden" charges and the extent of my involvement in the intricate network of the Resistance increased each day. Dr. Hogenholz, who had so kindly attended to me when I was sick with the flu, left a message with Tom Kruizinga that he needed my help. When I came to see him at his office, he first complimented me on my work and then he had a favor to ask of me:

"Could you supply me with twenty-one food ration cards each time that they are issued? My source went *kaput*, is no more."

Without question I promised him that I would arrange it for him. It meant that Dr. Hogenholz had twenty-one hidden people whom he was taking care of, and until the end of the war I supplied him with whatever he needed for his people.

Our food situation became increasingly disastrous. Finally the Swedish Red Cross succeeded in persuading the Germans to allow two ships with food to be sent to the Western provinces. It was a happy day when we received the rations of 800 grams of white bread and the 125 grams of margarine.

Together with Hans and Phil, Black Vic ingeniously "organized" a considerable amount of bread to be distributed by us as extra nourishment to very weak and starving individuals. The people accepted the unexpected gift with genuine happiness, as if it were more precious than diamonds.

I had just come out of the house of the Rietvelds on the Rijnsburger weg, where I had delivered some special rations for my charges. Walking my heavy-laden bike, my mood was one of elation to be able, at last, to bring something extra to brighten the miserable existence of those in hiding. Suddenly I heard steps behind me and I felt a hand on my shoulder. I stopped in my tracks . . . mortified . . . I turned around, anticipating with fear the consequences of being found out by the Nazis . . . and there, unbelievably in front of my eyes stood my friend, Ann, who had worked together with me as a student-nurse in the Joodse Invalide Hospital in Amsterdam.

We embraced each other joyfully, happy to see each other again. I asked her:

"How did you spot me?"

"It is really a miracle," she answered. "I heard the whistling of a sonata by Beethoven and I was curious to see who it was. Following the sound I recognized you. Thank God we are still alive! How are you? Where are you living now?''

I hadn't noticed that I was whistling; I had been so happily occupied with my bread deliveries. I told her what I was doing and my involvement in the Resistance. I promised to visit her soon. We had so much to talk about and she needed my help in something important.

My next stop was at Nora's parents on the same wide avenue where seventeen of my people were hidden in six homes.

I had seen the Kramers several times before, having arranged for them, as I did for my other charges, ration cards for food, financial aid, which was paid to their hosts for their room and board, plus some other little extras.

They were a very strange couple, always quarreling or arguing with each other and complaining about the people in whose house they were taking refuge. From the moment I came into the room, Mrs. Kramer did not stop her incoherent tirade in a mixture of Dutch, German, Yiddish, and Polish. She yelled at her husband and complained. She was suspicious of her hosts, saying that they did not give her a full amount of rations, all the while gesticulating and pacing nervously. Mr. Kramer scoffed at her, shrugged his shoulders and said in German: *"Ach, sie ist ja ganz verrückt"* (''Oh, she is completely crazy'') and he laughed mockingly.

What a difference from Terry and Johnny Naber, whose love and understanding for each other carried them through the most excruciating period of their self-imposed imprisonment. Apparently claustrophobic shut-in feelings could often produce negative reactions in people.

For a moment I observed this middle-aged couple. They looked like prisoners; their faces were waxen and pale, their clothes dirty grey and shabby. Both the Kramers were educated people, but this close proximity to each other over the past number of years of hiding had aggravated their differences. After meeting her parents, I understood Nora's personality as being the result of their unfortunate influence upon her.

Mrs. Kramer immediately started eating the bread I had

brought for them. Mr. Kramer tried to take it away: "Leave it for later, we just ate lunch," he said.

"No, I'm hungry now. I must have it. Leesha will bring more. She has to. I'll find out where she lives and then I'll come and get it myself," she boasted.

I paid no attention to this childish, silly talk. Mr. Kramer turned to me:

"Really, Leesha. We are so hungry. You must bring us more food! The Underground Resistance has so much money, they could buy it for us on the black market!"

I had kept my calm up to that point; after all, their quarrel was their own. But his last remark really provoked me. I looked into his eyes and said emphatically:

"You are getting no less than any one of the *onderduikers*. Instead of being grateful for being kept safe and alive and appreciative of what others are doing for you, you fight and bicker with each other and with your hosts. Now, you are going to tell the Resistance how to handle its affairs. I had already heard from Reinier that you had to change hiding places because of the trouble and unpleasantness you caused. I tell you, if you want me to continue to take care of you, you'll have to quit this bickering!" With that I picked up my bike and left to visit Will and Joop a few blocks down the avenue.

I looked forward to seeing this nice and friendly couple. They were just a few years older than I and we had a lot in common. They were from Amsterdam, where she had studied law before the Nazis forbade Jews to attend the University, and he was a highly successful partner in his father's business firm. As a hobby she had taken up drawing during hiding and he played chess with whoever was available, myself included. It was a pleasant relief to be able to communicate with them in easy and refreshing conversation. I finished my mission and again I was on my way.

At first I did not pay attention but when I strained to listen, I could hear short running steps and then a pause. I had learned never to show fear or suspicion of being followed. I stopped to make sure that the bundle in back of my bike was well-fastened, quickly I mounted and made a sharp U-turn on the avenue, just in time to spot Nora's mother, Mrs. Kramer, hiding behind a tree. I caught up with her, took her by the arm and steered here toward her house as inconspicuously as I could.

"What are you trying to do?," I asked her. "Don't you realize the danger in which you put yourself, your family, the Resistance, the people you live with and myself? If the Germans catch you, they will make you talk and then we are all lost. Why did you leave the house?"

She tried to get loose, but I held her firmly with one hand while holding on to my bike with the other. Fortunately, the lady of the house had not noticed Mrs. Kramer's disappearance, for she would have thrown her out of the house. Mr. Kramer woke up from his sleep when we entered the room. He took one look at his wife and understood what had happened. He shook his head and said sadly:

"Now you know what she is always up to. She did the same thing to Reinier. Our former landlady made us leave; Reinier had the same trouble."

Mrs. Kramer got her nerve back and turned on me: "You can't control me. Wait. I'll find out where you live and where the Resistance meets. I'll get as much food as I want." She kept talking foolishly. I went to the door, took out the key and held it in front of Mr. Kramer:

"You are responsible for keeping her inside. This door has to be locked always. She is not a reliable person. You will go with her even to the bathroom to make sure she won't repeat this again.

"I will have to report this to the Resistance, since I am sworn to report any irregularities that may harm the safety of the organization. She may succeed in doing something foolish or be caught by the Germans and get us all into trouble.

"Mr. Kramer, this is a warning. You are responsible for keeping her indoors at all times."

I put the key in his hand and left their house for the second time that day.

In the evening I related the Kramer incident to Vic and Hans as we sat at the supper table with the Kruizingas. I knew it was a serious problem; for that reason I did not want to carry the sole responsibility, but I was not prepared for the shock I got when Black Vic pushed his plate away and exploded:

"That woman is a menace and a danger. She has to be taken care of. You just give me the address and I'll go and get rid of her myself! I'm not joking. Where does she live?"

I was sick with fear. Could he force me to tell him? I had expected that he would want to threaten her and to warn her. But to go to the ultimate, to do away with her! I was terrified at the turn of events. Tom, being the older and more mature man, saw it with a little more moderation:

"Let's give this woman another chance. Maybe you can lock her up, Leesha?"

"I put her in her husband's care. He has the key to the room and he won't let her out of his sight," I told them.

Hans, who had a quiet intellectual way of speaking, offered his opinion:

"We put our lives on the line every minute of the day and night to save people in hiding. The irresponsible behavior of this crazy woman could arouse the suspicion of the Nazis. Our whole organization and all our work could collapse right into their hands. I am inclined to agree with Vic. 'Soft doctors make stinking wounds'—the dangerous infection has to be cut out, drastically."

I looked at blond, sophisticated Hans pleadingly:

"But she is Jewish. She wouldn't . . . ."

Vic cut in angrily: "There is no other way, Leesha. We must get rid of her!"

I turned away completely upset. Logically they were right. She could be the downfall of hundreds of people—maybe more. But how could I be party to this drastic action? I wouldn't have a moment's peace, my whole life long! I faced Vic, feeling like David meeting up with Goliath, and I said with determination:

"I have been with the Resistance for a long time in many places, sometimes working day and night even beyond the call of duty because my conscience dictates it to me. You called me from Heemstede to take Reinier's place. I walked a whole day in pouring rain following your instructions to get here as fast as possible. I know there must be discipline to ensure safety and efficiency.

"But I am sorry, Vic. I cannot comply with you now. I will not knowingly cause a person's death. I cannot!"

I looked at him fiercely, but I could not control the embarrassing tears that sprang into my eyes.

Vic was on the point of another outburst, but abruptly changed his mind. With a dismissing gesture of his hand and with disgust on his face he blurted in rage:

"Ah, women. . . .But I want you to know, we can't possibly let it go on! I'll consult with some others, you'll hear from me tomorrow!" He left the room. It was evident that he was not accustomed to being contradicted.

Before going to bed Tom talked to me and as always I could feel his concern for me. His wise words had a calming effect on me:

"Leesha, could you stay away from here for a couple of nights? You told me about these nice friends, stay there. This Kramer woman and our safety, that's your responsibility."

Tom had shown me the way. He did not have to say anymore about the matter. Then as if to change the subject he continued:

"Oh yes. You mentioned to me that you needed some warm blankets and sheets for some of the people. I spoke to the director of the mental hospital, Dr. van der Steen. He is expecting you and he is ready to help."

That night I lay awake analyzing the consequences of my opposition to Vic's verdict. The awesome responsibility weighed heavily upon me. How I missed the reassuring decisiveness of Reinier! His compassionate feeling for the persecuted race would never allow him to consider such drastic measures. Of one thing I was sure: I would not tell Vic where to find Mrs. Kramer! My decision was made.

Because I wanted to leave promptly at 6:00 A.M. when curfew ended, I fought off falling asleep. The night was endless. Every few minutes I awoke with a start thinking it was time to get up. Frightening images troubled my mind. I was cold and tired and sick to the very core of my being. A powerful loneliness enveloped me.

"Will this ever end? Will blackness and hopelessness ever give way to life, bright and promising?"

Oh, how I yearned for a sunny corner of my own! What a relief and luxury it would be not to be afraid! To be unencumbered by alien restrictions and rules! I felt as if we were cut off from the world, except for the sky immediately above our heads.

"Why so long? How long will we have to endure this suffering? Will I ever enjoy life?"

When I saw the first rays of light breaking through the dark, I started moving quickly and soundlessly. Assembling a few personal things, a bundle of ration cards and some other papers I needed for my work into my bag, I dressed and in my stocking feet I left through the back door without having made a sound. I walked my bike through the grassy meadow in order to avoid the noise of the gravel on the pathway.

On my way to Leiden I made sure that nobody was following me. I backtracked to the Rijnsburger weg where the Kramers lived. They were alarmed to see me so early in the morning and were evidently impressed with the seriousness of the visit. I told them what had transpired the night before—Vic's verdict and my trying to save Mrs. Kramer's life. I had no other recourse but to scare them out of their lives.

"Mr. Kramer, if you want your wife to live and at the same time not to endanger your own life, not to mention the lives of hundreds of other people, you must observe the following rules. At no time may you step out of the house during the coming week. You are not to look out of the window; as a matter of fact, you must draw the drapes tightly. Under some pretext, I'll persuade the landlady not to open the door to strangers. You must obey these instructions, do you understand? Mrs. Kramer, if I hear of any trouble, I'll personally go to our leader in the Resistance and tell him about you. And you, Mr. Kramer, you will have to account for her. If you must, tie her to the bed or knock her unconscious, but keep her inside. Your very lives are at stake!"

229

I told the landlady about a suspected informer on the loose and implored her not to let anybody in, nor the Kramers out, and I left the place as fast as I could; it had been a scene of painful aggravation.

After freshening up and eating breakfast at Terry and Johhny Naber's I finally began to recover. In a few short sentences, I told them what had happened without revealing names and addresses. They were so eager to please me, even offering me a second slice of bread, which was their evening ration, but of course, I refused. I had to go, but I promised to sleep over at their house on the following night.

The mental hospital on the Endegeesterstraat weg in Oegsgeest was completely surrounded by a mesh-wire fence. Entrance was granted only to people with a permit, whether they were employed there or relatives of the inmates. When I approached, the guard asked me to state my business. I told him that I wanted to see Tom Kruizinga. While I waited I saw groups of men inside the grounds, walking, running, and behaving like immature playful children. One man ran as fast as he could from one tree to another hiding from an imaginary pursuer.

Tom met me and we walked together to the doctor's office. Several times one of the inmates would approach us and touch me or let out a yell. One man had a tree-branch in his hand ready to strike with it. Tom quietly took the piece of wood out of his hand and told him to go and water the plants. The patient smiled and left. I was full of admiration.

"Tom, you know exactly how to talk to them. How could you be sure that he wouldn't lash out violently? These poor people . . . ."

"That's my profession. I have been here more years then I care to admit. I know every patient. It is pitiful to see them in such a mental condition. But on the other hand, they don't realize a thing about the agony of war, about the risks, the danger nor the hunger. They live in a world of their own. Here we are, Dr. van der Steen."

The elderly, pleasant-looking doctor extended his hand to me and before I could even say a word, Dr. van der Steen took a piece of paper, sat down behind his desk and matter-of-factly inquired:

"How many blankets do you need? Sheets? Beds?"

Touched by this ease and generosity, I started to answer, but he continued:

"Come on now. Don't be shy! If I ever need your help I will ask for it too. Speak up. Tom told me about you and I like what I see."

In no time at all I had four blankets tied on to the back of my bike and an invitation to come back for more. Tom saw me out and for a few minutes we discussed the Kramer case. He approved of my action of the morning.

The gift of a blanket would be greeted with great happiness by the needy recipient, since the weather was cold and raw.

With bent head and legs peddling forcefully I fought my way against a strong wind. Suddenly I was overcome by an overwhelming exhaustion. I got off the bike and stood resting in the shelter of the entrance of a flower shop.

The main shopping street in Oegstgeest was empty of traffic. No one had business to transact. The stores were empty, locked up; the large store windows protected by tape and blackout paper. There was nothing to sell. The grocery store, where the meager rations were to be redeemed in exchange for the few allotted coupons, had a sign on its door: "We're out of everything. Maybe there'll be something tomorrow."

"What poverty. What emptiness in our land of plenty!"

The effects of the sleepless night had caught up with me. I also realized I had not eaten anything since the cup of imitation tea and the slice of "saw-dust" bread early in the morning at the Naber's. I walked into the flower shop. I felt I had to sit down.

The owner was very kind; he brought me something warm to drink and said:

"It happens very often now that people faint in the street or don't feel well. Don't be ashamed, young lady."

My eyes were drawn to the most precious sight I had seen for a long time—a small bunch of yellow and white crocuses. How innocent and tender they looked! They were on the point of

231

opening their colorful crowns. Suddenly I felt better. I bought the flowers, put them under my coat to shield them from the wind and with seemingly inexhaustible energy I jumped on my bike on my way to my friend, Ann.

Every once in a while I got a whiff of the delicate fragrance of the flowers inside my coat. My everlasting awe and love for nature knew no bounds.

"There is so much beauty in the world to be enjoyed and to be admired," I mused. "That's the feeling of oneness with nature . . . that's happiness . . . that's freedom . . . ."

Freedom . . . something clicked in my mind. Food and ration cards, financial aid, and safekeeping were necessary to keep my people hidden, but how could I provide a little freedom for them, even now, during the war under the Nazi occupation?

A plan started to take form. The initiative had come from a colleague in the Resistance branch of "Fighting Netherland"— *Strijdent Nederland.*"

I was advised to contact Cor van Wijk, an official at the Leiden city hall registry, the *Bevolkings Register*, who was part of their operation.

I would do so in the morning without fail.

Cor van Wijk, who performed important Underground activities in the Registry of the Leiden City Hall.

Speciaal bulletin voor Leiden's omgeving.   Zaterdag 28 April   No.215.

RUSSEN EN AMERIKANEN ONTMOETEN ELKAAR/

Officieel is in Londen,Washington en Moskou bekend gemaakt dat de Russen en
Amerikanen elkaar op 26 April om 20 minuten voor vijf in Torgau ontmoet heb-
ben.Churchill,Stalin en Truman hebben ieder ter gelegenheid van deze gedenk-
waardige gebeurtenis een korte verklaring afgelegd.Churcill zeide:"De taak van
de geallieerde legers is de resten van de Duitse militaire macht geheel te
vernietigen.Truman:"De laatste vage hoop van de tot wanhoop gebrachte Hitler
en zijn boevenregering is de bodem ingeslagen.Volkeren ide samen plannen kunnen maken en samen kunnen vechten,kunnen ook samen een vrede opbouwen.Stalin
bracht hulde aan de geallieerde legers en verklaarde dat het hun plicht is
de vijand volledig te vernietigen.
Het grote nieuws van de historische ontmoeting is overal in de wereld met grote vreugde ontvangen.In de Londense dagbladen staan foto's waarop men Russische en Amerikanse soldaten elkaar de hand ziet reiken op een brug over de
Elbe.De soldaten van beide legers boden elkaar sigaretten aan en dronken op
elkaar's welzijn.De soldaten deden alle mogelijke moeite om elkaar te verstaan
zoo vertelt een correspondent.Dit is het grootste moment van mijn leven zei
een Russisch soldaat.In Moskou werd het feest gevierd met 24 salvo's uit 324
kanonen en met het spelen van de Volksliederen.
                              -o-o-
Nederland: In verband met de plannen voor hulp aan de bevolking van bezet Nederland is Radio Oranje gemachtigd het volgende mede te delen:
Alles wordt in het werk gesteld om alle practisch uitvoerbare mogelijkheden
te benutten om ten spoedigste voedsel te brengen aan de drie hongerende pro-
vincies.
Duitsland: De Russen hebben Rathenau veroverd,op 20 km.afstand van het 9e Am.
leger,terwijl zij Wittenberg stormenderhand genomen hebben,waardoor zij het
9e Amerikaanse leger tot op eveneens 20 km.genaderd zijn.In een dagorder maak-
te Stalin bekend dat Spandau en Potsdam gevallen zijn.Het Tempelhof vliegveld
is in Russische handen.DeRussen staan op 1 km.van het hart van Berlijn.Een
meer bekend generaal,nl.de radiocommentator van de nazis von Dittmar is Woens-
dag de Elbe overgestoken en zich aan de Amerikanen over te geven.Hij heeft nog
geen commentaar geleverd op deze militaire gebeurtenis,maar wel verklaarde
hij dat Hitler nog in Berlijn was en zelf de legere aanvoerde.
Bremen is geheel gezuiverd en er wordt verder opgerukt naar de mond van de
Weser.De Schooten werden in de stad door Franse en Nederlandse dwangarbeiders
begroet.
Generaal Patton heeft de Oostenrijkse grens overschreden,3 km.ten Z.van het
punt waar Tsjecho Slovakije,Oostenrijk en Duitsland samenkomen.De Amerikanen
staan hier 240 km.van de Russen verwijderd...andere eenheden van het 3e leger
rukken Tsjecho Slovakije verder in.Regensburg is veroverd,evenals Ingolstadt.
Het 7e leger is München tot op 40 km.genaderd,terwijl ook afdelingen van het
6e leger naar die stad oprukken.De Duitsers die ingesloten zitten in het ge-
bied ten Z.W.van Stuttgart worden opgeruimd.De Fransen hebben Constanz aan het
meer van dien naam veroverd.
Zuidelijk Front: Radio Milaan heeft bevestigd dat Mussolini gearresteerd werd
bij een poging om de Zwitserse grens over te komen.Behalve de Duce zijn ook
Graziani,Pavolini en Farinacci in handen der patriotten gevallen.In Italie
wordt overal gefeest en in vele bevrijde steden wapperen de geallieerde vlag-
gen.Het 5e leger heeft het Gardemeer bereikt na de verovering van Verona,waar-
door de vlakte van N.Italie in tweeen is gesplitst.Zowel het 5e als het 8e
leger zijn over de Adige heen.Het 8e leger rukt op naar Venetie.De Amerikanen zijn Genua binnengerukt.Italiaanse patriotten zijn bezig het N.W.deel van
Italie te zuiveren van Duitsers.Fransen troepen hebben Ventimiglia en Borg
dighera veroverd.
Verre Oosten: Super Vliegende Forten deden een aanval op Kioe Sioe,het Z.ei-
land van Japan,waarbij één bommenwerper verloren ging.
Luchtfront: Uit luchtfoto's blijkt dat het huis van Hitler ""t Arendsnest"
drie keer getroffen is bij het jongste bombardement.
Ter zee: Een Engelse eskader deed een aanval op een krachtig geescorteerd duits
convooi onder de Nederlandse kust.Een schip werd tot zinken gebracht.Het eskader keerde onbeschadigd huiswaarts.

Underground news bulletin.

234

After Liberation, V.E. Day, in front of the Naber's house on the Emmalaan in Oegstgeest. Left to right: Sidney (the driver); Leesha; Johnny Naber, holding his daughter, Emily; Capt. I.B. Rose; and Terry Naber.

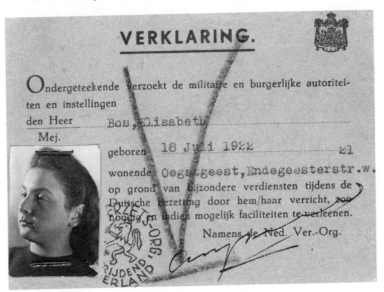

Declaration and recognition card, presented to me by the Resistance Organization, ''The Fighting Netherlands,'' for special accomplishments during the Nazi occupation.

Newspapers across Canada carried headlines, the story, and picture of my marriage to Dr. I.B. Rose, the former Capt. Rose of the Canadian Army.

24

"How would it feel to be one's self again and to live normally? What were our chances of doing so now?"

These were the questions that Ann and I were busy discussing during most of the night of our first visit together.

We were so happy to see each other, we just couldn't get over the miracle that had brought us together again.

"Actually it was Beethoven!," Ann exclaimed. "If you hadn't whistled his sonata I wouldn't have followed the sound of the music."

Her infectious laughter reminded me of our days together in Amsterdam in the Joodse Invalide Hospital in 1942–1943. We recalled incidents, the patients, our mutual friends, and wondered what had happened to all of them: "Will they come back...?"

After she had left the hospital the evening before the Nazis had deported the invalid patients to concentration camp, Ann had gone into hiding and had come out again. She had been picked up by the Germans and after escaping, she went into hiding permanently in Leiden in November 1943. Her mother and sisters were hidden in Amsterdam. Her father, who had been a professor at the Groningen University, was sent to concentration camp in 1941 because of his critical, outspoken writings against the Nazis.

Ann consulted me about our mutual friend, Suzanne, also a former nurse at the Joodse Invalide hospital, with whom she was still in touch.

"You know Suusje, shy and dreamy. She is hiding at the moment in a very unsafe place, her identity card is false and can be easily detected. Leesha, could you help her?," Ann asked.

"Of course!," I promised. "I'll need a day or two to arrange a place for her. When she comes here I'll provide her with a new identity card. I'll let you know the moment I have a safe address for her."

Throughout the evening we played records on her little record player, which had to be cranked up manually—Mozart, Beethoven, and the *Harpsichord Concerto* by Johann Christian Bach, which I favored in particular. For supper we had boiled sugar beets, drank ersatz coffee and adored the crocuses I had given to Ann upon my arrival. My parched soul drank in the music.

"Flowers, music, friendship," I was thinking, "isolated drops of happiness in the midst of so much suffering . . . ." They would quickly evaporate in the unrelenting pressures of urgent responsibilities and lurking dangers.

On parallel tracks my mind was already jumping to tomorrow—Leiden Registry—identity cards—will it work out? I could not allow myself to relax from my duties, for too many people depended on my help.

Every minute counted!

The entrance to the registry and filing office of the Leiden City Hall was guarded by a German policeman. I joined the line of people at the door and calmly offered my card for identification while my heart beat in my throat. Although I knew that my card was new and legal since I had received it officially from the Heemstede registry office, one could never be sure what the Nazis might find to be wrong. The German handed it back to me and waved me on. With breathless relief I ran up the stairs and there I asked for Cor van Wijk.

I was referred to a tall, slim, dark-haired young man of about my age. His intelligent eyes behind the horn-rimmed glasses quickly acknowledged my mention of Henk, our mutual contact. He motioned to me to move two windows further away, out of earshot of his neighbor. I handed him my identity card and said: "I'm Leesha Bos; Henk suggested that we cooperate."

Cor looked directly at me. Hardly moving his lips and audible only to me, he spoke quickly and clearly:

"Don't talk. Just write down an address where I can meet you tonight an hour before curfew. I will provide you with new identity cards, a fingerprinting kit, the necessary legal stamps, and I'll show you how to handle the procedure. You have to supply me with the personal facts and data of the person who needs the identity card, the rest you can leave up to me."

I could hardly believe my ears. Everything was turning out to be so quick and easy and I had been so apprehensive. Did I dare ask him for more?

The idea of providing personal freedom to my people left me no rest. I had to try.

"Cor, I hope you won't mind my question," I asked modestly. "Is there a way to register the hidden people legally, under their assumed names so that they can move freely outside? I . . . ."

"That's done automatically," he interrupted me. "I'll explain it to you this evening. We are talking too long. Goodbye."

It was the beginning of a most wonderful and cooperative association that very naturally turned into sincere friendship. It was an almost impossible goal that I had achieved for my hidden people. With the good services of Cor van Wijk, the illegal status of many of my hidden people could be legalized by registering them in the official registry—the *Bevolkings Register* of the City Hall of Leiden. New identity cards were provided by Cor in case the old ones were of a suspicious nature. Afterwards he registered all the particulars on special filing cards, corresponding with those on the identity cards, including fictitious names of parents and their birthplaces, which Cor made up himself and which the people had to memorize. The reason given for the replacement of a new identity card was either loss of same or the torn and illegible state of the old one issued somewhere in the north, south, or east of Holland. Since we were completely cut off from those areas, no further checking was possible.

It was my task to assemble all the personabilia for Cor, fingerprint the people, make sure of proper assumed signatures, affix the legal stamp, and then bring the cards back to Cor for the final city stamp.

After this procedure the individual's identity could be scrutinized by even the most efficient Nazi and he would find nothing wrong.

I immediately brought up the question of the Kramers and Cor arranged for their legalization. This fact minimized the extent of jeopardy that Mrs. Kramer could bring upon herself or the Resistance.

Black Vic was full of praise for my display of efficiency and resourcefulness.

"I don't have to worry about you anymore. When you take care of people, they are well off," he said. The matter of Mrs. Kramer was dropped. There were more important and urgent matters that claimed his immediate attention.

I found a suitable place in Oegstgeest for Suusje, whereupon Ann went to Amsterdam to help her move. They walked their heavily loaded bicycles, with wooden tires, the entire distance. Halfway, a policeman asked them for their identity cards. Knowing the fatal consequences if found with a falsified card, Suusje pretended to be deathly ill. Ann told the policeman that she had to bring Suusje, who was a T.B. patient, to a sanitorium. The policeman was afraid of infection and quickly disappeared. Suusje's problems concerning a safe hiding-place and legal identification were thus resolved.

Cor introduced me to his group of the Dutch Resistance *Strijdent Nederland*, Fighting Netherland, of which I became a member. Together with Koos, Lex, Bernard, and others, they sometimes provided food packages or wood for cooking or heating for my people. Once we even distributed two-hundred pounds of rye kernels that could not be milled because of the lack of electricity. Cor assisted me with the distribution and transportation of the packages to my hidden charges.

Another person who was indispensable to me was a man called Schiller, a representative of the N.S.F.-*National Steunfonds*— The National Aid Fund. The N.S.F. provided the Resistance with the funds necessary for all their illegal activities. The Dutch government-in-exile in London authorized the disbursement and guaranteed the reimbursement of funds, which consisted of loans and voluntary gifts by various banks and financial institutions. The N.S.F. was organized by an Amsterdam banker, Waalraven van Hall, under the very eyes of the Nazis.

Every month I submitted a list of names with amounts of cash I needed for the people in my care, which amounted to fl. five-thousand a month. Not all of my one-hundred and eighty hidden people needed financial aid. In the beginning I introduced myself to Schiller as Miss van Dorn. We met by special appointment, after first receiving a short note from him at the Naber house. Our association was very pleasant and efficient, full of mutual trust and respect. After each transaction, the list was destroyed for fear of detection. Only after the war did I submit a detailed list of all my charges to be entered in the official records of the N.S.F.

The Naber's place became my second home. Terry and Johnny accepted me as a member of their family. I could drop in at any time, stay for the night, or make appointments with my colleagues for meetings at their house. Whenever it was possible I contributed something extra to the household. I loved being there with them, it made my busy but lonely existence more bearable. The little we had to cook had to be prepared on a small Mayostove, which looked like a large can that sat on top of a regular stove to benefit from the drafts of the chimney. Every few minutes, small matchlike pieces of wood had to be put on the fire. We grated sugar beets or kohlrabi and tried to fry them in a pan without oil. It tasted horrible and in our undernourished state we suffered even worse after-effects. But we had to satisfy the growling hunger pains in our stomachs.

During one of my visits with the Nabers, we heard about the terrible disaster that had befallen The Hague, my hometown.

The Allies, intending to destroy the V-2 rocket sites directed at England, had bombed The Hague instead. Because of faulty navigation, a densely populated area, the Bezuidenhout, was destroyed. More than five-hundred people were killed and thirty-thousand were left homeless, without a roof over their heads, and all their possessions were lost.

What a calamity! It was as if my own home had fallen in on me. The strong urge to go there to help compelled me and Henny, another member of *Strijdent Nederland* and also from The Hague, to make our way to our stricken, beautiful city by bicycle.

The highway from Leiden to The Hague was clogged with people: on foot, pushing carts, riding bikes. They did not talk very much and their faces were grim. They were eager to get to The Hague as quickly as possible in order to find out whether their families had survived the bombing. Many came to offer help.

From afar, a sea of fire colored the horizon; we saw buildings crumbling and suffocating smoke filled the air. The entire stricken district of Het Bezuidenhout was cordoned off by the police.

Most of the survivors had already been brought to another part of the city for shelter or treatment. Children and adults were running from the fire, their faces streaked with soot, dirt, blood, and tears, clasping some prized item in their hands.

I had never witnessed such devastation, anguish, and confusion! It looked to me like the destruction of the world!

Het Bezuidenhout had been a residential section where many Jews had lived before they were deported to concentration camps, and I had visited many of my friends there. The School of Fashion Design, which I attended for one year, was only a few streets away from where I stood. Everything had now been reduced to smoldering ruins.

People around us were outraged and bitter at the suffering and bereavement caused by the bombing of an innocent city. Later on, the British apologized for the horrible mishap that resulted from the irresponsibility of a few.

Henny and I found ourselves consoling the children, helping people carry packages, and running back and forth with messages from hospital orderlies.

In the late afternoon we returned to Leiden, tired, bitter about the fate of The Hague, and with pain in our hearts because of the innocent victims.

The Underground bulletins carried glowing reports about the progress of the war. Everyone read them eagerly and followed the battles on the maps of Europe:

242

"The Allies have crossed the Rhine."
"Five Allied armies have pushed into Germany."
"The biggest push since the Invasion!"
"Russians thrust toward Austria."
"Allies in complete air mastery over Italy."

"The combined Allied offensive struck right at the heart of Germany." Yet western Holland did not seem to be affected by the promising developments on the other war fronts.

German soldiers were still marching in the streets singing about the *Heimat*, the Fatherland, even though there was not much left standing in their Fatherland. Nazi street raids were still continuing and we were extremely watchful for spies and informers in the service of the enemy.

The notorious SS officer and police leader, Hans Rauter, was seriously wounded in an action of the Underground army, the B.S., *Binnenlandse Strijdkrachten*, the Netherlands Forces of the Interior. In reprisal, four-hundred people were executed by his deputy Schoengarth in a fit of revenge and the bodies were not allowed to be taken away from the street.

Each week people died by the hundreds from hunger and disease; there was no longer any gas and electricity. The water pressure was low and there was a danger that there would be a serious shortage of water.

In Amsterdam the people plundered empty houses in the Jewish quarter, using whatever furniture, doors, and window-frames they found to stoke their stoves.

Individual German soldiers began to run away, stealing bicycles, watches, jewelry, clocks, and food in their flight. Nobody knew where they were running, since the Allies were over most of Germany, which faced definite defeat.

My preoccupation with my never-ending work left me little time to engage further in the activities of Vic's L.K.P. actions group. However, I was obliged to attend the special secret meetings of the L.K.P. All the young men were members of the B.S.—the Underground Forces of the Interior—and had to undergo military training in case of active confrontations with the

243

Germans. We were afraid that in sheer vindictiveness they might blow up the utilities and other large buildings in their final battle. The closest vigilance was exercised by the B.S. to make sure that any such attempt would have little chance of succeeding.

Vic was riding around in a motorbike now. He showed us how to use the rifles and guns that he had stowed away in his apartment where we had met. A special way of entering and leaving through the front and back entrances was devised in order not to arouse suspicion, and our bicycles had to be parked on a neighboring street.

Vic told us about an exciting scheme that would focus on two most important purposes of the L.K.P. actions group: first, to take advantage of the Nazis and then, secondly, to destroy them.

Many of the German military personnel, in trying to avoid imprisonment, were seeking help from the Resistance in order to go into hiding. The Germans obligated themselves to supply uniforms, guns, ammunition, motorbikes, and fuel to the Resistance in exchange for hiding places until the end of the war.

Vic was excited: "Can you imagine such a windfall! We are in dire need of supplies. Who knows how much longer we will still have to fight in order to smoke out the Nazis. The motorcycles are of the utmost necessity to us in the B.S. Underground forces."

While he was talking I glanced at the people around the room: Hans, Kees, Phil, and others whom I did not know as well.

Anger, revulsion, and disappointment welled up within me. "That we of the Resistance should assist the Nazis to hide? No matter what we get in exchange, no matter what the stakes, the whole idea is repugnant to me. Never!" I forced myself to listen further.

"But, do you think we are really going to hide those blasted Nazis?," Vic continued savagely, striding up and down in his black boots. "Here is what I propose we do. At our first encounter the Germans will be told what to deliver and we will set an appointment for them to go into hiding. When they bring the agreed-upon items, we drive them into a wooded area—and that's the last anyone will see of them."

244

He stood there, his head poised defiantly, ready to pounce on anyone who dared to contradict him. His announcement had the effect of a bomb explosion. Everyone started talking all at once.

"That's only the beginning of our revenge for all the murder and bloodshed—the hostages killed in the streets, the deportations to concentration camps—all the destruction they have caused; the hunger and the suffering."

Vic took out a bottle of Dutch gin, poured some in his coffee cup, and said encouragingly:

"Come on, each of you. Take a snifter! This bottle comes from a German; he stole it in this country. Now it's back to its rightful owners."

Now everyone was excited and listened to Vic in rapt attention.

"We need your fullest cooperation, since we have the opportunity to contact many Germans. We need the supplies badly and time is of the essence. Through the special contact man who sought me out, I'll arrange the meetings. You will soon be notified of the time and place schedule. You will have to inform the Germans about the date of the final delivery."

He turned to me. "Leesha, I did not see you drink. However, I will not excuse you from your obligation in this mutual venture."

Embarrassed, I said, "I don't drink gin. It makes me sick." I could not stand his patronizing attitude.

Not long after this session I was instructed to meet a German soldier on the outskirts of Oegstgeest not far from the main highway at 4:00 in the afternoon. Phil would cover me from a distance, just in case the German would attempt to trap me instead of seeking refuge.

Checking my gun first and then the message for the German, I started on my way. "Here was my chance to inflict revenge for the torment that I was suffering, to destroy one of the Nazis who had deported everyone who was near and dear to me. The German who considered the Jew to be his arch-enemy worthy only of being annihilated, was now in my hands. And I had instructions for his ultimate destination."

With beating heart and extremely nervous, I jumped off my

bike when I saw the Nazi in uniform. He turned and there stood—a boy, not more than eighteen years old, light-brown hair, frightened blue eyes, and a painful expression on his face. His eyes never left my face, searching, grateful for the act of humanity he anticipated from me. Instead of giving him the message and leaving immediately, I asked him in German:

"How old are you? How long have you been in the army?"

"Seventeen and a half," he answered in a stammer. "I came to Holland a few months ago."

"What will you deliver to us?," I inquired.

"Three uniforms, ammunition, two guns, a machine gun, a helmet, gasoline, and boots. I tried to appropriate a motorbike, but I did not succeed. I am sorry," he apologized profusely.

Something beyond my control took hold of me and I said brusquely, "We can't stay here any longer. You are to come to this spot with all your supplies the day after tomorrow at 6:00 P.M. Now leave quickly!" He stammered a quick thanks and goodbye and then left.

I took the opposite direction and rode on furiously, trying to collect my thoughts, trying to understand what I had done just now. Instead of telling the German to come at 4 o'clock when the members of the L.K.P. actions group expected him, I had instructed him to come at 6 o'clock. I knew if he would not be there promptly at four the Resistance would not wait for him; it would be too dangerous.

"Why did I do that? Why did I prevent this German from being killed? Surely every German was responsible for the bloodshed and killings of so many millions of innocent people. At least I should take the opportunity to avenge the fate of my own family!"

Tears of frustration streamed down my face. I was so angry with myself!

"Why was I that weak? This was their rightful punishment!"

Then I recalled the frightened eyes in the young face of the German soldier.

"But they are guilty! The Germans would not think twice about killing an innocent Jew! Think of the concentration camps, the lives lost in vain, the excruciating suffering inflicted upon humanity, the five years of near-death!''

I was ashamed for not being able to be as cold-blooded as I was expected to be, but the minute I saw his frightened young face, the German had become a human being to me.

"How could I become the judge and executioner of a human being? I could never go on living in peace with my conscience. Those eyes would pursue me in all my active and leisure moments.''

A week after this happened, I ran into Vic at the home of the Kruizingas. He was boasting of the great supply of guns he had secured. He said that all the male members of the L.K.P. actions group were equipped with motorbikes and that he had easy access to gasoline. Only one German had not shown up. He looked at me with a curious expression, but did not say anything. Toward evening I packed some of my belongings and decided to stay with Terry and Johnny for a while.

Our patience and tension were tested to the utmost. We learned that the Allies were making swift progress and that they were slicing through Germany taking town after town.

The provinces of Friesland and Groningen, in the north of the Netherlands, were freed by the Canadian army, which forged ahead into the eastern provinces bordering Germany.

But in the Dutch provinces along the west coast the German army was caught in a deadly trap and four million Dutch people were suffering a far worse fate. The population was starving; even the soup kitchens had closed because of lack of food. For Easter the Swedish Red Cross was again permitted to distribute a loaf of bread and a ration of margarine to the badly undernourished and hungry population.

We knew the end was near. However the question was: "Would we make it to the end? Food and medicine and with them our strength and time were running out on us.''

The bread ration was reduced to one pound a week, without much other food available.

Food Commissioner Louwes announced there would be no distribution of food as of May 1st, since there was no supply left.

To prevent the Allies from easy access into the western provinces, *Vesting Holland*, Stronghold Holland, the Germans ordered the opening of the locks *(sluizen)* of Muiden and Ijmuiden, to allow the waters to flood the area. As a result, the water line between Amsterdam and Utrecht—the Grebbe line from Rhenen-Ijselmeer to Amersfoort stood under water. The last spiteful order of the German general Blaskowitz put the low level area, the Wieringermeer polder, which was reclaimed land from the Zuider Zee and the pride and success of the Dutch, under sixteen feet of water. It would take a long time to cultivate this area again.

The water became our enemy now for the land was completely water-logged. Our isolation made us envious of the French and the Belgians, who had been liberated so quickly.

The sad news of the death of the American President Franklin D. Roosevelt affected us all; we prayed that the new President Truman would end the war quickly.

We learned that the Americans and the Russians had met at the River Elbe and had divided the German Reich into two parts.

In the Underground news bulletin we read of the report by the British and American delegations on the conditions they had found in the concentration camps. Such atrocities had not been perpetrated even in the Middle Ages. The Allies forced the German P.O.W.'s to march through the concentration camps to see with their own eyes, so that they would not be able to say: "It is not true!"

Truman, Churchill, and Stalin warned that the people responsible for the atrocities would be brought to justice, and reported that millions of human lives had been brutally terminated by the Nazis.

This devastating report short-circuited in my head. I did not allow its significance to penetrate my brain, yet an icy coldness sank into my heart. I worked indefatigably, grateful that the many activities in which I was engaged demanded my complete attention.

The distraught "hidden people" needed my strength more than ever. My encouragement helped them to hold on just a little longer and not to give up hope. "The final hardships are the heaviest to bear!"

Then finally, toward the end of April 1945, we saw the beginning of our redemption.

25

In an official broadcast by Dutch Radio Oranje from London, the Netherlands government-in-exile declared that:

"In the name of the Allied High Command it is announced that airplanes will transport food for the three provinces who are now in a state of starvation: North Holland, South Holland, and Utrecht. The planes will leave England as soon as weather conditions permit."

I will never forget that sunny Sunday morning of the 29th of April, 1945. We had already become accustomed to the sound of planes, so we paid little attention to the drone of bombers overhead. But the planes did not continue eastward!

Those gigantic, beautiful birds—hundreds of Lancasters and Liberators—flew overhead in low circles as if they deliberately wanted to touch the city. The pilots were easily visible inside.

What a beautiful, almost unreal experience! We ran into the streets, we waved enthusiastically to the pilots, we shouted to them, we laughed, and we cried.

The pilots waved back. Then we saw the bombers open their holds, and suddenly the sky was full of crates and packages dropping at the nearby airport of Valkenburg!

A tremendous shout went up from the people at the unbelievable sight! The planes were actually bringing us food and dropping it right in front of us, while the enemy looked on with silent guns! Those were not bombs being dropped—it was food for us! Tons of it!

We had nothing to fear! Children and grownups danced and hugged each other for joy. Now we knew the war was ending! We would be free soon!

The people were as excited as on that Mad Tuesday in September 1944, the *Dolle Dinsdag*, when we had mistakenly expected the arrival of the Allied forces.

Some people even stayed out after curfew. Radio Oranje warned the Dutch population to be careful and avoid premature demonstrations. The war was not really over yet; the German "Green Police" were still riding through the streets and opening fire on the demonstrators. The Germans were acting as if nothing had happened, and nothing had changed.

Negotiations concerning the air drop of food into occupied Holland had been held with the participation of Prince Bernhard of the Netherlands, Commander of the Princess Irene Brigade, Lt. General Smits, and some high ranking Dutch officers. The Germans were represented by Seyss-Inquart and high-ranking officers of their army and navy.

An unofficial truce had been in effect since negotiations had started. Specific instructions had been issued for efficient, swift, and even-handed distribution of the food stuffs, which had required more than five weeks to prepare for transportation.

On the second food drop, on April 30, four-hundred and fifty RAF bombers dropped one-thousand two-hundred and fifty tons of food in ten different places. Cheese, meat, potatoes, flour, vegetables, tea, coffee, chocolate, and sugar were among many other welcome items distributed to the starving population. Our gratefulness was beyond words. We recognized the American Flying Fortresses and greeted them like welcome friends with love and enthusiasm.

In the first three days, the American and British air forces dropped three-thousand six-hundred and fifty tons of food into occupied Holland. Canadian and British cars delivered thousands of tons of food from the free areas. The Allies made two-hundred and fifty trucks available for the transportation of the foodstuffs. Even supplies of coal were brought in for heating and for use by boats.

We began to realize that other people really cared about what happened to us! We were finally being linked up with the living world outside the borders of the Netherlands.

The heady atmosphere was exciting but it also bred much confusion. Rumors flew that peace had been signed, which were later denied. Peace was near but the Allies were waiting for the Germans to surrender unconditionally.

Then we heard—Hitler was dead! An air of mystery surrounded the cause of his death. But our long-awaited wish was finally fulfilled!

We heard that Radio Milan had acknowledged the arrest of Mussolini while attempting to cross the Swiss border. He had been shot by Italian patriots and his body, together with that of his mistress, had been hung gruesomely for everyone to see.

At long last these two criminals had left the world to which they had brought so much suffering, death, and destruction, leaving a bloody trail behind them.

Many of the high-ranking Nazi leaders were reported to have committed suicide. Admiral Doenitz was now in power and he ordered the German army to continue its fight against the Allies.

Stalin announced the fall of Berlin and the Russian flag flew from the *Reichstag* building!

We were almost drunk with anticipation. The end was in sight. We were both happy and relieved—but the enemy was still among us. There were still clashes between German troops and the Dutch people. The German "Green Police" were still riding in the streets and opening fire on demonstrators.

We still had to be patient and wait for the official signing of the German surrender.

For me it became crystal clear that this was the point in time to go to look for my friend Reinier van Kampenhout, the much-respected and beloved underground leader, who had been caught and imprisoned by the Nazis at the beginning of January.

As if I had planned it far in advance, I knew I had to search for him immediately so that he, together with us, could experience the first moments of sweet liberty. I could not bear the thought of his remaining in prison any longer, now that the Germans were on the point of surrender. It was his right to be released at once!

I began to inquire about the prisons to which he might have been taken. Tom Kruizinga told me that the Rotterdam prison was possibly the place to which he had been taken. Vic suggested Utrecht or the infamous Amersfoort prison.

Then I realized that I could not make such a reconnaissance tour on my bike and I began to look for other possibilities. Would Vic or Kees or Phil take me on their motorbikes? I saw that they were too involved with the B.S., the underground Dutch Forces of the Interior, which had become the official Dutch Force now and which was ready to meet any military challenge.

There were no means of public transportation. Buses, trains, and intercity trams were not in service because of the lack of electricity and gasoline.

How could I accomplish my mission?

The solution to my problem came very unexpectedly. My friend, the grocer with whom I had discussed my problem, informed me that he knew someone, Mr. van Sand, who would be willing to help me.

I lost no time in contacting Mr. van Sand. His villa was magnificent! I was shown into a beautifully decorated living room, where delicious real tea was served by Mrs. van Sand from a silver teapot in bone-china cups. I could sense an air of elegance and abundance.

Mr. van Sand offered me the use of his car, a Citroën, which he had stashed away in a boarded-up garage since the *Dolle Dinsdag* in September 1944. He had been afraid that the Germans would confiscate it.

"But I have no gasoline and no way of getting any. Maybe you could request some from the Resistance? I will take it upon myself to get the car serviced and I am prepared to be your driver."

I was most impressed with his cooperation in my difficult mission and I expressed my appreciation and thanks to him. Leaving his house I had but one single thought in mind: how could I get gasoline for the car?

Upon discussing these new developments with Vic and Tom I found out that Mr. van Sand was known to have been a German collaborator and that now he most probably wanted to cover himself against retribution by the Underground by offering his services to a member of the Resistance. This would help to white-wash him of any previous wrong-doings. Now it dawned on me why I had felt so luxurious in his house; he had never lacked for anything and for him there had been no privation during the war. Through his connections with the Germans he was able to get everything he and his French wife needed.

"Well," I decided, "I need him now. What will happen to him later on will be the responsibility of the government. Vic, how can I get some gasoline?"

He told me that he could not supply gasoline at the moment but perhaps in a few days there might be some available.

However, I was impatient. I could not wait! Where could I get gasoline? Who else had some?

Suddenly it struck me! That's it! How could I have overlooked the most obvious source? Surely, the Germans had gasoline! Now that there was an unofficial truce I would risk it and ask the German Officers-Obersturm-führers-Command, who had requisitioned the nicest homes in Oegstgeest, to supply me with some gasoline.

My strong determination triumphed over my wavering apprehension. I approached the sentry at the door of the German headquarters and requested to see the officer in charge. After a few minutes he showed me inside and I found myself facing an important-looking officer across a large desk. I spoke in German and stated my business in an official and resolute manner:

"I represent the Dutch Resistance and I request that you assist me in the following. I am about to embark on an important search mission and I need gasoline to fill up the tank of my Citroen car. If you help me I will guarantee you a certificate stating that you helped the Resistance. However, if you intend to harm me, I want you to know that my colleagues are covering this house. They are ready to retaliate in case I don't come out of here safe and sound, within fifteen minutes."

"There is no question of harming you. The war is over," the German answered, evidently surprised. "We don't have too much gasoline ourselves, but I can give you ten to twelve liters.

Will that help you? I'll send someone to get it while you wait."

I thanked him. When I came to the door a German soldier handed me a large jerry-can of gasoline and even helped me to place it on the back of my bike.

It had gone so smoothly that a feeling of elation came over me. I almost danced with my bike on the way back to Mr. van Sand to bring him the gasoline. I successfully executed the same performance two more times with good results.

Terry and Johnny were astounded but proud of my resourcefulness and bravery in entering the lion's den.

The moment Terry heard of my intention to search for Reinier and go as far as Amersfoort she became very excited and tearfully implored me to take her along:

"Leesha, I must go and bring my baby home. Johnny and I haven't seen her since she was hidden two years ago. Please, do me this great favor and let me come with you. If you only knew the pain and heartache a mother and father feel in not being able to care and love their own child. The nights we stay awake trying to imagine what she looks like and whether she is safe and sound. We want her so badly! Leesha, you are going to Amersfoort. That's not far from Apeldoorn. Emily is hidden with farmers about ten kilometers outside of Apeldoorn. Please, let me go with you. I am not asking for Johnny to join; he has to remain with the B.S.—the Dutch Forces."

Naturally I could not refuse her and it was decided that we would begin our mission early the following morning, Thursday, the third of May.

That night I saw a vision of Reinier van Kampenhout vividly before me as if he were there in person. Honesty, strength, compassion, and determination—his outstanding qualities radiated from him. I missed him so!

"Oh, God, let him be alive!" My whole heart and soul willed him to be within reach of my search tomorrow. I could feel the tension and anticipation building up within me.

Mr. and Mrs. van Sand proved to be very pleasant company and gracious hosts. Terry and I spoke French to her since she did not speak any Dutch.

On our way to the Rotterdam prison, the first stop on our

itinerary, we saw parts of the farmland on both sides of the highway, standing under water. Now we saw with our own eyes the results of the inundations of the low-lying areas behind the dykes, carried out by the vindictive Germans. How much time, effort, and money would now have to be applied by the farmers in order to render the soil productive again!

When we reached Rotterdam and parked in front of the entrance I jumped out of the car and rushed into the prison office. After introducing myself as a representative of the Resistance, the officials agreed to check the registry to determine if Reinier van Kampenhout was in prison.

"No," they shook their heads. "No such name in this prison."

"Maybe under his alias, Fritz van Dongen or Fritz van Kampen?," I insisted.

Again they checked, but without results.

"Try the Utrecht prison," they suggested. "Maybe they took him there." Disappointed and sad, I left the office. When she saw me, Terry put her arm around me protectively. I was completely dispirited.

"I was so hopeful we would find Reinier here. This prison is near to Leiden; it would be the logical place," I said disconsolately.

"Let's not give up. We still have more ground to cover. Perhaps we'll have better luck in Utrecht," Terry consoled me.

But we did not have better luck in Utrecht. The prison officials explained that Amersfoort would be the only place where we could possibly find Reinier, since it was a large prison where they kept political prisoners. This, plus the fact that after the Allies had captured the eastern provinces, the western area was cut off and no prisoners could be transported to concentration camps further east.

And so we sped on to Amersfoort prison, our last chance to find Reinier. Mrs. van Sand kept urging us to partake of her inexhaustible supply of sandwiches and coffee. We drove through parts of the countryside where the landscape resembled lakes with trees, shrubs, and farms rising above the water. There was bitterness in our hearts to see the extent of the damage that the Germans had willfully brought upon our poor land.

As we approached the highway leading to the Amersfoort prison we found ourselves flanked on both sides of the road by German soldiers marching in single file, looking haggard and disheveled. They were disarmed both literally and figuratively. Here and there, groups of Dutch citizens yelled at them and cursed them. Some spit at them and raised their fists and implements in a spontaneous expression of a rage, which had been contained for five years of hatred and frustration.

The marching of the soldiers resembled a funeral march. This was German defeat! Another facet of this senseless war!

Did the German soldiers now accept that they had lost? Or had the years of indoctrination with Nazi poison destroyed their common sense? Some of them still believed they were being sent back to Germany to reorganize, regain their strength, and then fight Communism and the Russians!

At the Amersfoort prison registry office we heard the devastating truth. Reinier van Kampenhout had been tortured and finally shot to death. His wife had died from the excruciating suffering of ileitis. She had been screaming from pain and starvation, a state shared by all the prisoners.

As if a sledgehammer had struck me, I reeled from the impact of this information. I could not believe it to be true and so final.

"Are you sure?," I kept asking, going in and out of the office. "Is he registered as dead?"

"Look here, young lady," the official in charge was becoming exasperated. "He came here; he is not here anymore and they did not transport him anywhere. They shot him."

"It cannot be. It's impossible," I cried out. "Not Reinier; he can't be dead. He was so strong, so full of life!"

How could I ever accept the inevitability of this loss? Why Reinier? He had put aside his own safety and comfort in order to help and safeguard others. His integrity and his honesty were so urgently needed in the immediate future.

Before long a number of just-released political prisoners gathered around us. They desperately wanted to get to their

257

homes, but there was no public transportation and they were too weak from their imprisonment to walk a long distance. Mr. van Sand agreed to take along two Resistance members, one of whom lived in Groningen in the north and the other in an eastern province. They were emaciated, waxen in appearance, and very weak. They had suffered torture and interrogation at the hands of their Nazi captors and had been subjected to long periods of starvation.

Terry, I, and the two young men squeezed into the back seat of the little Citroen. With my head on Terry's shoulder I poured out my unhappiness and misery and disappointment at the loss of Reinier. I would have given or done anything to see him alive and well. How utterly bitter I felt about his fate!

We were again driving alongside German army units as they were retreating from their Dutch bases. It was late afternoon and we were heading toward the farmer couple in Vaasen, about ten kilometers from Apeldoorn, where Terry would finally regain her little daughter. She had been hidden there since her birth about two years ago. The road led alongside a wooded hilly area called the Veluwe, which lay on our right. A number of times we had to detour because stretches of the highway had been closed to traffic. Beyond the hills of the Veluwe we could hear the sound of machine-gun fire.

We approached a road block and two British soldiers motioned us to stop. This was the first time we had come face to face with our liberators, our Allies! When we realized this, we got out of the car and ran up to them excitedly and started shaking their hands and thanking them. The soldiers acknowledged our sentiments but immediately became very businesslike:

"Ladies and gentlemen. I am afraid you'll have to turn around. This road is closed to civilian cars."

"Why? What's the matter? The war is over!," we argued.

"Some isolated German units are still continuing to fight and we are in the process of smoking them out. Therefore, no civilians are allowed into this stretch of road," one soldier explained.

Taking one look at Terry's grief-stricken face I began to plead with the two soldiers in English:

"Gentlemen, I represent the Dutch Resistance movement. Today we embarked on a very painful mission to find one of our leaders who was imprisoned by the Nazis in January. We searched for him in three prisons and in the last one we were informed that he had been shot to death by the Nazis. These two young men are political prisoners whom we are helping to return home after imprisonment. This is a Jewish lady whose baby is hidden with farmers about one hour away from here. Please let us through so we can return the baby to its natural parents. They have suffered so much during the war on account of the Nazis. Please let us go through!"

The two soldiers looked at each other and then waved us on saying:

"Proceed at your own risk!"

We expressed out thanks, piled into the car, and off we went, proud at having overcome such a formidable obstacle.

Dusk began to fall and Mr. van Sand had to be increasingly careful of the road conditions. At times, we held on to each other, shaken by the impact of the nearby sounds of firing.

Suddenly the car backfired, slowed down, and stopped as if reluctant to climb the long hill ahead. We offered to get out and try to push the car but Mr. van Sand gave us the bad news. We had run out of gas.

What were we to do now?

"Let's stop an Allied army car, they are the only ones who can help us," I suggested. The idea was accepted and we waited on the side of the highway hoping to flag down a kind driver.

It would be dark soon and the shooting was still going on. Unfortunately, there were few cars on the road and the few vehicles that did appear drove past us at such a high rate of speed that our hair and clothes blew wildly in the wind and clouds of dust swirled behind the disappearing vehicles.

We began to become anxious; the thought of being attacked at night by a desperate band of Germans was not very comforting. Something had to be done!

Then from afar we saw a large staffcar approaching with what appeared to be the Allied star affixed on the front of the radiator.

"This one must stop!," Terry called out. All of us began signaling wildly trying to flag down the car, when Terry in desperation, jumped right in the middle of the road, barely missing being hit by the car.

That did the trick! The staffcar stopped. We rushed to it eagerly and a Canadian Captain stepped out.

"What's the matter?," he asked. Everyone started talking at once. He turned to Terry:

"Young lady, you almost caused an accident!"

In my most persuasive manner I explained our situation.

"Please forgive us for this inconvenience to you. But soon it will be dark and we are stuck here on this lonely road because we have run out of gasoline, with the Germans still fighting nearby. We are tired, hungry, and frightened. Could you please help us with some spare gasoline so that we can reach Apeldoorn tonight?"

He looked at us and shook his head.

"Sorry but we have received strict orders not even to stop for anyone. This could be a trap since the area has not been completely cleared of isolated German fighting groups. I don't know who you are. You could be part of some anti-Allied action!"

I tried to persuade him: "Sir, nothing could be further from the truth! Let me introduce myself. My name is Leesha Bos. I am a member of the Dutch Resistance in Leiden and Oegstgeest and I am responsible for hiding and caring for many people who are in great danger.

"Today we have completed a search of three prisons hoping to find our dearly beloved leader who was caught by the Nazis in January and we learned the heartbreaking news that he had been shot to death by the Nazis.

"Now we are continuing our trip in order to help Terry here. She is Jewish. Soon after birth, her baby girl was hidden with farmers about 10 kilometres outside of Apeldoorn. It is now more than two years since Terry and her husband have seen the baby. Can you imagine the pain and deprivation they have felt all this time because they have not been able to care for and love their own child? Please help us. Once we get to Apeldoorn, I can go to the Dutch army headquarters and see to it that all the gas we borrow is returned to you."

The Captain was not listening to me anymore. He turned to Terry and called out in amazement:

"Are you Jewish? I am Jewish, too! My name is Captain Rose. I am a Jewish Chaplain in the Canadian Armed Forces Overseas!" They embraced each other spontaneously and Terry started crying on his shoulder. The captain too was overcome by emotion.

They stood there in the approaching darkness with the tall trees in the background standing like guardian angels. Two souls finding each other. It was a most heart-rending sight. We all felt part of their unique experience.

He turned to me: "Are you Jewish too?"

I nodded. It was the first time since I had changed my identity that I had admitted publicly to being a Jew and I saw a warm expression light up his face.

The Captain quickly took charge of the situation.

"Come. Let's go. It's getting dark. Sidney!," he called to his driver. "Come out and meet the people here, and let's get some gasoline and whatever else they may need."

Suddenly everything became possible. The strong feeling of human charity had overcome strict army restrictions and the fears of sabotage.

Since the staffcar did not happen to have gas for our little Citroen, all of us, except Mr. and Mrs. van Sand, were moved into the staffcar, which also towed the Citroen into Apeldoorn. The two young men to whom we had given a lift from the Amersfoort prison bid us goodbye and continued on their own. The van Sands went with Sidney to fill up the Citroen. While awaiting their return, Terry, the captain, and I strolled up and down the park area where we had stopped and became more closely acquainted. I could sense Terry's excitement in anticipation of seeing her baby again. She kept on talking incessantly about the war, about the persecutions of the Jews, about the raids and the transports to concentration camps. She described their period of hiding, the activities of the Resistance, and to my great embarrassment she kept on praising me for my accomplishments in the Resistance. I implored her to stop but she would not listen.

It seemed as if every ounce of lifeblood had seeped out of me. The defeat and pain I felt at Reinier's death together with the day's ordeals left me drained of all my strength. I longed to retreat within my own shell, to be left alone. I had done whatever I had demanded of myself. I could do no more.

The night was clear and balmy, fragrant with blossoming shrubs and flowers, yet I shivered as if shaking off something foreboding.

Then I became aware of a soothing hand touching my arm, clasping my hand with tenderness and warmth. I knew it was the Captain. The gesture coming to me so unexpectedly when I needed it most, touched me deeply. I could not see him in the dark, but I remembered the trim athletic figure of medium height, an intelligent face with deep-set dark eyes and dark hair. We passed the edge of the park lit up by the street lights and as I glanced up, shyly, I met his eyes which expressed the same tender understanding, compassion, and strength that I had felt with the clasp of his hand.

I was oblivious of Terry who walked between us and who was still holding forth.

"What are your plans, Leesha, now that the war is just about over?," Captain Rose asked me directly.

"Plans for myself?" I was strangely disturbed by the question. I haven't given it a thought yet. "There are so many things to be done for my people to get them back into normal life. It will be difficult for them to return to their hometowns since there is no transportation."

"Maybe I can be of help to you with their repatriation," the Captain said.

Then we heard the horns of the Citroen and the staffcar; they had spotted us. As Terry was writing down her address for the captain, he asked me:

"And where can I reach you? Can I see you soon?"

"I have no permanent place of residence," I answered non-commitedly. "In any case, I'll be very busy for the time being."

"Don't worry, Captain," Terry interjected. "When you visit with us, she'll be there. We want you very much to come and see our baby once we get her back. After all you helped us get to her, you must come see her. Promise to come!"

Terry and I were already in the car when Captain Rose and his driver, Sidney, started loading us down with boxes of cookies, crackers, matzot, cans of salmon, sardines, butter, kosher corned beef, bars of chocolate, and cigarettes.

"What is this?," we gasped. We laughed and we were flabbergasted. There was so much food there was hardly any room left for us. It seemed like magic, like a fairy tale! We had not seen such luxury and plentitude of food in years!

"That's enough!," we called out almost in tears.

"Eat, eat, my child," said the Captain, quoting a well-known Yiddish expression. "I'll see you soon. Good luck to you all!"

We fell back in our seats too exhausted to talk. I felt embarrassed that war conditions had forced me into a situation where I had to be grateful to accept gifts of food. The only redeeming features were the sentiments and the sincerity with which the gesture was offered by the Captain and his assistant.

We were on our way to the farmer's.

"Leesha, you know what I think?," Terry asked in the dark. "I think the Captain has an eye for you. He is very impressed with what he saw and heard about you. I saw him looking at you."

"You are talking through your head. That's nonsense. Just because he looked at me, you are reading a special meaning into it. I have neither the time nor the inclination for anything personal. To me, he was the first soldier in uniform whom I did not hate or fear. Oh, Terry I am so tired!," I exclaimed.

Terry had opened a package of Sweet Caporal cigarettes and was smoking them nervously one after the other. We were approaching the little farm village of Vaasen where her little daughter was hidden. It was nearly midnight. After inquiring at a number of farmhouses, we finally knocked on the door of Farmer Hendriksen and awakened the entire household. Reluctantly we were shown into the living room. Terry, who had met Mr. and

Mrs. Hendriksen when little Emily had been brought to them, apologized for the lateness of the hour and explained the delay caused by our running out of gas.

The farmers and their grown children sat around the table listening silently. The atmosphere became more tense with each passing minute. The Hendriksens knew that Terry had not come at this time of night to pay a social visit. Terry spoke with feeling:

"On behalf of my husband and myself I have come to thank you sincerely from the depth of our hearts for all that you have done for our daughter, Emily. We know the danger to which you subjected your entire household by taking her in and thus saving her life. We will be forever indebted to you for the wonderful care and the good home you have provided for her. But now that the war is over, we are not able to wait a minute longer. We yearn to have our own child back with us. I was fortunate that I had the opportunity of getting here by car with my friend. Now we can take her home. Where is she?"

The Hendriksens were stiff and unyielding. There was hostility in their eyes; their faces became grim. Mrs. Hendriksen drew herself up from her chair and said vehemently:

"You can't take her away from us. We are too attached to her. She has become one of the family. She doesn't know you. She wouldn't want to go with you. You are a stranger to her."

Mr. Hendriksen underscored his wife's sentiments. Their sons and daughters moved about restlessly and said with great emotion:

"We will never let her go! She is ours now!"

"That's the thanks you get . . . ."

Terry was beside herself. She never dreamt that her coming to retrieve her own child would provoke such furor and opposition.

"But she is my flesh and blood. During the war the Nazis wanted to kill us. But now the war is over. Your refusal to give her back will kill me. Can you possibly imagine my suffering and heartache all this time in not being able to hold my own baby in my arms and to take care of her needs? I was deprived of the most natural and pressing maternal instincts . . . ."

She went down on her knees before Mrs. Hendriksen and cried

264

as if her heart would burst: "Please, give me back my child. She is flesh of my flesh . . . ."

I had stood by silently while this drama was being played out but when I saw Terry in a state of near collapse, I could no longer restrain myself.

"No court, no judge in the world would ever agree with what you are trying to do to this mother. You agreed through the goodness of your hearts to safeguard Emily's life for the duration of the Nazi regime here in Holland. For what you have done in looking after the child, the Nabers will be forever grateful to you.

"But now it is their right, as natural parents, that their daughter be returned to them. I am a leader in the Resistance. I personally took care of many Jewish people during the war, among them many children. The danger is over now. The Jewish people are free to go to their own homes and families and wherever they want to go.

"I can understand that you came to love the little girl like your own. But now, please, give the child back to its mother. Otherwise, I assure you, you are headed for a lot of trouble."

One of the Hendriksen daughters had left the room and now she came in with sleepy Emily in her arms. Terry's face lit up at the sight and the tears flowed again. Her arms went out to take Emily but the little girl turned away from her and leaned in the direction of Mrs. Hendriksen as if wanting to be picked up by her. Terry had been rejected. She fell into a chair holding her head in her hands.

Mrs. Hendriksen took a little jacket from a bundle of Emily's clothes on the table, put it on Emily and placed her on Terry's lap. The child became alarmed and began screaming and striking out at poor Terry, who held her close and tried to soothe her with loving words. Terry promised to keep in touch with the Hendriksens, who reluctantly allowed us to leave with the little girl.

Emily kept on crying hysterically during the entire trip home no matter how many chocolates and cookies we offered her.

"Don't be despondent, Terry," I tried to console her. "Love and time will work wonders, you'll see."

Terry kept looking helplessly at her little daughter.

"It will be difficult for her to become adjusted. I only hope she will feel that our every heartbeat is full of love for her," she sighed. "At least our family is together again."

I looked out into the dark night. Dare I think of my own loved ones? Will we ever be together again? Uncertainty, dwindling hopes, and fear filled my body and soul.

During the next few days world-shaking events followed each other with breathtaking rapidity and excitement.

On May 4, 1945, the Germans unconditionally surrendered Northwest Europe to Field Marshal Bernard Montgomery of the Allied High Command in a tent on the Lunenberger Heide.

On May 5, 1945, at the hotel The World, General Foulkes, commander of the First Canadian Corps, and Prince Bernhard of the Netherlands were witness to the signing of the complete capitulation of the German army in the western part of the Netherlands.

The now legal *The Free Press* of Leiden printed a special bulletin number 43. The bold letters across the page read:

"THE BEST NEWS OF THIS WAR"

"Unconditional surrender by the Germans"

"Netherland shall rise again!!!!"

Suddenly Dutch flags appeared everywhere! People began to celebrate and to express their thanks to the liberating Allied armies.

Finally we were free of the German yoke. Gone were the constant fear, the brute force, the hunger and death, the persecutions and shootings.

"Can we become ourselves again?," the thought came to me speculatively. The conditions brought on by the war were still with us. One could not easily forget what had happened to us as if it were a bad dream.

On May 7, 1945, General Dwight D. Eisenhower announced the unconditional surrender of the Third German Reich to the United States, England, and Russia at Allied headquarters in Rheims.

The Second World War in Europe had finally come to an end!

May 8, 1945, was declared as Victory Day, or V.E. Day, and it was greeted with wild jubilation!

What a beautiful day! With tears of joy we welcomed the victorious Allied troops as they arrived in our towns and cities. Thousands of Dutch girls and boys hung on to their vehicles and sprawled all over their tanks. They kissed the soldiers and covered them with flowers. They waved and cheered and sang the Dutch national hymn, the *Wilhelmus* and the song *Oranje Boven,*" "the House of Orange we hold high."

How we welcomed the Canadian troops, who were friendly, natural, and easy-going, as were the British soldiers! We were fascinated by the colorful Scots in their kilts. Later on, when we met the Americans, we were captivated by their cheerfulness and handsome appearance.

How proudly and enthusiastically we applauded our own Dutch Princess Irene Brigade, which had fought so valiantly alongside the Allies!

However, my most moving experience came when I first encountered the soldiers of the Jewish Brigade from Palestine, who had fought as a unit of the British 8th Army. I was stirred to tears by a profound sense of awe, happiness, and kinship as I noticed the emblem on their sleeves: a golden star of David on a blue and white field.

I had to touch it to make sure it was real. My heart was bursting with pride knowing that Jewish men from our Promised Land had been free and had fought victoriously against the very Nazis who had so diabolically planned the annihilation of the Jewish people in Europe.

We welcomed all of our liberators with profound gratitude.

Peace had finally come! We had waited five long, agonizing years!

Queen Wilhelmina addressed the Dutch nation for the first time after the war had ended:

"Our language cannot express the feelings we have in our hearts in this hour of the liberation of the Netherlands.

"The enemy is defeated! Finally we are once again masters of our own house."

That very night we celebrated V.E. Day at the Nabers', where a group of our friends had gathered; they were the young couples whom I had taken care of. Everyone brought along something that they had saved from their rations for the long-awaited and hoped-for occasion. We were in the midst of our preparations when suddenly we heard a screeching of tires and the sound of a car coming to a stop in front of our house.

Terry ran excitedly from the kitchen to the door and called out to me:

"Leesha, I'm sure it's the Captain. I had a premonition he would come today."

There was a lot of commotion in the hall and then Johnny led the way into the kitchen:

"Yes, here she is. Leesha, you remember Captain Rose?" There he was, smiling happily; in back of him was Sidney, his driver, surrounded by our guests.

Introductions were made all around and a festive spirit began to permeate the little house.

"Wait," said the Captain. "We also brought something as our contribution to the party." And with these words they began to bring in all kinds of wonderful surprises. There seemed to be no end to the supply of foodstuffs that they showered upon us. It surpassed by far the amount they had given to us in the car, the likes of which we had not seen for five years. They even brought several dozens of fresh eggs that they had exchanged at the farmers for cigarettes. To top it all off, they had brought along a large battery, knowing that there was no electricity, and like a miracle, suddenly:

THERE WAS LIGHT!

That evening marked the end of an era that none of us would ever forget.

I was proud to have been part of the struggle. Ours had been a fight of people without weapons, without power, and lacking favorable geographical terrain. Our resistance to the Nazis had proved that we were willing to sacrifice our lives and property for the moral values of freedom and justice. We had remained true to our principles and to ourselves throughout all our failures and successes in our long struggle for our very existence.

The humanity, the stamina, and the spiritual power of the wonderful Dutch people had been vindicated! We had survived!

People slowly began to rebuild their broken lives. So much had been destroyed, especially in the cities of Amsterdam, Rotterdam, The Hague, Arnhem, Nijmegen, Oosterbeek, and Wageningen.

Houses had been stripped of their contents, trees had been cut down, great parts of the land had been inundated.

The coming of victory found the Netherlands without telephone or telegraph service, gas, electricity, buses, trains, trams, cars, or gasoline. So much had been stolen or wantonly destroyed by the Germans that it would take time and hard work to repair all the damage.

But we were free and we could say whatever we wished! We were no longer afraid of raids, killings, imprisonment, bombardments, thefts, and the terror of war. There were no more blackouts and we could once again walk the streets at night.

Dutch traitors, members of the N.S.B.—The Dutch Nazi party—were arrested and dealt with severely.

The return and resettling of my many *onderduikers*, the Jews who came out of hiding, in their hometowns required all my energies, and in this work Captain Rose was extremely helpful, because of the many facilities that he put at my disposal.

Then suddenly, I found myself without obligations, without activities—alone.

People began to come back from their hiding places in Holland and other free countries, from concentration camps and from prisoner-of-war camps. Many, if not all, were weak, ill, emaciated, and frightened. Some were maimed for life. Most were seared with the memories of experiences that would haunt them forever.

My fervent hope of finding my family after the war became a

moving force in me. However, deep-seated fear began to take root, making me feel restless and cold.

Desperately we scanned the daily published lists of concentration camp survivors, each one trying to find the members of his family. We flocked to the International Red Cross office, which kept a registry of all the war casualties, to discover some news about our next of kin. I put my name and address on numerous lists requesting relatives to contact me. The Jewish Coordinating Committee in Amsterdam, which had been established after the war to aid the surviving Jews, was as helpful as possible and filled a tremendous need.

One of the few rays of sunshine I personally experienced came shortly after the war ended. In recognition of my active participation and achievements in the Resistance Movement, the Dutch government granted me a six-year scholarship to study medicine at the University of Amsterdam and I began to make plans for becoming a medical student.

The cafes, restaurants, officer's clubs, and yacht clubs all began to cater to the fun-starved nation and its Allied liberators. People danced to the tunes of ''Bessa me mucho'' ''Symphony of Love,'' ''Don't Fence Me In,'' and ''Saturday Night Is the Loneliest Night of the Week.''

It seemed to me as if everyone wanted to hide his personal sorrows, and the youth wanted to make up for the loss of five precious and important years of their lives. It was as if the nation's hilarity after the war was meant to quench their restlessness and loneliness and to temporarily cover up the depths of their needs.

Then one day came the verdict that I had anticipated with dread and trepidation. The International Red Cross handed me a list with the following statistics:

Father: Arrived in Camp Westerbork   January 2, 1943
        Deported to Auschwitz   November 16, 1943
        Died in Auschwitz   March 31, 1944

270

Mother:	Arrived in Camp Westerbork	April 1, 1943
	Deported to Auschwitz	November 16, 1943
	Died in Auschwitz	November 19, 1943
My brother Jackie:	Arrived in Camp Westerbork	April 1, 1943
	Deported to Auschwitz	November 16, 1943
	Died in Auschwitz	November 19, 1943
My brother Paul:	Arrived in Camp Westerbork	April 10, 1943
	Deported to Sobibor	May 18, 1943
	Died in Sobibor	May 21, 1943

Just three lines for each one of them as their epitaph. As I looked at the paper a surge of wild hatred rose within me. The letters and figures ignited within me a fire that I felt was consuming me with an agony such as I had never believed possible.

Someone pulled me away from the wall against which I had beat with my hands until they had become bruised and hurt.

How could I bear this pain?

How could I go on living knowing that they are no more?

How could such young and beautiful lives be snuffed out so senselessly?

I saw them all before me: my learned, respected, and charitable father; my sweet, lovely, and sensitive mother; my two young, innocent brothers—I could not absorb this torment.

"God why did they deserve such a fate?"

"For what did they have to sacrifice their lives?"

"Why, God. Why?"

"Where were You when all this happened?"

I fought with myself and with my belief as I tried to understand; I fought for my sanity. I fought for my life.

Did the world outside know about these atrocities? Were they not guilty of the gravest sins of omission in not making every effort to put a stop to the atrocities, the moment it became known that Hitler had decided to make real his "final solution" of the Jewish people in Europe?

I could not understand this injustice! I could not absorb such an evil situation!

A heavy, impenetrable, and protective shell closed in on this throbbing cameo of excruciating torment. It opened only at night, in tear-drenched moments and haunting nightmares, in the loneliness of my room.

But from the depths of my grief and mourning for my lost ones, I felt a resolve stirring within me. As it was during the war, so the necessity to act constructively and to help humanity became my purpose in life and at the same time helped to assuage my ever-present sorrow.

I determined that I would study medicine and after completing my studies I would serve my people in Palestine.

More than ever, I now felt inevitably bound up with my Jewish people.

I saw our Jewish existence as a strong, gnarled, life-giving tree rooted in the rich heritage and traditions of the past, which stressed the responsibility of one person for the other. Its strong branches reached far and wide and made its life-giving fruits available everywhere.

Heavy storms might break a branch here and there; intentionally set fires might char many branches; murderers might chop off a great part of the tree—but the loving and life-giving powers of the remaining branches would heal the bleeding tree and their lushness and fertility would make up for whatever was lost, for the roots of the tree remained indestructible.

EPILOGUE

For twenty five years I was silent. My experiences, my pain, my feelings of loss were hermetically locked up within me as in a vault. I could not talk or read about the history of the Holocaust nor relate in depth to its tragedy.

I wanted so much to enjoy a normal life, to study, to work, to accomplish goals, to meet and enjoy the company of good friends.

When World War II ended in 1945 I submerged myself in my medical studies at the University of Amsterdam. Simultaneously I helped smuggle Jewish displaced persons across the Dutch-Belgian border on their way to Israel (then Palestine). A year later I undertook the supervision of a pioneering training-center that prepared youth for a life in Israel. I worked hard to forget the painful past; my energy knew no bounds.

In 1947 I gave up my studies and flew to Canada to marry the same Captain Isaac B. Rose who had stopped to help me on the highway between Amsterdam and Apeldoorn, near the war's end.

I remember that on my wedding day I walked down the aisle without the loving presence of my parents and brothers; I felt my heart bursting with yearning for them.

In the height of the pain of childbirth, I remember crying out for my mother and not finding her consoling and helpful hand.

I had an instinctive desire to shelter my children from the horrors of the Holocaust; therefore, I did not relate my past experiences and pain to them. They knew the superficial facts only.

Then there is that unaccountable feeling of envy when I attend a funeral and console the mourners. My parents and brothers had no burial with the traditional rituals and respects afforded to the dead. I had never been consoled by sympathetic friends for seven days as are all mourners in Israel. I cannot visit their graves—for there are none. My prayer for the dead, my Kaddish, has never left my lips.

The drive to involve myself in the cause of freedom and education of my people has always governed my life, be it as a social worker in Israel, working with the newly arrived Yemenite Jews of "Operation Magic Carpet" or as president of charitable and educational organizations.

After many years of teaching, I began to realize that the Holocaust as an event in Jewish history was being commemorated in a most pitiful manner. There was ignorance of its historic, national, and religious significance on the part of leaders, students, teachers and parents alike. I began to be consumed by a flame of awakening, and the hermetically closed vault of my memories began to open up slowly but painfully. However, it was my son's intense interest in my personal experiences that finally convinced me of the necessity to relate my own story in full.

I began to lecture at school assemblies and teachers' seminars. I staged Holocaust commemorations. I wrote and directed plays stressing the heroism during the Holocaust. I began to delve into the history of anti-Semitism and Nazism, into the mechanics of the "final solution" of the Jews in Europe, and I became more and more astounded at the unbelievable monstrosities perpetrated against the Jews. I also found to my great dismay that thirty-five years after the Holocaust books are being published denying that the Holocaust ever took place—some even denying that Hitler knew or was responsible for the systematic extermination of the six million Jews. The Neo-Nazi movements claim the Holocaust is but a figment of the Jewish imagination. All this, despite the millions of personal, eyewitness reports, the vast Holocaust literature, and the official German Nazi records.

Therefore, we, the eyewitness survivors, the last link to the Holocaust, must tell our personal stories, no matter what pain and anguish we suffer in doing so. That is why I have written this book—so that present and future generations will never forget the Jewish agony. Only then will they prevent it from ever happening again.